TRYING TO MAKE DECISIONS
CAN DRIVE YOU CRAZY!

Life simply will not let you off the hook. The need to decide is inescapable. To *act* is to decide. And *not* to act is to decide. You can't win.

How often have you wished for some clear-cut path, some obvious, familiar way of choosing what needs to be done?

Finally, with this guide, you can improve your decision-making skills. By understanding and managing the inevitable conflicts involved in most important personal decisions, you'll cut through the maze of insecurities and doubts—and make the choices that are right for you!

Making DECISIONS

by Dr. Andrea Williams

Illustrated by Benjamin W. Lawless

ZEBRA BOOKS
KENSINGTON PUBLISHING CORP.

The examples given in this book are based on real-life decision dilemmas, but all names have been changed to prevent identification.

ZEBRA BOOKS

are published by

Kensington Publishing Corp.
475 Park Avenue South
New York, NY 10016

First printing: July 1985

Printed in the United States of America

This book is dedicated to
Martha
and her brothers and sisters

Acknowledgments

To MMY, who taught me how to drink from the well

To Ben, who encouraged, inspired, and teased me into writing this book

To Wendy, who found a penny in the snow and saved it

To Dennis, who kept my feet on the ground

To George, who loved and loved

Table of Contents

At the beginning of human history, man lost some of the basic animal instincts in which an animal's behavior is embedded and by which it is secured. Such security, like Paradise, is closed to man forever; man has to make choices.

—*Viktor Frankl*

Chapter I. The Universal Dilemma

Trying to make decisions can drive you crazy. There seems to be no area of life which causes as much confusion, as much pain, and as much uncertainty as decision making. More than any other reason I know, people turn for help to family, friends, clergymen, and therapists, because they *don't know what to do.* Life simply will not let you off the hook! The need to decide is inescapable. It lasts all day. Every day. To *act* is to decide. And *not* to act is to decide. You can't win. To be alive means you are in the act of making constant decisions—some easy, some painful, some momentary, and some whose effects may last a lifetime. How often have you wished for some clear-cut path, some obvious, familiar way of getting done what needs to get done? If only life could be simple for us . . . as it is for the animals.

11

Take squirrels, for example. The red squirrel of Central Europe has a perfectly sensible way of hiding nuts for the winter. With the nut in its mouth it looks around until it finds the base of a tree trunk, then scrapes out a nice hole. Laying the nut down gently, the squirrel pushes it into the hole with its nose and then scrapes back the loose earth with its paws, packing the soil firmly back over the nut. So far, so good.

But now, let's change that squirrel's environment a bit. Take that same squirrel, put him on a tiled kitchen floor, and give him a few nuts. "No problem," he thinks. Having eaten a few nuts, he takes one carefully in his mouth and looks around until he finds a corner. Running to it, he scrapes with his paws until he has "dug" a suitable "hole." Then he lays the nut down gently, gives it a push with his nose, again scrapes with his paws, and pats down firmly, satisfied that the nut is safe.*

Because the squirrel's environment is *usually* stable and predictable, his behavior *usually* works, and he can count on being fat and sassy in the spring. But let some major change come into his life, and those very same actions turn out to be totally ridiculous. Squirrels can't *change* because squirrels can't *choose*. Fortunately, they don't usually have to.

You are not quite so lucky. Your life has been full of changes, some of them intentional and fun, many of them unexpected and unwanted. Like most people, you found that with each *change*, you had to *decide* something or other. By and large you were able to

* From Eibl-Eibesfeldt, Irenäus, *Love & Hate: The Natural History of Behavior Patterns*, (translated by Geoffrey Strachan). Holt, Rinehart & Winston, New York, 1971, p. 11.

meet the challenge. But more often than you'd like to admit, you wished you had some guidance, some rule, someone to figure out the mess and *tell you what to do*. What happened instead? You sat for hours carrying on long, imaginary conversations inside your head. You turned to friends and family, only to find that you ended up more confused and uncertain than you were in the first place. You procrastinated and delayed, hoping that a miracle would take place, that some turn of events would relieve you of possible blame and point to a clear, easy way out.

You are not alone! Not knowing what to do is the greatest dilemma human beings face. At one time or another, we have all experienced the paralysis of being unable to decide. An indecisive person has been called "an engine with sand in its crankcase, broken piston rods, water in its fuel lines. In spite of great effort and noise, nothing much happens."* Why is this experience so common? Why is decision making so difficult? Because your mind craves what is simple, clear-cut, and obvious. It tries desperately to avoid what is indefinite, unpredictable, or complicated. Your mind wants to *know*, and you are asking it to *guess*.

A decision is always only a guess. Instead of accepting the fact that most of the time you do not—and *cannot*—know exactly what effects your decision will have in the future, you torment yourself in advance with visions of disaster and punish yourself afterward with waves of regret. By thinking about decision making in the usual way, you are asking yourself to do the

---

* Pearce, Joseph Chilton, *The Crack in the Cosmic Egg*, Simon & Schuster, New York, 1973, p. 13.

impossible! You are trying to make decisions *as if*:

(1) You "should" know exactly how everything is going to turn out. (You don't.)

(2) There is a perfect, right answer. (There isn't.)

(3) All loss, pain, or discomfort you or those you care about experience could somehow be avoided *if only* you could figure out which is the "right" choice. (You can't.)

Decision making is usually confused with problem solving. However, a problem occurs when you know how things should be, when you can identify the source of the difficulty, when someone or something could resolve it, and when your purpose is to restore things to *the way they were* before the problem came up. Say your hot water heater springs a leak. You know exactly what's wrong. You know exactly what will happen if you don't do something pretty soon. And you know that someone has the knowledge, the expertise, and the willingness to "put things right." Perhaps you've been going through life thinking that your difficulties, like the hot water heater, can somehow be "fixed" once and for all. You *want* to solve problems. What you *must do* is make decisions.

Decision making is not problem solving! Problems are meant to be solved for good. The purpose of "solving a problem" is to make sure that a sticky situation never comes up again. Usually there *is* a right, or best, solution—the one that prevents that problem from occurring again.

Decision making, however, is more like paddling a

canoe down a winding river. Yes, there is a current which guides you (a desire for happiness), and you get better at rowing as you go along (experience). But at each fork you must choose a specific branch of the river, *without knowing or being able to know exactly what lies around the bend*. You turn right or left depending on which one *seems* more inviting, based on what you have learned from similar forks.

The purpose of deciding is to *find out how things are* in the place you've reached. If you are displeased with what you discover there, sometimes you can paddle back upstream and take the other fork. But sometimes you can't. Sometimes you find weeds and alligators and can only push on, hoping to get through in one piece.

And so it goes, one branch continuously leading into another, continuously flowing, continuously surprising you. What you find is never *completely* right and good, but it's usually not completely wrong or bad either. What is certain is that opportunities for experimenting, for learning, and for discovering exist along each and every branch.

Decision making is a continuous and creative process, a constant seeking to know both the river and the rower—to learn what *life* and *you* are all about. And it is a process that never ends. You can use problem solving to repair a leak in the boat, but you must use imagination to figure out what you want and decision making to figure out how to get it.

Here are the differences between the two:

Problem Solving	Decision Making
Usually depends on complete and accurate information	Is *always* based on incomplete or unknown information
Tries to arrive at permanent solutions	Is essentially temporary—a working principle
Deals with right and wrong	Deals with trade-offs and compromises
Is inflexible and unchangeable	Is flexible and changeable
Focuses attention on the end result	Focuses attention on what you can *learn* about life and about yourself
Aims for "perfect" resolutions	Aims for "satisfactory" results
Works toward *eliminating* contradictions to reach *definiteness*	Works toward *managing* contradictions to reach *balance*
Is usually designed to prevent such events from ever happening again	Is designed to *prepare you* for similar events which will very probably happen again

You can learn to make up your mind without losing your mind!

A well-known executive was once asked the secret of his success. "I make the right decisions," he replied. His questioner probed further. "And how did you learn to make the right decisions?" "By making so many wrong ones!" he responded. *Decision making is a skill*, and it is a skill that can be *learned*. To learn it requires some ability to organize, a little time, and some willingness to take risks. The more willing you are to admit that the results now taking place are unfavorable, and the sooner you are willing to switch to another alternative, the more quickly your decision making will improve.

A decision is a tool. It is a tool used to get and evaluate information. You use it to *learn* what is suitable for *you*. You learn to become sensitive to what you think and feel as outcomes—positive and negative—begin to take place. They provide you with the information you are seeking, and it is this information which automatically guides you into making future decisions that are more and more satisfying to you and to those around you.

In this book, you will learn to use a few simple steps that will improve your decision-making skills. These procedures are based on a strategic diagram called the *Road of Life*. It works. By using the *Road of Life* procedures, you will learn to *understand* and *manage* the inevitable conflicts involved in making most important personal decisions. These techniques cut through the maze of information and doubt and allow the essence of your decision to become crystal clear.

- You will learn the FOUR MAJOR OBSTACLES to successful decision making and how to use the *Road of Life* to remove them.

17

- You will learn an EFFORTLESS PROCESS for discovering your hidden desires and hidden fears.

- You will learn why there are only THREE BASIC DECISION DILEMMAS

- You will learn what your particular DECISION DILEMMA reveals about your personality.

- And you will learn SEVEN SPECIFIC STRATEGIES for dealing with the painful contradictions and tensions that are a part of most personal decisions.

The *Road of Life* procedure has been used successfully by deciders of all ages, in situations of all kinds. You will meet dozens and dozens of them in this book. For example:

Eddie, who decided whether to date beautiful Jody or fun-loving Kate

Mary, who decided whether to continue teaching at a school where she had poor faculty support or to quit

Frank, who decided whether or not to take an early retirement

Amy, who decided whether to join the marching band or the track team

Margaret, who decided whether to send her children to public school or to private school

Vince, who decided whether to remain in his home city or to move out West

Sarah, who decided whether to end her thirteen-year-old marriage.

You will meet boys and girls, men and women—people who wrestled with issues of work, money, self-image, change, and intimate relationships. No one's situation will be exactly like yours, but no one's will be entirely unlike yours either. All will help to teach you how to decide what is best for you.

An old proverb states, *"Experience is a hard teacher. It gives you the test first and the lesson afterwards."* This is the *reverse* of the way you would like things to be. And this is the reason you are having trouble making up your mind. As we move through the decision-making procedures and strategies, keep these three cardinal rules in mind:

(1) Making decisions is a way of GETTING IN-FORMATION.

(2) Each alternative is likely to have very important ADVANTAGES *and* very important DISAD-VANTAGES.

(3) You will never be able to tell whether a decision was beneficial until *after* you have made it and had a chance to EXPERIENCE the outcomes.

Chapter II. Stopping the Merry-Go-Round

Sarah, thirty-seven, a pretty brunette with two sons, five and three years of age, had been trying for over a year to decide whether to leave her husband when she came in for help. I asked her to tell me what was on her mind.

"I can't understand it," she said. "I care a lot about Doug, and I think he cares for me. But we argue about *everything*, and it seems to be getting worse and worse. Mostly, we're having trouble over the children. Doug criticizes my handling of them, and he's so nasty about it I don't want to have anything to do with him, if you know what I mean. I'm not even sure I love him any more.

"I think I have what it takes to make a fresh start, but I haven't worked for over six years, and I'd be hard pressed to make it financially on my own. Of course I'm afraid of what effects a divorce and all that turmoil would have on my children . . . and on me too!

"I suppose every family has its problems. But sometimes his temper really gets out of hand, and he gets pretty nasty. He hit me once." Here, Sarah was quiet for a while, and her eyes filled with tears.

"On the plus side, Doug is a good provider, and we have a very nice house. I'd hate to give up our standard of living. And my parents are conservative; I'm afraid they'd put the blame on me. Doug's parents are even worse. They'd never forgive me. I threatened to leave once, and Doug screamed at me, 'Look around. Do you see anyone much better off than we are?' It's terrible. I'm so lonely and depressed I cry myself to sleep almost every night. I just don't know what to do!"

I asked Sarah whether she now felt any closer to making a decision regarding divorce than she did a year ago. No, not at all! I must have spent a hundred hours thinking about this and another hundred talking about it. No sooner do I come up with a good reason to leave than I come up with an equally good reason *not* to. I just keep spinning around in circles. The whole thing is driving me out of my mind!"

Sarah was trapped. Round and round went her thoughts, bobbing up and down like horses on a merry-go-round, never getting anywhere, never catching up. ^{Yes} But ^{Yes} But ^{Yes} But. Sarah was trapped on the merry-go-round of spoken words.

OBSTACLE ONE: YOUR DECISION MAKING IS NOT SUCCESSFUL BECAUSE YOU ARE ASKING YOUR BRAIN TO PROCESS INFORMATION IN THE *WRONG WAY*.

The gift of speech is a mixed blessing. On the one

21

hand, our ability to use language is what makes us human. Words allow us to understand and communicate complex and subtle ideas. On the other hand, words have a built-in problem. They move. They're oh so slippery. You try to grab hold of a thought, and it slips through your fingers. You try to remember an idea, and it disappears into the shadows of your mind. No sooner is one sentence created than another jumps in to take its place.

Spoken words are like musical notes, constantly changing, constantly fluid—beautiful and interesting while they're there but gone in an instant. Because words cannot be pinned down, they are *powerless* and *inefficient* tools for reaching decisions. Your ideas need to be *fixed in time and space* so you can review them with the full power of your mind. In order to keep your thoughts from whirling around endlessly, you must switch from your ears to your eyes. You *must* STOP talking and *start writing*.

The "Yes-But" List. Right now, while you're thinking about your decision, grab a pen or pencil and a piece of paper, and start writing. *Work as quickly as you can.* Don't censor anything, don't argue with yourself, and don't try to judge whether an item is good or bad. What are *all* the things that might happen if you made either choice? Write as many outcomes as you can possibly think of—the goods, the bads, the favorables, the unfavorables, the "Yeses," and the "Buts." Don't try to put them in any particular order. To make your list usually takes ten to twenty minutes. When the ideas slow down a bit and the

"Yes-But" List feels more or less complete, take paper and pencil in hand, stand up, and walk. Yes, *walk!* You are going to take a FANTASY WALK right into each alternative.

Try to find a location which lets you walk at least twelve or fifteen feet before you must turn around. Keep a steady, rhythmic pace. If you can, dim the lights or pull the curtains. Let your eyes roam; do not focus on anything in particular. If your eyelids feel heavy, let them close a little.

As you get into the flow of walking, your mind will begin to wander. Gently now, create a scene that might exist if you actually chose one of the alternatives. Put rooms, furniture, people, grass, and trees in it. What do you see? Whom do you meet? What are people saying? Are there background noises? Are you indoors or outdoors? What is the weather? Are you warm or cold? Do you smell or taste anything? What are you doing? Are you talking? Listening? Working? Dancing? Crying?

As you mentally experience WALKING into each alternative, ideas will begin to come very fast once again. *ADD THEM TO YOUR LIST IMMEDIATELY. DO NOT TALK TO ANYONE!* At this stage of the game, conversation is the enemy of thought!

OPTION: Some people prefer to sit while having the FANTASY. Just be sure you're comfortable and will not be disturbed. Also, you may find that while you're occupied with other activity—walking to the bus, driving, doing dishes—

more items will come. Take a moment to write them down . . . unless you're driving.

OPTION: It might be easier to get a free and fast flow of ideas by having someone do the writing for you. But do not let the person speak. That will come later.

When this new batch of items slows down or stops, your "Yes-But" List is basically finished. Still, don't be surprised if items come up hours or even days later. Items can be added at any time until the very moment you make your decision.

The Diagram. As soon as the "Yes-But" List is finished, your next step will be to prepare the *Road of Life* Diagram. The diagram should contain all of the following: two big boxes for alternatives, the words *Choice*, *Advantages*, and *Disadvantages* written in each box, the figure at the crossroad, and the question mark. (For the time being, limit the number of alternatives to two. If necessary, the "winner" can be matched against other alternatives later.)

Road of Life Diagram

Choice: *Advantages*:	*Choice*: *Advantages*:

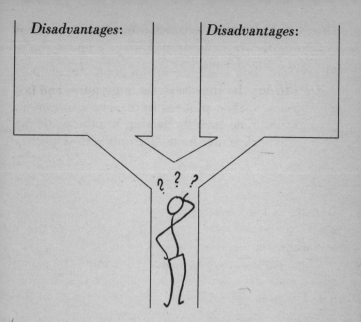

Disadvantages: *Disadvantages:*

All of the words, thoughts, and ideas that have been making you dizzy are about to quiet down and line up within the boundaries of this diagram. You have *stopped* the MERRY-GO-ROUND and overcome the first major obstacle to successful decision making.

TIPS

DO: Have enough paper handy. Your "Yes-But" List will probably be longer than you think.

DO: Walk around (pace), or sit quietly and comfortably, with your eyes unfocused on something in the far distance.

DO: Take as long as possible to complete your list—a day, a week, or a year, if you can.

DO NOT: Judge or criticize any item. Just put it down.

DO NOT: Talk to anyone at this point. It is important for the success of the procedure that you follow each step in sequence. There will be an appropriate time for talking to others and an appropriate time for talking only with yourself.

Chapter III. Won Tu Many: The Chinese Menu Panic

You sit down in a bustling Chinese restaurant, and the waiter hands you an enormous menu. Column after column, choices begin to parade before your eyes: pork . . . beef . . . chicken . . . shrimp . . . noodles . . . pork and noodles . . . chicken and shrimp and vegetables . . . beef and pork and vegetables and noodles and . . . on and on. Within five minutes you are expected to *notice*, *understand*, *remember*, *compare*, *evaluate*, and *select* from a staggering amount of information. The waiter returns, eyebrows lifted expectantly, pencil poised. You are hit with Chinese Menu Panic. With some hesitation, aware that you haven't the slightest idea how to order the exquisite, flaming dish just brought to the next table, you *simplify*: One pork dish, one chicken dish, one shrimp dish, fried rice, wonton soup, and egg roll for everyone. Or, secretly grateful that the restaurant has already done the choosing for you, you say with confidence, "Family dinner for four."

OBSTACLE TWO: YOUR DECISION MAKING IS NOT SUCCESSFUL BECAUSE

YOU ARE ASKING YOUR BRAIN TO PROCESS *TOO MUCH* INFORMATION.

Hundreds and hundreds of research studies have been done to find out how the brain handles information. Some have tried to discover how many things people can remember. Others have tried to find ways of reducing information to a manageable amount. One of the earliest reports summarized dozens of studies which investigated people's ability to remember different quantities of information. Dr. Robert Miller* discovered that the brain can remember, without assistance, about seven (or at the very most nine) separate, *unrelated* pieces of information.

A typical example is the shopping list. It is fairly easy to remember three items, but once you reach four or five, it is almost certain you will forget one unless you connect them by using some mental trick. Let's say your list is: milk, bread, bananas, shoe polish, and a birthday card for Mother. You might try to remember it by repeating to yourself, "Pour the milk on the bread, stuff it into a banana skin, polish it, and send it to Mother." But as the sheer amount of information grows, and as the information becomes more complex, your mind will reach its *information-processing limit* and give up in exhaustion.

Dr. Miller offers a variety of suggestions on how to simplify or reorganize large amounts of information. The purpose of reorganizing information is to bring it *within the range* of what your brain can handle. And that is about seven items. Miller calls each individual

* Miller, Robert, The magical number seven, plus or minus two. *Psychological Review*, 1956, *63*, 31–96.

piece of information a "bit." He says that bits can be combined into groups (he calls these groups "chunks"), and each group can be given a name. Then, instead of trying to remember individual bits, people can simply remember the name of each group.

For example, suppose I asked you to name all your aunts, uncles, and cousins. But to make it more difficult, I asked you to name them *out of order*, that is, no name should belong to the same family as the one before or after it. Tough to do. You would be stretching your brain's capacity to process this information by selecting isolated, unrelated bits. Anyway, I know how you would really do it (you little devil, you). You would picture each family group in your mind (a chunk) and you would give me one name (a bit) from each family in turn. In so doing, you would automatically have used a mental device called RECODING. Recoding is organizing *unrelated* pieces of information by creating *meaningful groups* or categories in which to place them.

If you are trying to make an important decision, it is very likely that you have come up with more than seven outcomes—total Yeses and total Buts. Count the number of separate items on your list. Are there more than seven? Then you have *gone past* your brain's information-processing limit. You need to re-organize the information. You will use the *Road of Life* Diagram to recode the separate items on your list into four meaningful groups: two sets of Advantages and two sets of Disadvantages.

Two of my clients, Linda and Tom, had asked for assistance in deciding whether to buy a house (Choice 1) or to stay in their apartment (Choice 2). After some discussion, they came up with their "Yes-But" List:

A house is a better investment in the long run.

The monthly costs of a house would be tremendous.

We like our present neighborhood.

The landlord could switch to a condo at any time.

A house gives you a great sense of independence.

A house is fun to fix up.

There is a loss of mobility with a house.

There's the time and energy for upkeep.

There are no tax benefits in the apartment.

We might be even better off financially if we paid less monthly and used the extra money for some other form of investment.

We might be happier using the extra money for things other than housing.

We like the neighbors.

Our apartment is too small.

A house gives you privacy.

We can't do what we want in decorating the apartment.

Clearly, the amount of information Tom and Linda were trying to process *at once* was far too much to handle. By using the *Road of Life* Diagram, we easily recode the information into four logical units:

- the *Advantages* of buying a house

- the *Disadvantages* of buying a house

- the *Advantages* of staying in the apartment

- the *Disadvantages* of staying in the apartment

First, consider each item separately and see where it would belong in the *Road of Life* Diagram. In Linda and Tom's list, the first item given (a house is a better investment in the long run) is an *Advantage* of buying a house. The second item (the monthly costs of a house would be tremendous) is a *Disadvantage* of buying a house. And the third (we like our present neighborhood) is an *Advantage* of staying in the apartment.

Second, shorten the items whenever possible. From now on, the idea is to *reduce the amount* of information with which you have to deal. See whether a long statement can be expressed in four to six words. And try to keep the items more or less the same length.

When Tom and Linda finished filling out their diagram, the items had been considerably shortened and looked like this:

Choice: Buy a house	Choice: Stay in apartment
Advantages:	**Advantages:**
sense of independence	cheaper
fun to fix up	like the neighborhood
long-run investment	like the neighbors
have it any way you want	use extra money for other investments
tax advantage	

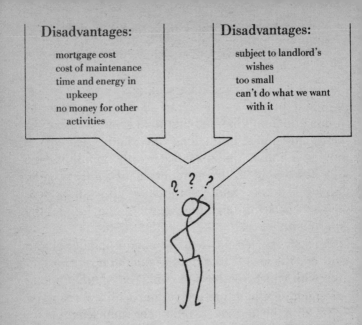

Although the decision itself was still far from being made, Linda and Tom already had a much better idea of exactly what they were dealing with and what the trade-offs might be. The outcomes were now *fixed* in time and space. And the recoding, the reorganization, allowed them to review each category in a meaningful, systematic way.

Sarah, another client who was trying to decide whether or not to get a divorce, made up a "Yes-But" List that was even longer and more disorganized than Linda and Tom's.

marriage is supposed to last forever

the children's lives would be very disrupted

it's terrible living with someone I don't trust

doesn't support me in the way I discipline the children

I don't have many skills for a good job

I think I could make it if I had to

I was able to take care of myself in the past

my friends would be supportive

divorce is against the teachings of my religion

it would be hard for my parents to take

it would be very hard for Doug's parents to take

end constant fighting in front of the children

never listens to what I have to say

walking on eggs all the time

could avoid turning everyone's life upside down

might never meet anyone better

my standard of living would be lower

don't know if I could hand it

no one to do things with

I'm lonely and afraid in my own house

big hassles—legal and otherwise

lots of turmoil

he's making me lose my self-respect, which was never terrific

could have a chance for greater happiness

stability for children

I love my house

I enjoy being a mother and homemaker

would hate to admit to my mother that I'm having problems

at least I know what I've got

has hit me and has threatened to hit me again

if I stay, I could avoid dealing with the turmoil

I love him (I think) but I don't like him right now

Although leaving the marriage was at the back of her mind, Sarah selected "Move out" and "Stay at home" as her choices. Moving out was, she felt, an intermediate step, after which she could make the more final decision.

We filled in the *Road of Life* Diagram one item at a time. As each item was used, we crossed it out. Each was put in the category where it "felt right." Some items balanced each other, for example, "The children's lives would be very disrupted" and "stability for the children." But sometimes they did not exactly balance. For example, Sarah felt her friends would be supportive no matter what she did, but their support would be much more meaningful to her in case of a separation. Therefore, that item belonged as an Advantage under "Move out," but not really anywhere in "Stay at home."

After using up all the items, Sarah's *Road of Life* Diagram looked like this. Again, notice how each item was shortened to at most seven words:

Choice: Move out

Advantages:

think I could make it
able to take care of self
in past

friends would be
supportive

have a chance for
greater happiness

end fighting in front of
children

Disadvantages:

children's lives very
distrupted
few skills for a good
job
against my religion
don't know if I could
handle it
hard for parents to
take
very hard for Doug's
parents to take
might never meet
anyone better
standard of living
lower

Choice: Stay at home

Advantages:

marriage supposed to
last forever
stability for children
love my house
enjoy being a mother
and homemaker
know what I've got
avoid turning every-
one's life upside down
avoid dealing with the
turmoil
I love him (I think)

Disadvantages:

has hit me—threat-
ened to again
terrible living with
someone I don't
trust
never listens to what I
have to say
walking on eggs all the
time
lonely and afraid
making me lose my
self-respect
afraid he might hit me
again
don't like him right

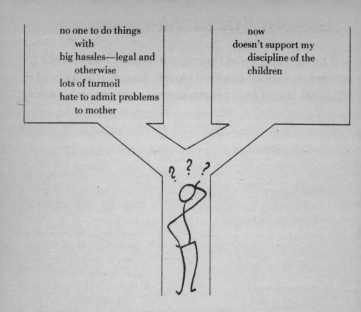

no one to do things with
big hassles—legal and otherwise
lots of turmoil
hate to admit problems to mother

now
doesn't support my discipline of the children

Sarah's decision was a complicated and difficult one. To resolve it we had to use all of the strategies you will learn in this book. We will return to Sarah's decision dilemma in detail in Chapter IX. Meanwhile, let's continue with the *Road of Life* procedure step by step.

If you followed directions carefully, you have done a lot of thinking, a lot of writing, and a lot of organizing. It is time now to turn to another excellent source of information—the experience and creativity of other people. You may now turn to a trusted friend, relative, or counselor and ask for further imput into your diagram. But this suggestion carries an *important caution:*

THE PURPOSE OF INQUIRING IS TO GATHER *MORE INFORMATION*, NOT TO

ASK ADVICE ABOUT WHAT TO DO!

The importance of finding someone who can take a neutral, impartial position cannot be overemphasized. An ideal friend for this purpose is someone who asks *nothing more* than, "Have you considered, or have you thought of (a potential item goes here)?" You are looking for someone who can help you add meaningful items to your diagram, not someone who begins to judge, evaluate, and argue with the items you have. *Now is the time to be very, very careful.* If anyone has tried to help you before, you know how hard it is for people to avoid giving advice—especially since that's probably what you've been asking for!

Put simply, advice is what *that* person would do in your place. It's not necessarily what *you* should do in your place. You'll definitely find out what's right for you soon enough. But at this point what you need is information, not advice, suggestions, or criticism. You don't need someone blowing that kind of smoke in your face.

> Warning: The Author Has Determined That
> Comments Like These
> are Hazardous to Your Decision

"Why don't you? . . ."

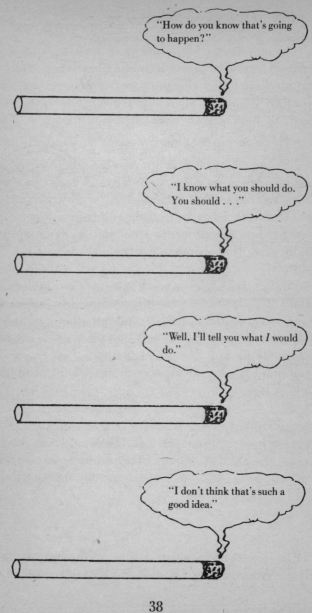

38

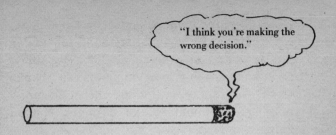

PUT AN END TO THE SMOKE!

Say "I appreciate your suggestion" or "That's an interesting idea, but what I need is help in coming up with some items. Can you think of anything I might not have considered?" You may have to repeat this many times. If your friend is a good friend, he or she will eventually get the message. But you will still have a judgment to make. If the new item hits home or feels right, put it in. If it doesn't, *leave it out*!

Lastly, I recommend that you do a quick review of each category. Have you considered: (1) the Advantages to yourself, (2) the Disadvantages to yourself, the (3) Advantages to others, and (4) the Disadvantages to others.

TIPS

DO: Try to use positive, not negative, statements to describe your Choices. For example, instead of:

Go to the party / Not go to the party, you might select: Go to the party / Stay home and watch TV. If you're *not* going to be doing one thing, what *are* you going to be doing instead? Sometimes, you simply have to use the word "not"; nothing else would fit, for example, Have a baby / Not have a baby.

DO: State your Choices as if the word "to" could be the first word. For example, Buy a stereo is a better Choice statement than Buying a stereo.

DO: Use words that describe an *action* rather than a condition or a characteristic, for example, Keep the kitchen clean, instead of A clean kitchen.

DO: Use the present or future tense for all Choices and items—for example, Likes me, or Would like me, instead of, Didn't like me.

DO: Use enough paper, so there will be clear space around each item. Better to have too much space than too little.

DO: Write legibly. Print if you have to.

DO NOT: Abbreviate. Use only a few words to express each item, but be sure they are *complete* words.

Once you have completed your diagram, you will have overcome Obstacle Two. Your decision is now beginning to take shape. Your thoughts are no longer going around in circles. Your information is organized, and you are gaining a sense of control. The next step in the *Road of Life* is a little different. I am going to ask you to take a five-minute break. After your break, bring your diagram, your pencil, and yourself to a place that is quiet, comfortable, and private.

Chapter IV. Wishes and Worries

I had to give up shopping with Francine years ago. Francine found it just about impossible to choose between two simple items. Should she buy the dark green blouse with ruffles or the apricot pullover with pearl buttons? (Invariably she ended up with neither.) At a restaurant, unable to decide whether she preferred the seafood in a pastry shell or the tenderloin tips on rice, she ended up with a hamburger. At home, faced with the choice of using the good china or the everyday dishes when she had company for dinner, she ended up asking her husband to decide. In most aspects of her life Francine found herself totally paralyzed whenever she was forced to choose between items of approximate value. Many people, like Francine, find that their decision making is brought to a screeching halt by the third obstacle:

OBSTACLE THREE: YOUR DECISION MAKING IS NOT SUCCESSFUL BECAUSE YOU DON'T KNOW WHAT YOU WANT *MOST*.

Not only do you not *know* what you want, you

haven't a clue about *how to find out* what you want! In this step of the *Road of Life* process you will easily and effortlessly discover what is most important to you. For a few moments you are going to allow the analytical critical, judgmental part of your brain to rest. Instead, you will call on the ability of your mind to create, to imagine, and to sense.

You are now in a quiet comfortable place and have your *Road of Life* Diagram (filled out) in front of you. I suggest that you read the following instructions twice before doing this step:

Put your pen or pencil down, turn the diagram over, and close your eyes for at least sixty seconds. Longer is fine. Bring to mind an image or scene that you find peaceful and beautiful. Let there be some rhythmic movement in it—a flowing river, trees swaying in the breeze, a gentle surf on the beach. Soft background music will help. Breathe slowly and evenly. Feel your muscles become warm and relaxed. Stay with the scene. Now, open your eyes and turn the diagram face up.

Let your eyes wander gently around what you have written. In a little while you will notice that certain items are beginning to stand out or vibrate, or you will notice that your eyes keep returning to certain items. When this happens, pick up your pencil and circle those items.

LIKE MAGIC, YOU HAVE HIT THE SPOT! YOUR *MOST IMPORTANT* VALUES HAVE JUST POPPED OUT!

OPTION: Instead of a peaceful scene, you may be more comfortable using this directed breathing technique. Close your eyes. Breathe slowly and evenly to a count of four: *One*-two-three-four, out-two-three-four; *Two*-two-three-four, out-two-three-four; *Three*-two-three-four, out-two-three-four. Do this a total of *ten* times or more. As you breathe in, picture each breath as a light, bright color: yellow, pink, apple green. As you breathe out, picture the breath as having picked up stress and tension, which makes it a deep, full color: dark green, navy blue, deep purple. If other thoughts come, let them pass on through, but continue steadily to count your breaths.

OPTION: Instead of imagining the peaceful scene or counting breaths, you may enjoy this very simple procedure. Close your eyes and picture our national flag waving gently against a bright blue sky, as puffy white clouds drift by. Hum the national anthem to yourself. This will take almost exactly sixty seconds. (You may want to hum the words, but I don't recommend it. The purpose of this exercise is to stimulate the *nonverbal* part of your brain, the part that is more in tune with art, music, and intuition, rather than the part that responds more to words and logic.)

If you are relaxed and spontaneous, and if you are completely willing to accept whatever "pops out" during this step, then you can be certain that the circles accurately pinpoint the WISHES (Advantages) and WORRIES (Disadvantages) that are most important to you.

HOW TO UNDERSTAND
YOUR WISHES AND WORRIES

Exactly what did you discover you wanted most out

of this decision, and what kinds of things were you afraid might happen? With surprising regularity, a few major categories of values appear in people's *Road of Life* Diagrams over and over again. By comparing the items that popped out in your diagram with the actual examples given below, you will come to understand your values precisely. (You will find a more complete listing of examples in the *Mini-Manual for Pinpointing your Wishes and Worries* (page 406.)

The first set of examples contains five major categories: Brass Tacks, Companionship, Pledges, Pleasures and Comforts, and Enhancers.

CATEGORY ONE: THE BRASS TACKS

The Brass Tacks are items which demonstrate that *practical* considerations are quite important to you: matters like employment, living arrangements, money, transportation, or education. Decisions involving work or school often contain items in this major category. If any of the following items appear in your diagram, you have a practical streak.

more assurance of a good job

gives real-life experience instead of being in school

price is right (or, costs too much)

takes too long

would have to break the lease

more (less) dependable (reliable, durable)

near public transportation

it's practical

CATEGORY TWO: COMPANIONSHIP

Being and working in the company of others is a nearly universal desire. While it is sometimes overshadowed by certain other strong desires, such as money or success, it is a very important factor in many personal decisions. Items in the Companionship category deal with human contacts. While some people show a desire for more contact, others are looking for greater privacy or independence. If you circled items like these examples, it shows that the opportunity to be *with* (or *without*) other people is quite important to you.

afraid of being alone (isolated, cut off, left out, out of place)

chance to be with my friend (friends, family, parents, relatives, buddies)

comfortable (uncomfortable) with those kinds of people

give me a chance to get to know her/him/them better

enjoy friendly competition (team sports)

gets me away from him (her, them) for a while

CATEGORY THREE: THE PLEDGES

Items in this category reflect the sense of social obligation, moral obligation, or duty you feel when you give your word or make a promise. In order to belong here, the wish or worry must imply, "doing something because *I said* I would," *not* because someone else would approve, disapprove, get angry, etc. (That situation is dealt with later.)

In some situations, the *pledge* is not actually stated but is a matter of general understanding. For example, when you register for a guitar course, there is an understood pledge that you will attend the classes; If you decide to have children, there is an understood pledge that you will take care of them. When you become a member of an organization, there is an understood pledge that you will support its purposes by contributing your time, money, or skills.

Circling items like these shows that you place great importance on living up to your word, keeping commitments, agreements, and promises you have made.

I promised (said I would, gave my word, made a vow)

agreed to take on the responsibility

wouldn't be able to follow through

paid (registered) for it

counting on me to finish in time (be on time)

CATEGORY FOUR: PLEASURES AND COMFORTS

Pleasures and Comforts are the kinds of experiences that make life rich, flowing, and fully enjoyable. For some people, enjoyment is expressed in terms of simplicity, certainty, lack of friction, or ease of accomplishment. Others find great pleasure in novelty, excitement, or mental stimulation. If you circled items like the ones below, you place a high value on some or all of these things: fun, excitement, comfort, ease, certainty, novelty, variety, simplicity, beauty, orderliness, and sensory pleasure.

wouldn't have to think too hard (worry about it, make decisions, keep track of things, keep things in order)

would have a good chance (or be sure) of getting the type of sofa (car, stereo system, teacher, washing machine, lover, etc.) I've been wanting

fun, entertaining

boring after a few minutes (hours, months, years)

like (don't like) any boss (studying, the atmosphere, my mother-in-law, that kind of music, vegetarian food, my boyfriend's dog, etc.)

In General

$$\text{I} \left\{ \begin{array}{l} \text{love} \\ \text{like} \\ \text{don't like} \\ \text{hate} \end{array} \right\} \text{the way} \left\{ \begin{array}{l} \text{it} \\ \text{he} \\ \text{she} \\ \text{they} \end{array} \right\} \left\{ \begin{array}{l} \text{looks(s)} \\ \text{feel(s)} \\ \text{sounds(s)} \\ \text{taste(s)} \\ \text{smell(s)} \\ \text{work(s)} \\ \text{acts} \end{array} \right\}$$

CATEGORY FIVE: THE ENHANCERS

The Enhancers are items which show concern with the quality of life in its deepest sense. People want very much to like and accept themselves, to feel worthwhile and good. They want to respect themselves and to be respected by others. These powerful wishes (and the worries that they might never be realized, or that once attained they might be lost) are found in all people, regardless of whether they are recognized or expressed. Items in this category reveal the greatest aspirations and hopes of mankind: to make meaningful contributions, to create, to master life's challenges, to be true to oneself, to express oneself honestly, to care about others, to be cared about, to give and receive love.

Look hard at what is behind words that may seem simple or common, because among the Enhancers you will find decisions with the greatest potential for affecting personal growth and the well-being of society.

respect myself more (lose respect for myself)

doesn't put pressure on him/her/them

not what I really feel (fake, hypocritical)

don't want to hurt her/him/them

gives me (does not give me) emotional support

able to try my wings

feel needed (feel useless)

don't want to be confined (tied down, inhibited, restricted, pressured)

get needed rest

not right (bad, not nice, doesn't feel good/right)

good place to raise a family

THE TROUBLEMAKERS

The second set of examples contains four categories. They illustrate common, but powerful and potentially harmful, goals:

(1) to acquire *Prestige*

(2) to acquire *Power*

(3) to *Please Others*

(4) to *Protect* yourself from trouble

Troublemakers are actually positive behaviors which have gotten out of hand. Sometimes, they cause you to have problems with *other people*. They don't like you as you are (No. 1 & No. 2). Sometimes, they cause you to have problems with *yourself*. Then *you* don't like you as you are (No. 3 & No. 4). Because one or more of these Troublemakers may be having a strong, hidden influence in shaping your decisions (and therefore your happiness), it is important for you to understand each one clearly. You need to understand how they develop, what the Advantages and Disadvantages of each Troublemaker are, and how other people reinforce *your* troublesome behavior. You need to understand exactly why a Troublemaker may be satisfying to you but also how it produces a specific set of problems in your life.

In order to understand the Troublemakers, we need to look first at the purpose of *all* human behavior. What is the bottom line? Why do we do what we do?

Chapter V. The Troublemakers: Prestige, Power, Pleasing Others, and Protection

Many psychologists, myself included, believe that the two ultimate purposes of all behavior—the two greatest human desires—are for self-fulfillment (developing all of one's potential) and social belonging. Your needs and the needs of others are deeply intertwined, neither being dominant over the other. Each is *required* for the other to be fulfilled. You cannot meet your needs, grow, and develop without the good will, participation, and cooperation of others. And a social group cannot grow and develop without *your* good will, participation, and cooperation.

Alfred Adler, one of the first social psychologists, believed that a satisfying and lasting feeling of belonging comes primarily from one source, from making a *meaningful contribution* to one's social group. That group may be as small as two individuals or as large as the population of the earth. And the contribution may have obvious value at the time it is made, or it may benefit people in the future. Constructive participation (making a meaningful contribution) is fulfilling for two reasons: first, because the power to do so lies *totally within you*; and second, because you can *always* contribute in a way that is appropriate to the situation. A baby, for example, contributes by learning to amuse itself and not to make undue demands. And people in a concert audience contribute by remaining seated and quiet.

When you consistently act in such a way that you make meaningful contributions, you are revealing certain underlying attitudes toward life. Adler was specific about these:

- you desire harmony, smoothness, and progress in your life

- you are willing to put creativity and effort into making things better

- you are willing to take responsibility for your actions and their consequences

- you feel that your contributions are worthwhile

- you like yourself

- you like other people

Above all, psychologists find that the single attitude present in happy and self-fulfilled people is *trust*. These people have a feeling that others have their best interests at heart (as they do for others). People who trust appreciate how closely their behavior and happiness is *intertwined* and *interconnected* with the actions of others, how everyone's welfare is in some way tied to that of everyone else, how their ability to make it through even one day would be impossible without the willing cooperation and labor of thou-

52

sands of other people.

The idea of trust, confidence, and mutual welfare is nowhere better expressed than in this segment of a poem by Buckminster Fuller.* In it, he is describing a man sorting mail on an express train:

> with unuttered faith that
> the engineer is competent
> that the switchmen are not asleep,
> that the track walkers are doing their job,
> that the technologists
> who designed the train and the rails
> knew their stuff,
> that thousands of others
> whom he may never know by face or name
> are collecting tariffs,
> paying for repairs,
> and so handling assets
> that he will be paid a week from today
> and again the week after that,
> and that all the time
> his family is safe and in well-being
> without his personal protection.

Out of a sense of trust and a willingness to contribute come all the qualities of the well-adjusted person. He or she values, and is responsible about, meeting the needs of the situation; has close friends; is capable of giving and receiving love (not necessarily sexual); is able to play and relax; thinks of him/herself as a good

* Fuller, R. Buckminster, *Untitled Epic Poem On the History of Industrialization*, Simon & Schuster, New York, p. 61.

and capable person; and has come to peace with the question of the meaning of life.

WHEN YOU WERE A CHILD

We find over and over again that certain needs must be met if a young child is to grow up into the kind of person I just described. Some of these are: being wanted, being able to express opinions and ideas freely, having his/her ideas taken seriously, being thanked for his/her contributions to the family's welfare, being respected for his/her accomplishments, and being made to feel successful at mastering life's physical, emotional, and social challenges. In other words, a child needs to hear, "Thank you," "You did a good job," "That will really help us out," or "I enjoyed being with you today."

Naturally, this is an ideal state of affairs, which rarely occurs in actual practice. When you were a child, chances are the times you *did* pick up your belongings without being asked, played nicely with your brother, did *not* spill the milk, and worked hard to bring home *B*s and *C*s went unrecognized and unappreciated. Instead of feeling capable and important, you may have concluded that you were small, that what you thought or said usually didn't count for much, that you were slow, or clumsy, or dumb—that in some important way you simply could not live up to your parents' expectations.

Here is just a small sampling of the kinds of statements your parents may have made, statements which discouraged you from trying to belong in a cooperative, useful way. "Don't bother me now; can't you see I'm busy!" "You could do it if you would only apply yourself." "Stop acting so stupid." "Be nice." "You look terrible." "You did a pretty good job, but it could have been better." "You bad boy." And, of course, the *always discouraging*, "Why can't you be as smart (generous, friendly, good, hard-working) as your older sister (younger sister, older brother, younger brother)!"

When you were young, if your immature and inexperienced efforts to contribute and belong were criticized, ridiculed, punished, ignored, or didn't live up to expectations, you began to turn to other, *partially successful* ways of finding a place for yourself. These limited ways of belonging are the Troublemakers. Let's examine each one in turn.

PRESTIGE SEEKING

How It Gets Started. One of the most common ways you may have tried to belong, and perhaps succeeded by doing so, was to *call attention to yourself*. By keeping people busy and occupied with you, you made yourself feel *important* and *valuable*.

Most children deserve and get a great deal of attention. They quickly learn which behaviors get attention and which do not. Generally speaking, children will continue to demonstrate behaviors that get a strong, positive reaction from their parents. And many children will continue to demonstrate behaviors that get a strong, *negative* reaction from their parents. They will tend *not* to repeat behaviors that get a mild or disinterested reaction.

If you were lucky, you may have had a particular characteristic or ability that was much valued by your

55

parents. Maybe you were the only girl or only boy. Maybe you had dimples or were athletic, musical, or artistic. Maybe you were unusually intelligent, brave, sweet, or good. If you were unlucky, you had these characteristics in reverse! You may have been clumsy, unattractive, a slow learner, cowardly, temperamental, or bad. Negative behavior gets even more attention and concern! Regardless or whether your behaviors were considered good or bad, what you may have been trying to communicate is, "Be interested in me. Be concerned with me. Show me that I count. Show me that my presence matters to you. Show me that I am too important to be ignored."

From this point of view, it is easy to see that it didn't particularly matter whether your parents' reaction was positive or negative, just as long as it was strong and showed interest. When your parents used such statements as, "Look, dear, isn't he/she cute (adorable, clever, smart)," or "Show Grandma how high you can count," or "I'll bet you're the best reader in the whole class," they reinforced the idea that you *counted*, were *important*—that people were noticing and admiring you.

But attention is not enough. For *Prestige Seeking* to develop, the element of *competition* must eventually creep in. If you think that gaining prestige or status is important, you probably were brought up in a home where there were open or hidden comparisons between you and someone else. *Comparative words* were probably used often, words like *better*, *best*, *as good as*, *as smart as*, *worse*, *worst*— in fact, *any* words ending in *er* or *est*. You may have been compared to a brother, sister, or cousin; to children in your school or neighborhood; or even to one of your parents. Maybe you heard, "Why can't you be as (fill in the blank with a quality) as (fill in the blank with a person's name)!" Don't be fooled. This is not a question! What it means is, "I am disappointed in you." "You are failing to live up to my expectations." "I am embarrassed by your behavior (or lack of achievement)."

On the other hand, maybe *you* were the high achiever, the one with the accomplishments, and someone else was being compared unfavorably with *you*. The point is that you were especially praised for your accomplishments when they were *better than someone else's*. And you were criticized and blamed when your shortcomings were *worse than someone else's*. As a result, you concluded that in order to find a place where you could belong, you would have to acquire status and position in whatever area you could. Here are some possibilities: the best income, the highest academic degree, the most precision, the most possessions, the best position in the company, or the most accomplished children. You might even want to be recognized as the best *sufferer*—the person who wants to be *admired* for his or her patience and forgiveness.

Some people who, in fact, have little confidence in their own abilities acquire a sense of superiority or prestige not through their own accomplishments or achievements but by putting down or belittling the achievements of others. In this way, they appear to themselves to be "better" or "higher" by comparison.

Personality Profile of the Prestige Seeker

If you are a Prestige Seeker, you have begun to measure your accomplishments not in terms of how they contribute but in terms of *how well you compare with other people*. You want to be, or think you may already be, better than others or the best (at least in some ways). You want to be *admired* and to be sure that your accomplishments and contributions are adequately recognized. You are full of good ideas and suggestions about how people can do better, be better, or accomplish more. These suggestions are not always welcomed with enthusiasm, which confuses and upsets you. You enjoy being *right* and feel comfortable when guided by clear rules and procedures. You live by high moral standards and may even be "too" helpful or "too" forgiving. (Only a person in a morally superior position can "forgive.") It bothers you very much to be ignored, proven wrong, unappreciated, or not given enough credit for your efforts. You are likely to be a perfectionist and impatient with your own mistakes and those of others. When things go wrong, you want to blame someone else and will go to great lengths to avoid being criticized or found wrong.

Are You a Prestige Seeker? Most people's decision diagrams do *not* contain Prestige Seeking items, but to test whether Prestige-Seeking could be a factor in your decision making, as yourself these questions:

> Could it be that I very much want recognition or admiration for the things I do?
>
> Could it be that I want to impress others with how good (patient, accomplished, rich,

58

strong, intelligent, etc.) I am (or my children are)?

Could it be that I want people to acknowledge that I am right?

If you answered yes to any one of them, then some of the items below may belong in your *Road of Life* Diagram. If they did not actually appear, *should* they have? Do they "feel familiar"? Are they asking to be circled? (Go ahead and do it. I won't tell.)

want them to know (to impress them/him/her with) who I am (what I can do, what I own, what I have achieved)

want to be one of the best (the best, the top) salesmen (students, drummers, mothers, etc.)

show (prove) that I can take it (that I'm tough, strong, capable)

makes me look "cool" (like I can take things in stride)

would be disappointed (I expect/deserve more, better treatment)

would have to admit that he/she/they were right

need to have their mistakes pointed out (shown where they're wrong)

shows that I forgive him/her/them

The words "show," "prove," "impress," "right," and "wrong" are typical Prestige Seeker words. Prestige items show that you want or need to be *noticed*, *looked up to*, or *agreed with*. If your accomplishment or achievement is enjoyed for its own sake or for what it contributes, then it belongs in the Enhancer category. But if you must show off the accomplishment or prove the point, and this has become *more important* than contributing, then the item is a Troublemaker.

Prestige Seekers Are Afraid

Every Troublemaker stems from *fear*. If you are a Prestige Seeker, you have come to believe that belonging and coping *require* status and superiority. The worst situation, therefore, is one in which you feel insignificant, humiliated, or unrecognized. The Prestige Seeker is terrified of being *ignored*. His or her great accomplishments and achievements are, in large part, designed to ward off that horrible, intolerable feeling of being ignored.

Your special fear can get you into big trouble. While status and achievements may *seem* to be strengths, they are in fact your very weakest spots and the areas in which you are most vulnerable should anyone have the desire to defeat or manipulate you. The key to understanding how Prestige Seeking acts as a Troublemaker is to realize that:

- In order for you to feel *superior*, someone else has to appear *inferior*.

- In order for you to appear *right*, someone else has to appear *wrong*.

- In order for you to be in the *spotlight*, someone else has to be in the *shadow*.

Few people are willing to be put in the position of feeling inferior, wrong, or unimportant. They will retaliate in subtle ways—by being argumentative and picky, by poking holes in your ideas, or by trying to make you look ridiculous. Or, they may simply withhold the admiration and agreement they sense you crave. They can reduce you to ashes by using such phrases as, "Big deal," "What a rotten idea," or, "I don't agree with you; I think you're wrong."

Why Prestige Seeking
Doesn't Lead to Total Happiness

Prestige Seeking has probably spurred you on to a position of achievement and success. And you *do* have a sense of belonging. Yet, it is a *limited* way of belonging. Why?

First, your attention is *primarily* focused on how likely your behavior is to lead to recognition and agreement. Your attention is only *secondarily* focused on meeting the objective needs of the situation. Other people feel "used," not respected. They think that you don't value their contributions. (Do you?) This leads to the reactions described above.

Second, if your need for prestige is great, you may be reluctant to participate when you are uncertain of receiving the recognition you desire or when you will be open to criticism. Therefore, you *limit your opportunities* for happiness since you cannot be the best, the most right, the most superior in every single one of your activities. You cannot *always* get the recognition you crave. People have other things to do.

Third, and most important, you are putting the control of your happiness in other people's hands by needing *specific* reactions from them, namely, admiration, agreement, or envy. You are allowing them to control your path to belonging and security as if they managed a tollbooth on the route. You drive up, put your "accomplishment" into the basket, and they judge how much it's "worth." You are allowing *them* to determine whether you get the green light: "Good enough. You may pass," or the red light: "Not sufficient. Pay more."

When you use your talent and creativity simply to make a contribution, you usually evoke genuinely good feelings toward yourself, you greatly expand your opportunities for happiness, and you take the means of achieving a feeling of belonging *back into your own hands*.

The Classic Conflict for Prestige Seekers

When people seek counseling or psychotherapy, they have usually come face to face with the Disadvantages which are the *direct outcomes* of their own particular Troublemaker. Without giving up its Advantages they wish, as if by magic, to make its Disadvantages vanish. Yet I want to assure you that the reason a Troublemaker is so persuasive and has such a powerful hold on people is that it brings very enjoyable *rewards* as well. The *Road of Life* Diagram which follows shows both the possible Advantages and Disadvantages of *Prestige Seeking*. A few, most, or all of them may apply to you. Or you may think of items

I have not included. Both sides of the diagram represent valid alternatives. Selections are strictly a matter of choice.

The Classic Conflict for the Prestige Seeker is:

BEING ADMIRED/BEING RIGHT *versus*
CLOSENESS/INTIMACY

Choice: Act mainly to gain prestige/ be right	Choice: Act mainly to meet the needs of the situation
Advantages	**Advantages:**
feel superior	contributions are valued as contributions, not monuments
feel "one up"	
feel important/impressive	associates become more creative in coming up with ideas and solving problems
have a position of status	
am looked up to	under less pressure to "perform"
am envied by some people	chance of being able to take criticism more in stride
get lots of recognition and approval	
have achieved/accomplished a great deal	chance of being better liked
feel knowledgeable	chance of feeling closer to people
feel self-assured	chance of being loved
am considered successful	can encourage and inspire others
have influence over others	

people feel respected
by me
chance of being better
able to show my
love

Disadvantages:

feel put upon
people say I'm aloof/
distant/righteous
people resent me and
my accomplish-
ments
am sometimes disliked
spouse (associates/
children) find
subtle ways to
"bring me down"
people feel they can't
live up to my high
standards
people get irritated,
annoyed, fed up
with me
feel pressure to "know
everything"
people feel I don't
trust them to do
good work
shattered by blame or
criticism

Disadvantages:

risk having to share
credit with others
for good work/
ideas
risk having other
people's mistakes
reflect poorly on
me
feel less important
risk feeling less certain
of myself
risk feeling less self-
confident
risk losing influence
over others (others
may follow their
own advice instead
of mine)
risk having to admit
that you were
wrong/made a
mistake

If you want what *Prestige Seeking* gets you, you lose the right to complain about its Disadvantages.

If you want what *Meeting the needs of the situation* gets you, you lose the right to complain about *its* Disadvantages.

POWER SEEKING

How It Gets Started. Every human being is born with a strong desire to master things, to accomplish, to make a mark on the world ("Kilroy was here"). As a growing child, you learned to manipulate your body and objects to make them do as you wished. If you discovered that these efforts to master or have control over *things* were not successful or did not lead to a feeling of belonging and security, you searched around for some other avenue of mastery and control. This may have turned out to be control of other *people*.

You quickly noticed that your parents seemed to have a good deal of control and influence over *you*! They picked you up and moved you here or there, they got you to do as they wished (through reason or force), and they had at hand a large store of techniques to "make" you do what they wanted you to do.

But one of the first ways *you* learned to "control" people was to say no. When you said no for the first time, you discovered a remarkable tool for self-assertion and exerting influence over others. The stage was immediately set for you to learn one of life's most important lessons:

IN OUR WORLD, THIS IS *WHO* GETS HER/HIS WAY (IS IN CONTROL), AND THIS IS *HOW* SHE/HE GETS IT.

The reaction your parents had to your first no (or second or three hundred and seventy-fourth) was critical in teaching you that lesson.

When you said no:

If your parents were intimidated, you learned: I can get my way (get Power) by refusing to comply. Parent backs down.

If your parents tried to distract you, you learned: Parent can get his/her way by taking my mind off the real issue.

If your parents used reason and persuasion, you learned either: Parent can get his/her way by being more clever and logical, *or* parent and I listen to each other and work out a suitable agreement.

If your parents resisted at first, then gave in under continuing pressure, you learned: I can get my way (get Power) by holding out long enough and refusing to give in. (Incidentally, this can produce an extremely stubborn and willful person.)

If one parent reacted one way and the other in a different way, you learned: I can get my way by approaching the right person.

If your parents responded with equal or greater force, either verbal or physical, you learned: The person who is the most violent wins.

These were powerful lessons but nowhere near as powerful as those you learned simply by keeping your eyes open. You figured out how to "win" by observing and imitating what was *really* important to your parents. You were an excellent observer (as all children are), and you were quick to pick up differences, if any, between what they *said* was important and what they actually *did*. Suppose you were punished for fighting with a brother or sister and strictly warned never to raise a hand against anyone. Then you *observed* what happened when they told *you* to do something . . . and you didn't do it. Suppose they told you that when people disagree, they need to sit down like rational human beings and talk it over. Then you observed what happened when Mom and Dad disagreed. How did that get settled? In a calm, rational way?

You were no fool. You learned that Power works! What you didn't learn at the time is that Power comes with a price tag. It only works when the other person is afraid of you. As soon as the other stops being afraid, you've had it.

If you found that *Power Seeking* is important in your life, it is likely that in your family there was a lot of "telling others what to do and not to do." And resistance to these commands produced strong, negative reactions. These reactions may have been obvious, such as threats or shows of force (spanking, grounding, taking away privileges), or the pressure may have been more hidden, as in silent anger, coldness, or "looks."

Personality Profile of the Power Seeker

If you are a Power Seeker, you have begun to measure your behavior not in terms of how it contributes but in terms of *who is winning and who is losing* the Power Game. You need to have things under control and are concerned about losing control. You like to make things happen and to have a strong sense of responsibility. You are likely to be in a position of supervision or leadership because you are good at keeping track of things and seeing to it that people do what they are supposed to do. You are not comfortable in situations where you cannot be the boss or be in charge.

It is hard for you to let loose or to show your feelings because you never know what might happen. And you don't like surprises. It frustrates you to no end when people won't do what you want; you hate to be contradicted. To you, "Because I said so," is sufficient explanation. You may even be tempted to *get even* with people who challenge you or disobey you.

Sometimes you are on the other side of Power. Maybe someone is trying to control or dominate *you*. You can be at least as strong as, and probably much stronger than, that person in fighting back or resisting. In fact, you are a *master of resistance*. You are willing to give up success, achievement, pleasure, and happiness in order to show someone, "you can't make me!" (Guess what. They can't.)

Are you a Power Seeker? Most people's decision diagrams do *not* contain Power Seeking items, but they should! Of all the Troublemakers, Power Seeking probably does more to harm relationships between people than any other. It is the King of Troublemakers. To test whether *Power Seeking* is a factor in your decision making, ask yourself these questions:

> Could it be that I am trying to make something happen (or to make someone do something) by applying pressure or force?

> Could it be that I want to show someone I can do what I
> want and he/she can't stop me?
>
> Could it be that I want to show someone he/she can't make
> me do what I don't want to do?

If you answered yes to any one of them, then some of the items below may have appeared in your *Road of Life* Diagram. If they did not appear, *should* they have? Do they "feel familiar"? Are they asking to be circled?

make him/her them:
get him/her/them to:
see to it that he/she/
they: } listen (obey, do as I say, show respect for me, do it my way, learn a lesson, get the message, go along with my plans/ ideas/ efforts)

my job/duty/responsi-
bility to make him/
her/them: } listen (obey, do as I say, show respect for me, do it my way, learn a lesson, get the message, go along with my plans/ideas/efforts

because I said so (because I'm the boss, in charge, the one who "wears the pants")

have something to bribe him/her/them with (hold over his/her/their head)

he/she/they would (might) take advantage of the situation

would get the blame (gets the blame onto someone else)

puts me in a situation for being (for getting out of being, for showing I won't be) manipulated

get back at (get even with) him/her/them

no one's going to push me around (force me to do anything)

The words "make," "get," "force," and "see to it" are the typical Power Seeker words. Power items show that what you want or need is to be *complied with*, to be *acknowledged as the boss*, or to be *obeyed* (preferably without a lot of hassle and with full understanding that you are The Authority).

If your leadership and influence are used in an encouraging way and for the mutual benefit of all involved, yourself included, then these items belong in the Enhancer category. But if you *must* be in a position of authority or you *must* feel in control, and these needs have become *more important* than contributing, then the item is a Troublemaker.

Power Seekers Are Afraid

If you are a Power Seeker, you have come to believe that belonging and coping *require* being in control, staying in command, and being responsible (for everything). You are terrified of feeling weak, powerless, out of control; of being disobeyed; or letting someone get away with something.

Your special fear can get you into big trouble. While control and command may *seem* to be strengths, they are your weakest spots and the areas in which you are most vulnerable to defeat. The key to understanding how *Power Seeking* works as a Troublemaker is to realize that:

- In order for you to be able to dominate, someone else has to be *willing to* submit.

- In order for you to be in control, someone else has to be *willing to* be controlled.

- In order for you to *win*, someone else has to *lose*.

- In order for you to have your way, someone else has to be *willing to* give in.

In fact, your "power" over others goes *only*, and *exactly*, as far as the other person's *willingness* to be in a subordinate position. And that person is willing to stay in a subordinate position only when he/she fully *agrees* with your right to dominate, or when the consequences of defying you are even worse. Most people, if they do *not* accept your "Right to Rule," will eventually find the subordinate position intolerable. *Power Seeking* is the King of Troublemakers because it undermines the King of Desires—personal freedom. In the worst cases, a deep hatred can develop between the controller and the person he or she is trying to control.

If you are a Power Seeker, you have probably found that people tend to respond to you in one of these ways:

(1) There are those who enjoy being told what to do and who are glad to be free of responsibility.

(2) There are those who will do as you say because they *enjoy* pleasing you.

(3) There are those who see obedience itself as a value and their way of belonging is to conform closely to rules and regulations.

(4) There are those who will do as you say because they are afraid of your anger or because they don't want to lose what you can take away from them.

(5) There are those who respond negatively, but in a passive way. They do a bad job, they make mistakes, they "forget." If you want them to do something *now*; they will move slowly and lazily, driving you to distraction. If you are intent on their getting good grades in school, they will bring home *D*s and *E*s. If you are fanatic about cleanliness and orderliness, they will leave messes in the most conspicuous and embarrassing places. Their behavior shouts, "You can't make me!"

(6) And there are those who respond negatively, but in an active way. They fight back. They are rebellious. They defy you in precisely the ways that will upset you the most. You give them a command, and they argue. You tell them to be in at eleven, and they saunter in at four. You tell them you can't stand those hideous, dirty, worn-out clothes, and they wear them every single day.

You are reduced to ashes when they say, "No, I won't," "You can't stop me," "You can't make me," or (silently), "Oh, yeah? I'll show you." Then they go ahead and show you.

Why Power Seeking Doesn't Lead to Total Happiness

Power Seeking has probably spurred you on to a position of leadership, influence, and responsibility. And you *do* have a sense of belonging. Why is it a *limited* way of belonging?

First, your attention is *primarily* focused on how likely it is that your behavior will lead to a feeling of control, to being in charge and getting other people's "cooperation." (Let's face it. What you really want is obedience.) Your attention is only *secondarily* on meeting the objective needs of the situation. Other people feel pressured, manipulated, powerless, trapped, and ineffective. This leads to the reaction described above.

Second, if your need for power is great, you may be reluctant to participate when you feel uncertain about reaching a dominant or controlling position. You especially don't like to play second fiddle to, or take orders from, someone whose authority you don't recognize. You have *limited your opportunities* for happiness, since you cannot be the leader, the head, the boss in every single one of your activities. You cannot always have the dominance you crave. Other people will resist you, defy you, and eventually overpower you.

Third, and most important, by needing a specific reaction from other people you are putting the power over your happiness in their hands. How do *they* really control your tollgate? You drive up, put your "authority" into the basket, and they judge it. You may get the green light: "Yes, I accept your *right* to tell me what to do. You may pass." Or, you may get the red light: "I do *not* accept your right to tell me what to do! Who do you think you are anyway?" As you turn around, you may get a swift kick in the behind for good measure.

When you see your organizational skills and leadership ability simply to make a contribution, you usually evoke genuinely good feelings toward yourself, you greatly expand your opportunities for happiness, and you take the means of finding a place for yourself *back into your own hands*.

The Classic Conflict for Power Seekers

Power Seekers *often* come face to face with the Disadvantages of their Troublemaker. But the Advantages are enjoyable and very hard to give up. They are . . . well . . . *powerful*! The *Road of Life* Diagram below shows both the possible Advantages and Disadvantages of Power Seeking. A few, most, or all of them may apply to you. Or, you may think of items that I have not included. Both sides of the diagram represent valid alternatives. It is strictly a matter of choice.

The Classic Conflict for the Power Seeker is:
BEING DOMINANT/IN CONTROL *VERSUS*
BEING LIKED/GAINING COOPERATION

| Choice: Act mainly to gain control/ dominance | Choice: Act mainly to meet the needs of the situation |

Advantages:

feel influential

enjoy freedom to make decisions

advance rapidly in my job

have my way

feel that things are "under control" (usually)

can avoid feeling controlled by others

have a strong sense of responsibility

capable of getting a lot done

able to intimidate others

feel well organized

have a good feeling for the "big picture"

have a good mind for details

make things work efficiently

Advantages:

chance of being genuinely liked

chance of being loved

decrease in stress and tension

feel relaxed/calm

opens avenues for true friendship

decrease in psychosomatic symptoms

others become more interested in helping than resisting

fighting, arguing, and deliberate incompetence of others lessens or disappears

feel less burdened with the whole load

potential for *sharing* work/responsibilities

chance of uncovering/developing skills, abilities, sense of responsibility in others

Disadvantages:

often not liked, even hated

often feel angry

sometimes feel defeated, persecuted, misunderstood

feel surrounded by

Disadvantages:

risk feeling less "on top of things" there may be mistakes

details may be overlooked

risk of being held responsible for

incompetents

often accused of manipulating

resisted and defied by others

associates, subordinates, spouse, children seem irresponsible

risk getting "fired" (from your job, marriage, responsibilities) because you are too hard to get along with

often feel hassled or blocked by other people

may be considered impatient, irritable, bad tempered, or "having no feelings"

fear that you, or things, may get out of control

often feel unrewarded, overburdened, unappreciated for hard work

may handle orders from others poorly or with resistance (but if you acknowledge the other clearly to have superior power, then may be extremely obedient)

prone to tension and psychosomatic symptoms (partic-

other people's mistakes

work may not be done as efficiently

people will want to do things differently (in their own ways)

risk feeling less useful/ needed

risk feeling controlled or manipulated by others

have to change style, using persuasion and requests rather than commands and intimidation

risk not getting as much done (pace of work slows down)

risk having to share feeling of influence

have to share decision making/have to compromise

may feel less organized

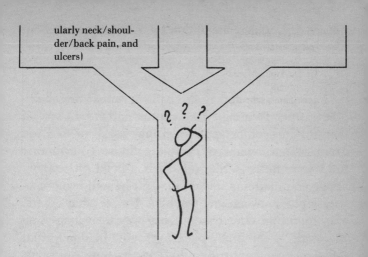

ularly neck/shoul-
der/back pain, and
ulcers)

If you want what *Power Seeking* gets you, you lose the right
to complain about its Disadvantages.

If you want what *Meeting the needs of the situation* gets
you, you lose the right to complain about *its* Disadvantages.

Pleasing Others

How It Gets Started. Pleasing Others is probably
the most common way of seeking a place of belonging
and security. And it is the Troublemaker most often
found in *combination* with the others. Few people *do
not* at one time or another sacrifice practical concerns, pleasure, their own self-respect, or even their
"word" in order to please someone. Pleasing pervades
human relationships. The fear of hurting, displeasing, or angering another is a very powerful factor in
most, if not almost all, decisions which have an impact on someone else. Some people feel the need to
please only one particular person. Others want to

please certain people but don't particularly care about the rest. Still others are terrified of displeasing *anyone*.

Parents value and praise behaviors that are obedient and conforming. It gave your parents a sense of control and competence when they asked or told you to do something and you actually did it! Your mother told your father, "She was such a good girl today." Your grandparents said, "Oh, isn't he well behaved—never gives anyone any trouble." By pleasing others, you found an effective and *easy* way to belong. You decided, "I can find a place for myself by doing what other people want me to do." At the time you made that decision, you were probably so young that your own personality, your own unique approach to life, had not yet developed. But it didn't matter then. You felt as though you had found The Way.

Your parents gave you the lesson that the most important thing about your behavior was what other people thought of it. They probably made statements like, "I'm so proud of you," "You're so sweet," "Isn't he a nice boy," "Don't do that, it will hurt Mommy's feelings," "That's naughty," "What will other people think?", or they resorted to the ultimate threat, "If you do that again, I won't love you anymore."

Personality Profile of the Pleaser

If you are a Pleaser, you find yourself choosing actions not for their genuine value, but for the *effect* they will have on others, especially on their *opinion of you*. You sometimes feel that you are in a cage, barred in by Fear: Fear of public opinion, Fear of displeasing someone, Fear of getting someone mad at you. You have your eyes closely fixed on people to judge their reactions to you. And you torture yourself endlessly with the question, "How am I doing?"

You work hard to "read" people so you can figure out exactly what they want . . . and then you do it. Even when your efforts to please are unsuccessful, you are reluctant to give up. You try and try and try. You are quite hurt by criticism and disapproval, and your usual reaction is to try to do better next time. You want to be thought of as a nice person and are devastated when someone whose opinion you value gets angry or upset with you. You realize how vulnerable you are to fear and disappointment, but you don't know what to do about it. You change your mind and actions often to meet the expectations of others and to gain their approval. You feel confused and unsure of yourself. You may even feel that you don't know who *YOU* are anymore.

You feel that people can easily manipulate you, and you often feel taken advantage of. You are surprised and bewildered when people deliberately or accidentally hurt you. You may think, "Why are they doing this to me?"

Are you a Pleaser? Many people's decision diagrams contain one or more Pleasing items. To test whether *Pleasing Others* is a factor in your decision making, ask yourself these questions:

> Could it be that I want very much to be liked, accepted, or approved of?
>
> Could it be that I want very much to keep people from getting angry at me?

> Could it be that I very much want people to have a good
> opinion of me?

If you answered "Yes" to any one of them, then some
of the items below may have appeared in your *Road of
Life* Diagram. If they did not appear, *should* they
have? Do they "feel familiar"? Are they asking to be
circled?

he/she/they will get angry at me (upset, mad,
furious, p——d off, hate me)

he/she/they might eventually like me (accept
me, approve of me, make me more popular)

might lose the friendship/love I have now

afraid of what people will think (say, gossip
about)

want to make him/her/them happy

want people to think of me as nice (don't like to
be the bad guy)

would (would not) be living up to his/her/their
expectations (image, what they want me to do)

he/she/they don't want me to do that (don't like
it when I do that)

don't want to put pressure on him/her/them

The words "will like," "won't like," "be mad at,"
"won't approve of," are typical *Pleasing* words. *Pleasing* items show that you want or need to fit in, to be
accepted and included, and especially to be liked. If
you do your Pleasing because it simply makes you feel

good to make others happy, then it probably belongs in the Enhancer category. But if you *must* be liked at all costs, if you *must* avoid being disapproved of or criticized no matter what, then it's probably a Troublemaker.

Pleasers Are Afraid

If you are a Pleaser, you have come to believe that belonging and security require figuring out what other people want from you and then doing it to their satisfaction. The message you give to others is, "You and what you think are more important than I am, or what I think." What's the problem with that? The problem is that *they believe you!* The longer you continue in this pattern, the more they increase their estimation of themselves and their desires/opinions and the less they value *you* and *your* desires/opinions. This is interesting. You are terrified of being rejected. But what is the logical outcome of the *Pleasing* pattern? You eventually feel completely worthless and—you guessed it—*rejected*.

Your special fear can get you into big trouble. People who wish to control or dominate you have an easy time of it. All they have to do is simply withhold their approval or pleasure. This will send you scurrying about to find some other way to please them. They can continue disapproving until the ante is very high indeed. In the worst cases, you end up not only *not pleasing*, but you risk losing the *respect* of others and, in some cases, respect for yourself.

The key to understanding how *Pleasing* works as a Troublemaker is to realize that:

- When you need to please, someone else acquires a false and inflated sense of importance.

- When you need to please, someone else acquires a false sense of power and control.

- When you need to please, others come to disrespect your ideas, opinions, and general worth.

Why Pleasing Doesn't Lead to Total Happiness

We have seen that a true and deep sense of belonging comes from an appreciation of the need for mutual contributions, contributions which benefit both the individual and the group. Prestige Seeking and Power Seeking tempt people to take unfair advantage of others (the group). *Pleasing* tempts other people to take unfair advantage of you. Pleasing doesn't lead to happiness because it puts you in a dependent position, it unbalances relationships, and it is unstable.

First, your attention is *primarily* on how your behavior is *being received*. (*Was it right*, did they like it, does he/she still want/accept me, are they talking about me?) Your attention is only *secondarily* on meeting the objective needs of the situation. Other people feel superior to you, manipulative, and disrespectful of you.

Second, since you often act as a mirror to other people, you find that you must literally change your personality from hour to hour. Or, you inevitably find that in order to please one person you may have to *displease another*. These challenges may be too great for you, so you try to withdraw from people or social situations when you cannot be absolutely sure of being

82

liked or accepted. You therefore greatly *limit your opportunities* for happiness because you cannot read everyone perfectly, because you can never simultaneously please two people who want different things from you, and because you are losing touch with what *you* want out of life.

Third, and most important, by *needing* their signs of liking and approval, you are putting the power over your happiness in the hands of other people.

How are you letting others control your tollgate? You drive up and put your "offering" into the basket for them to judge. You may get the *special* green light treatment: The gatekeeper actually *comes out* and gives you a pat on the head, saying, "I hereby approve. You may pass." But you will probably get the red light: "You *know* I can't stand purple. Now go back and see if you can find a blue one." (And so you do.) "Actually, now that I see it, I'm not really too fond of the blue either. Maybe . . . yes, maybe a green would do." (Back you go and return to try again.) "Green? Did I say *green*?" And so on. I'll tell you a secret. Some people's tollgates *cannot be opened up*! They have rusted shut from lack of use. There. Now you know.

When you use your understanding of people (which is great, because you've had a lot of practice) and your good will (which is abundant) simply to make a contribution, you produce genuinely good feelings toward you, you greatly expand your opportunities for participation and happiness, and you act to meet the needs of the situation without sacrificing your self-respect.

The Classic Conflict for the Pleaser.

Pleasers often come face to face with the Disadvantages of their Troublemaker later in life. It is as if they have been thinking, "Well, if I just persist long enough, surely I'll eventually feel happy." At some point they realize that years and years of failing to *respect themselves* is *not* bringing happiness. It's not that they *want* to give up pleasing others. They just don't know how to bring their need to do for others into balance with the need to do for themselves. The diagram below may help. It shows both the Advantages and Disadvantages of *Pleasing*. Both sides of the diagram represent valid alternatives. It is strictly a matter of choice.

The Classic Conflict for the Pleaser is:

PLEASING SOMEONE ELSE *versus* PLEASING OR ENHANCING YOURSELF

Choice: Act mainly to please others	Choice: Act mainly to meet the needs of the situation
Advantages:	**Advantages:**
am well liked	have a chance to express own true ideas and opinions
am considered an agreeable employee	can work toward own goals
usually produce satisfactory work	chance of accomplishing own goals
am accepted and welcomed into groups	chance of gaining self-respect
have a lot of friends	

thought of as sweet
and nice
others feel needed by
me
feel like a good person
am considered
thoughtful
am considered easy to
get along with

Disadvantages:

feel like a pushover,
marshmallow,
doormat
do things I don't want
to do (can't say no)
am often not listened
to
am easily led/influ-
enced
am overly conforming
am often not respected
by others
have a poor sense of
myself and what I
want
have a low self-esteem
may be physically or
mentally abused
feel that my destiny is
out of my hands

chance of gaining the
respect of others
have a better opinion
of myself
develop a sense of
inner strength
feel that destiny is in
my own hands

Disadvantages:

risk not being liked as
much (or liked at
all)
risk not being accepted
by others
risk people's getting
upset, angry,
argumentative
don't feel as needed
don't feel like a nice
person
feel guilty
people may resist my
attempts to assert
myself
people may consider
me disagreeable or
obstinate
people may call me
selfish

> If you want what *Pleasing* gets you, you lose the right to complain about its Disadvantages.
>
> If you want what *Meeting the needs of the situation* gets you, you lose the right to complain about *its* Disadvantages.

Protection Seeking:

How It Gets Started. Two different types of upbringings seem to be in the backgrounds of people who later find that their decisions are governed by the desire for Protection.

In the first case, you may have been overprotected and prevented from really spreading your wings and flying. A sense of competence comes from knowing what your needs are (knowing what will make you feel good and strong) and then having the *knowledge* and *confidence* to go after them directly. If your parents were exceptionally good at supplying your needs and were anxious to please you, you barely had enough time to realize you *had* a need, let alone to take the initiative to fulfill it. With this step, they accidentally, and with the best of intentions, prevented you from gaining *knowledge about yourself.* You weren't quite sure *what* you wanted, and you certainly would not know how to get it even if you *were.* As soon as you felt vaguely uncomfortable, some solution would magically appear.

In addition, your parents may have unwittingly given you the impression that you were delicate, fragile, or weak. "Here, honey, let me do that for you." "Be careful, or you'll hurt yourself." "You're too little to do that." "Now be sure to call as soon as you get to your friend's house. I'm afraid for you in that neighborhood." In this way, they accidentally, again with the best of intentions, prevented you from developing *confidence in yourself*. They accidentally gave you the messages: "You can't handle it." "That's too hard for you." "Life is difficult, dangerous, and painful, and I don't think you have what it takes to make it without a lot of help."

In the second case, your parents may have given you quite a different type of message. "You are great," "You are wonderful," "No mountain is too high for you to climb," "You can't fail." This type of upbringing denies that effort, struggle, mistakes, and yes, failure are absolutely necessary on any path to success and accomplishment. A Protection Seeker brought up in this kind of atmosphere comes to a specific conclusion. Let's see how it works.

As a child you first *evaluated* or *graded* the expectations that were made of you. Then you evaluated or graded how well you thought you were already living up to those expectations. (By the way, these evaluations often had no relationship to what was actually going on. They reflected only how *you felt* about the situation and about yourself.) Finally, if it seemed to you that you were falling short, you had to make one more judgment: "How *likely* is it that I *can* live up to their expectations and my own?" In other words, you had to estimate your *ability to improve*. Your final conclusion was based on the combination of these three elements.

Some possibilities are diagrammed on pg. 88-90.

Personality Profile of the Protection Seeker

If you are a Protection Seeker, you are fairly certain you can't perform as well as you would like to, or as well as others expect you to, and you'd just as soon not

HOW A HIGH ACHIEVER MIGHT SEE THINGS

My parents' expectations for me seemed:	I felt that my performance was:	I felt that my ability to improve was:	Conclusion:
extremely high	(superior)	outstanding	I can do it and do it very well.
(high)	excellent	(excellent)	
medium	average	all right	
low	below average	pretty low	
very low	poor	just about nonexistent	

HOW AN AVERAGE ACHIEVER MIGHT SEE THINGS

My parents' expectations for me seemed:	I felt that my performance was:	I felt that my ability to improve was:	Conclusion:
extremely high	superior	outstanding	I can probably do O.K., but I'm going to have to work for it.
high	excellent	(excellent)	
(medium)	(average)	all right	
low	below average	pretty low	
very low	poor	just about nonexistent	

HOW A PROTECTION SEEKER MIGHT SEE THINGS

My parents' expectations for me seemed:	I felt that my performance was:	I felt that my ability to improve was:	Conclusion:
extremely high	superior	outstanding	**I'll never live up to my parents' expectations, and I don't want anyone to find out, so I'll just try to be as inconspicuous as I can.**
high	excellent	excellent	
medium	average	all right	
low	**poor**	pretty low	
very low		**just about nonexistent**	

find out for sure. You often put yourself down in advance. You dread problems, especially personal conflicts and confrontations, and you try hard not to make waves. Your mottos are: "Leave well enough alone," "Let sleeping dogs lie," and "Better the mud is at the bottom of the puddle." Even if things are already bad, you believe they will get worse if you intervene or take direct action.

If pushed or pressed to take action, you find excuses why you *cannot* or *should not* be expected to perform. You may have frequent illnesses or accidents. You want constant reassurance that things are going to be all right. You don't make direct demands on other people, although sometimes they have to take over your share of the responsibilities. Your "demand" often is that others just leave you alone or that they don't bother you. You may be a procrastinator. You would like the good things of life, but not if you have to break your neck for them. You prefer work with low rather than high levels of responsibility.

Are you a Protection Seeker? To search for a permanent position of protection and safety is not a common way of seeking belonging, but it is a fairly persistent one. Some people limit their desire for self-protection to a certain few situations, which they try to avoid. For others it has become a total way of life. Some people find *Protection* items in their decision diagrams. To test whether *Protection Seeking* is a factor in your decision making, ask yourself these questions:

> Could it be that I want very much to avoid causing any trouble?
>
> Could it be that I want very much to keep from making waves or rocking the boat?

> Could it be that I want very much to keep people from finding out how inadequate I really am?

If you answered "Yes" to any one of them, then some of the items below may have appeared in your *Road of Life* Diagram. If they did not appear, *should* they have? Do they "feel familiar"? Are they asking to be circled?

don't want to cause trouble (a fuss, anyone to go out of the way, a conflict, a confrontation, an argument, a fight)

stirs up a can of worms (opens Pandora's box)

avoid having to think (worry) about it (deal with it)

may go away by itself if I don't do anything

whatever he/she/they want

he/she/they probably know what's best

would be embarrassed (noticed, self-conscious, ill at ease, mortified

probably turn out badly (wrong)

who needs promotions (good grades, friends, money, love) anyway

I'm no good at (I'm terrible) at driving (cooking, public speaking, saying how I feel, parties, managing money, etc.)

The words "can't," "no good at," or "who needs it anyway" are typical *Protection Seeking* words. If you declare yourself inadequate or inferior in advance, who can expect anything of you? If you claim you don't *need* or *want* something, who can expect you to work for it?

Protection items show that you want to keep things smooth at all costs, that you do not feel confident of having an impact on others, that there are some or many areas where you feel pretty sure you will fail to live up to expectations (yours or someone else's)—so it is probably better and safer just to avoid doing many things. If Protection-type items are present to a reasonable degree and are based on genuine dangers or difficulties in the environment, then they belong in the *Pleasures and Comforts* category. But if they prevent you from participating in a wide variety of activities, keep you from using your talents and abilities, or greatly limit your interactions with people, and if *Protection* has become more important than *participating*, then it is a Troublemaker.

The dotted lines show the *Protection Seeker's* usual paths. While the first type of upbringing leads the *Protection Seeker* to conclude, "I can't," the second type leads him or her to conclude, "I don't want to find out for sure that I can't, so I won't risk trying."

Protection Seekers Are Afraid

Protection Seeking shows that at some point in your childhood, you learned to be *overly cautious* or to *feel unable*. You could feel afraid (or unable) to meet new people, afraid (or unable) to assert yourself, afraid (or unable) to achieve at work or in school, afraid (or unable) to take chances when you could not be sure of the outcome. Regardless of what your specific fear is, the bottom line is the same: you are afraid to risk failure. You are afraid when you feel inadequate. You are afraid when you believe that you don't have what it takes to meet the needs of the situation.

Your Special Fear Can Get You into Big Trouble

You have learned successfully to avoid many situations which would reveal your inadequacies. But life just won't quit, will it? It keeps on putting challenges in front of you, daring you to meet the needs of some very complex and trying situations. No matter how carefully you structure your activities, you still never feel completely safe. Someone always seems to be looking at you, asking or demanding something of you. You are terrified of being *exposed*. Your efforts are designed to ward off that horrible feeling of being embarrassed or held responsible. You are reduced to ashes by someone's saying, "I'm sorry, but you'll have to do it yourself," "You'll have to go in and say something," or "That's not *my* job; it's yours."

The key to understanding how *Protection Seeking* works as a Troublemaker is to realize that:

- in order for you to feel *safe*, someone else has to be willing to *protect you* from challenge, confrontation, and discomfort

- in order for you to *avoid failure*, someone else has to be willing to *excuse you* from, or to take on, responsibilities which rightfully belong to you

- in order for you to *avoid taking risks*, someone else has to be willing to *solve your problems*.

These things make people tired. They feel trapped. They get fed up. Although they may feel sorry for you for a while, few people are willing to take on the position of permanent caretaker. When they finally give up and leave, you are left with few coping skills, little self-confidence, and little experience of the strength and security that comes from participating in a mutually supportive social network.

Why Protection Seeking Doesn't Lead to Total Happiness

Protection Seeking has worked by helping you to feel safe and secure. Yet it is a *limited* way of belonging. Why?

First, your attention is focused *primarily* on how likely you are to succeed in avoiding notice, embarrassment, or exposure. Your attention is focused only *secondarily* on meeting the needs of the situation. Other people may feel that you shirk your duty, that they have to pick up the slack, that you are a burden on their time and energy.

Second, if your need for Protection is great, you are quite reluctant to participate when you feel you may be called on to demonstrate competence, when you think you may be given more responsibility than you feel you can handle, or when there is a risk of failure. You *severely limit* your opportunities for happiness, since only a handful of situations (if any) will satisfy these conditions.

Third, you are putting the power over your happiness almost completely in other people's hands. Here is how you try to slip past them *and* the tollgate in an attempt to seek safety. If you approach the gate directly, you *suspect* that you're going to get the red light: "I'm sorry, but you cannot pass. You haven't put anything in the basket." "Right," you say, "but see what happened is:"

"I lost it."

"Someone stole it from me."

"I was sick in bed and couldn't get it."

"I had some once, but I didn't think it would be enough."

"I had to use it to get through the last gate."

"I had it right here just a minute ago . . . honest."

"How can you expect it from someone like me?"

"How can you expect it after what I've been through?"

Sometimes you'll score a reluctant hit: "Oh, all right, come on through." But usually the gatekeeper just says, "Sorry. No way." In that case, you wait in the distance until he bends over to tie his shoe and then quietly slip under the gate while he's not looking. If he notices and comes after you, you run into the woods and hide under your camouflage cape. Sooner or later he'll give up and go away.

The Protection Seeker's Classic Conflict
Protection Seekers often avoid facing up to the Disadvantages of their Troublemaker, especially if they have continuously found someone who is willing to

protect them and take on some of their responsibilities. Often, it is only when these excessive supports are removed that they are forced to confront the outcomes of their behavior. The diagram below shows the Advantages and Disadvantages of *Protection Seeking*. Both sides of the diagram represent valid alternatives. It is strictly a matter of *choice*.

The Classic Conflict for the Protection Seeker is:

SAFETY *versus* ACCOMPLISHMENT/PERSONAL
GROWTH/MASTERY

Choice: Act mainly to seek protection/ safety	Choice: Act mainly to meet the needs of the situa- tion
Advantages:	**Advantages:**
feel safe have a sense of privacy feel secure considered easygoing feel peaceful considered harmless people don't place a lot of demands on me feel comfortable with (able to handle) the level of responsibility I have now don't feel like I have to participate in activities I don't enjoy or feel com-	accomplish goals advance in profession have a sense of mastery have respect for self have support from friends and family feel competent greater sense of freedom feel in control of own life

fortable with
don't have to live up to
    high expectations
considered patient
can put up with a lot
    without complain-
    ing

Disadvantages:

sometimes feel anxious
    or afraid and don't
    know why
feel that I haven't
    accomplished
    anything worth-
    while
afraid of being over-
    whelmed
can't handle conflict
feel trapped
feel like a victim of
    circumstances
afraid of everything
feel ineffective
feel inferior
others don't value my
    ideas and opinions
feel that other people
    have control of my
    life
can't handle changes

Disadvantages:

people may ask too
    much of me
people will intrude
    with their demands
may not be able to
    handle additional
    responsibilities
risk failing
risk feeling and look-
    ing stupid and
    incompetent
risk feeling embar-
    rassed
quality of work may
    not be up to my (or
    someone else's)
    standards
risk getting into con-
    flicts or confronta-
    tions

If you want what *Protection Seeking* gets you, you lose the right to complain about its Disadvantages.

If you want what *Meeting the needs of the situation* gets you, you lose the right to complain about *its* Disadvantages.

You have nailed your thoughts down and organized them. You have pinpointed *and identified what is most important to you. And you have gained an understanding of whether a Troublemaker may be affecting your decisions—and how. As you go over your items, are you now able to choose in such a way that you get all your WISHES with no WORRIES attached? Can you choose so that you avoid everything you fear* without having to give up anything you *desire*? If so, you will be delighted to learn that your decision is made! If not, well, you have come upon the fourth and last obstacle to decision making.

OBSTACLE FOUR: YOUR DECISION MAKING IS NOT SUCCESSFUL BECAUSE STRONG WISHES OR WORRIES ARE IN BALANCE WITH OPPOSING WISHES OR WORRIES OF APPROXIMATE OR EQUAL VALUE ... AND YOU DON'T KNOW WHAT TO DO ABOUT IT.

You have discovered that you cannot be in two places at once. *YOU CAN'T SIT ON TWO CHAIRS WITH ONE BEHIND!*

Chapter VI. You Can't Sit on Two Chairs with One Behind: The Three Basic Decision Dilemmas

By following the steps in the last chapter, you were able to identify the source of *your* particular decision conflict. Maybe you found that in order to fulfill a pledge, you would have to sacrifice some freedom of choice. Maybe you learned that in order to go after a better job you would have to give up the pleasures of your home and neighborhood. Perhaps you were caught by one of the Troublemakers. For example, in order to take a step toward happiness you would have to admit to someone that you "were wrong," or in order to make a move toward independence you would have to risk someone's getting angry with you.

The Three Basic Decision Dilemmas
All decision conflicts occur for one of ONLY THREE reasons:
  (1) There is something important you are not yet *willing* to GIVE UP
  (2) There is something important you are not yet *willing* to ACCEPT
  (3) There is something you are not yet *willing* to give up AND there is something you are not yet *willing* to accept

---

In this chapter you will discover exactly what *type* of bind you have gotten yourself into. (Some fortunate people learn that they are not in a bind after all!) You will do this by creating a *Value Pattern* based on the WISHES and WORRIES you have already circled.

How to Make a Value Pattern

First, take your pencil and *lightly* draw a box around each *group* of Advantages and Disadvantages. Your *Road of Life* Diagram will then have four boxes, as shown below:

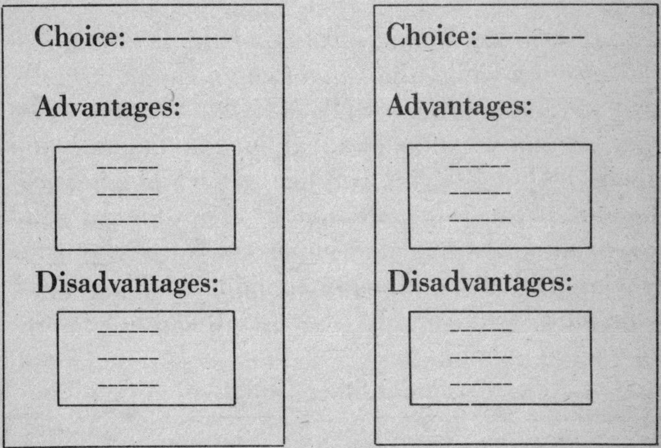

```
┌─────────────────────┐   ┌─────────────────────┐
│ Choice: ────────    │   │ Choice: ────────    │
│                     │   │                     │
│ Advantages:         │   │ Advantages:         │
│      ┌────────┐     │   │      ┌────────┐     │
│      │ ─────  │     │   │      │ ─────  │     │
│      │ ─────  │     │   │      │ ─────  │     │
│      │ ─────  │     │   │      │ ─────  │     │
│      └────────┘     │   │      └────────┘     │
│ Disadvantages:      │   │ Disadvantages:      │
│      ┌────────┐     │   │      ┌────────┐     │
│      │ ─────  │     │   │      │ ─────  │     │
│      │ ─────  │     │   │      │ ─────  │     │
│      │ ─────  │     │   │      │ ─────  │     │
│      └────────┘     │   │      └────────┘     │
└─────────────────────┘   └─────────────────────┘
```

Look over your diagram to see where the circles (your most important Values) are. Some boxes may have no circles at all in them. Some may have a few. Some may have a circle around every single item. No matter *how many* circles are in a box, put your pencil in the middle of it and draw *one* line to the middle of *every other* box that has a circle in it. Your line or lines may be vertical, horizontal, diagonal, or any combination of the three. Here are some examples:

101

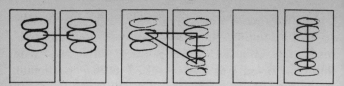

There are six possible *Value Patterns*. Only one of the Patterns shows instantly that a decision has been made. Each of the others points to a specific type of *Decision Dilemma*. If you use the *Road of Life* Diagram many times, you may be surprised at how often you find yourself in the same type of bind.

How to Tell What Your *Value Pattern Means*

Once in a while, the *Value Pattern* shows instantly that you have MADE A DECISION. When one and only one line appears, and that line is a diagonal, you are HOME FREE! I call this pattern the Leaning Ladder, because you are able to climb toward what you want *most* (your most important WISHES) while leaving behind, avoiding, or escaping what you *don't* want most (your worst WORRIES). It looks like this:

The Leaning Ladder

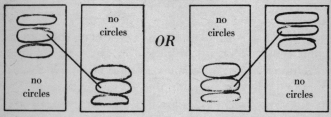

Ginny

A friend of mine discovered a Leaning Ladder when trying to decide which breed of dog to buy.

Ginny liked many of the qualities of each breed (otherwise, of course, she would not have been in conflict), but when the circles popped out it was clear that one breed was better suited to *her* particular needs.

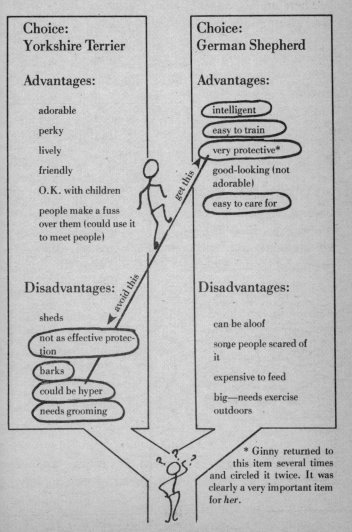

**Choice:
Yorkshire Terrier**

Advantages:

adorable

perky

lively

friendly

O.K. with children

people make a fuss over them (could use it to meet people)

Disadvantages:

sheds

not as effective protection

barks

could be hyper

needs grooming

**Choice:
German Shepherd**

Advantages:

intelligent

easy to train

very protective*

good-looking (not adorable)

easy to care for

Disadvantages:

can be aloof

some people scared of it

expensive to feed

big—needs exercise outdoors

avoid this

get this

* Ginny returned to this item several times and circled it twice. It was clearly a very important item for *her*.

Ginny chose the Shepherd. *You* might have chosen differently.

Ron

Ron was equally delighted by his discovery of a Leaning Ladder when trying to decide between jobs. He had been accepted for two positions, as a postal clerk and as a sales representative. His circles surprised him at first, but the more he thought about it, the more "right" the Leaning Ladder felt.

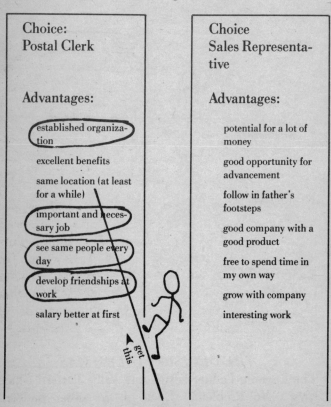

Choice:
Postal Clerk

Advantages:

- established organization
- excellent benefits
- same location (at least for a while)
- important and necessary job
- see same people every day
- develop friendships at work
- salary better at first

get this

Choice
Sales Representative

Advantages:

- potential for a lot of money
- good opportunity for advancement
- follow in father's footsteps
- good company with a good product
- free to spend time in my own way
- grow with company
- interesting work

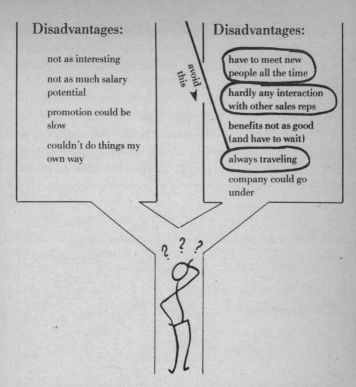

By using the *Road of Life* Diagram, Ron discovered how important it was to him to *see* and *socialize with* his co-workers. He was also more attracted to stability and security than he had previously thought. For Ron, pay, benefits, job interest, and freedom of choice were important but not *as* important as the items that popped out. If your values are in a different *order* of importance from Ron's, *you* will choose differently.

THE DECISION DILEMMAS
The Leaning Ladder is the only Value Pattern which says: "No Problem." Each of the other patterns

points to a specific type of Decision Dilemma. Each says something important about the decision which gives rise to it, and maybe about the way you look at life in general.

Dilemma One

In this pattern, one line connects the *Advantages* on one side of the diagram to the *Advantages* on the other side of the diagram. I call this dilemma *Monkey Bottles*. It looks like this:

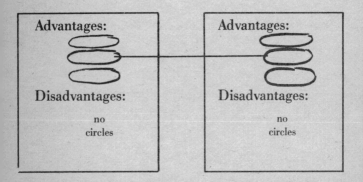

Why Monkey Bottles? Clever hunters in Africa can trap small monkeys quickly, easily, and without violence by taking a narrow-necked glass bottle, putting a piece of fruit in the bottom, and tying it to a stake in the ground. Along comes the monkey. Excited, he reaches in and grabs the fruit. But when he tries to get away, he finds that he cannot get his fist back out through the narrow neck of the bottle! *He refuses to let go of the fruit* and so becomes trapped by his own desires!

If this is your Value Pattern, it shows that like the monkey your attention is much more on your WISHES (what you *want*) than on your WORRIES (what you *fear*). *Monkey Bottles* are often found in the diagrams of powerful and successful people. If the pattern shows up frequently in your *Road of Life* Diagrams, you are probably an energetic, ambitious person, unwilling to settle for less than the most or the best. And when things don't work out well for you, you may feel frustrated and deprived—sometimes resentful that life is unfair.

Eddie

Eddie was a successful young professional, good-looking and personable, interested in developing a permanent relationship with a woman. He had been dating Jody seriously when Kate crossed his path. He found himself strongly attracted to both, for different reasons, and couldn't decide which one to date exclusively. When Eddie connected his circles, he came out with one line connecting *Advantages* only: *Monkey Bottles*.

Choice: Jody

Advantages:

- absolutely beautiful
- other men envious
- love the way she feels
- gives me a lot of attention
- chemistry
- love kissing her

Disadvantages:

- can't really talk
- different values
- doesn't read
- less intelligent
- disagree on child-rearing
- seldom laughs
- complains

Choice: Kate

Advantages:

- a talker
- more outgoing
- interesting person
- same values and outlook
- brighter, well read
- loves to have a good time
- laughs a lot
- a hard worker

Disadvantages

- wants children
- not as much chemistry
- touch not as pleasing
- above average looking

Eddie was in the same spot as the monkey—hardly free to enjoy what he already had, but quite unable (unwilling, really) to let go and look for another alternative. Both the monkey and Eddie got stuck because they were unwilling to GIVE UP *any* of what they wanted. They wanted it *all*.

Laurie, age sixteen, also discovered *Monkey Bottles* when she selected decision alternatives that are familiar to almost every young person: getting homework done versus relaxing and enjoying free time. Here is her diagram:

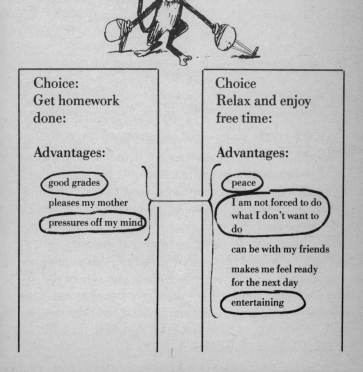

Choice: Get homework done:	Choice Relax and enjoy free time:
Advantages:	Advantages:
(good grades)	(peace)
pleases my mother	(I am not forced to do what I don't want to do)
(pressures off my mind)	can be with my friends
	makes me feel ready for the next day
	(entertaining)

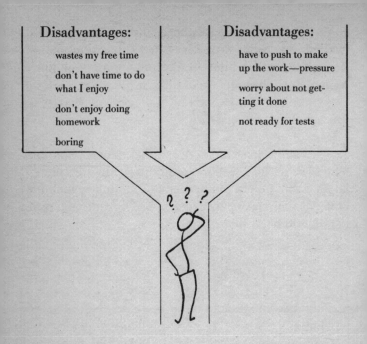

Disadvantages:

- wastes my free time
- don't have time to do what I enjoy
- don't enjoy doing homework
- boring

Disadvantages:

- have to push to make up the work—pressure
- worry about not getting it done
- not ready for tests

Laurie's choice contains elements that are of critical importance to many teenagers: being with friends, having fun, and avoiding pressure. At the same time, good grades are important to a good future if a child wants to go on to college, and she knows it! But working exclusively for top grades can mean sacrificing time spent with friends, and many teenagers are not willing to go *too far* in that direction. Like many of her friends, Laurie sometimes chose one side of the diagram, sometimes the other. To her parents she seemed inconsistent and unmotivated. But she was, in fact, managing to balance strong desires in *both* directions to her own satisfaction.

Walter's choice involved hiring a moving company or doing the moving himself. His dilemma was simple: money versus hassle:

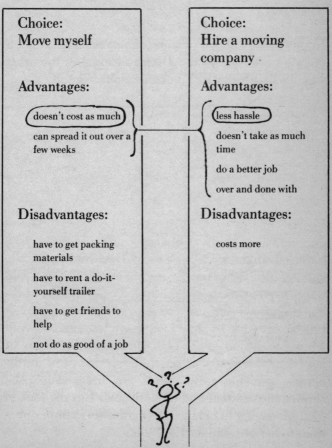

Choice:
Move myself

Advantages:

(doesn't cost as much)

can spread it out over a few weeks

Disadvantages:

have to get packing materials

have to rent a do-it-yourself trailer

have to get friends to help

not do as good of a job

Choice:
Hire a moving company

Advantages:

(less hassle)

doesn't take as much time

do a better job

over and done with

Disadvantages:

costs more

Walter was in a fairly comfortable financial position, and when he thought carefully about *what he would do with the money he had saved*, he decided that the peace of mind he would get from hiring a moving company would be a pretty good purchase after all.

If *your* financial situation is different, or if you enjoy the socializing that occurs when friends help you move, then you might have chosen to do it yourself.

Dilemma Two

In this *Value Pattern* one line connects the *Disadvantages* on one side to the *Disadvantages* on the other side. I call it Railroad Tracks. It looks like this:

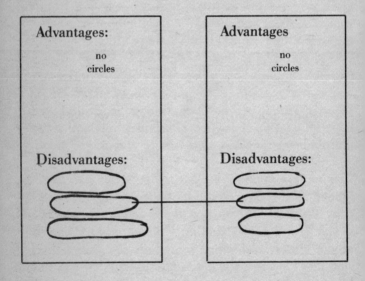

When your decision shows this pattern, it feels as though no matter which way you go, you are sure you're going to get hit by a train.

Railroad Tracks shows that WORRIES—the losses, discomforts, or pain you expect to experience—are most important to you regardless of which alternative you choose. If you regularly find Railroad Tracks* in your diagrams, you may be a person who focuses on negatives, for example: "Someone will disapprove," "Someone will be displeased," "Someone will blame or criticize me," "Someone will be hurt or inconvenienced," or "I will lose status (money, comfort, or power)." It may be hard for you to enjoy life and very hard for you to make decisions since you anticipate pain and trouble wherever you look.

Neil

Sometimes, Railroad Tracks will pop up unexpectedly. Neil found them when he tried to decide whether to stay on his present job in Washington, D.C., or to accept a more interesting job at his company's division in Charlottesville, North Carolina. He was not being promoted, so salary was not an issue.

---

* Everyone finds them once in a while.

Choice: Transfer to Charlottesville

Advantages:

more interesting work

cheaper to live

less of an urban area

something new

geographic change

some people would be happy to see me go

live closer to family**

better climate

Disadvantages:

some people would miss me

would have to train somebody to take the job

unknown management

have to move

leave friends

live closer to family**

don't know what to expect

family wants to stay in D.C.

Choice: Stay in D.C.

Advantages:

better chance of promotion

get along with boss

good schools

many cultural activities

family likes D.C.

Redskins

Disadvantages:

not happy with job

long drive to work

high cost of living

crowded

cold winters

* *This is not a mistake! It happens when you have mixed feelings about the same thing or person.

While moving to Charlottesville had risks and losses, especially the loss of good friends, the disadvantages of staying in D.C. were becoming less and less tolerable. Neil did something that made it much easier for him to make up his mind. He took his family to Charlottesville for a long weekend. Each member of the family had a chance to express his or her concerns about the move and to decide what he or she wanted to explore. His wife and teenage daughter wanted more information about schools and neighborhoods. They arranged meetings with a realtor, who showed them around, and with the vice-principal of one of the high schools. The younger boys wanted to know about soccer and swim teams, so they arranged a visit to a Y.M.C.A. and a local community center. And Neil, who was most worried about management, asked to meet with his potential supervisors to get their ideas on how he might fit into the organization there. (Actually, this was only partially true. He wanted to see whether or not he *liked* them.) The visit was successful, enjoyable, and informative because it was focused. The visit said, "I realize that this decision will affect all of your lives." It said, "I want to know what your concerns are, and I respect them." And it said, "Let's figure out what information you need to answer your questions, and let's get it." Neil had to borrow money for this trip, but later on he realized it was money well spent. It answered some of the family's questions, relieved their anxieties a little, and allowed them to feel more comfortable about finally making the transfer.

For Pauline, both sides of her diagram seemed to lead to loss; she just couldn't figure out which loss would be *worse*. Pauline had been dating Fred for about eight months. A few months before they met, Fred had broken up with a woman he'd dated for five years. It was a painful breakup. Pauline was willing and ready to make a commitment to the relationship, but Fred swore he would never let himself be hurt like that again, and he wanted the relationship to remain casual. When Fred left town for a week, he did not call Pauline when he returned. Pauline waited a day or two and then became frantic. She put in an "emergency" call to me, and we did this *Road of Life* over the telephone:

Choice:	Choice:
Call Fred	Not call Fred
Advantages:	**Advantages:**
find out what's going on	leave him free
show an interest in him	do not crowd or push
be assertive	give him the benefit of the doubt (he didn't get back, or is too busy)
chance of getting together	
Disadvantages:	**Disadvantages:**
he may feel boxed in, crowded, bothered	tired of crying and feeling this pain

Pauline's dilemma boiled down to the possibility that Fred might get irritated with her versus her own loneliness and uncertainty. She decided that the risk of his feeling bothered was a risk she was not willing to take, and that her best bet lay in being easy on him.

We explored ways for her to relieve her own pain in some way *other* than trying to be with Fred. She called some friends and was invited to a potluck supper with the family of one of them. It wasn't *exactly* what she had wanted, and it didn't ease that certain special spot of loneliness, but it was a good and satisfying experience. Mostly, it got her a bit unstuck from the feeling that she *had* to be with Fred, or all was lost.

Vicki

Vicki had a lot of things on her mind, things she wished she had the nerve to say out loud to her boss. Her imaginary Assertive Self would stride confidently into the boss's office, shoulders back, head high. Fixing him with a steady look, Assertive Self would say, "Mr. Johnson, I have been very unhappy lately about the way my job is going. You are giving me much too much work for the amount of time I have, and I'm not getting enough direction. Whenever I come in to ask you a question, I can almost hear you thinking, 'C'mon Vicki, can't you figure that out for yourself? Why do you come in here and bother me with such stupid little things!' And while we're at it, Mr. Johnson, this salary you're paying me really stinks. If I didn't feel a sense of loyalty to this place . . . which you don't even *appreciate* . . ." And so on. If you had to guess, about how many times would you say this kind of conversation actually took place? You've got it. Not one.

Vicki presented her decision alternatives during an assertiveness training workshop. The result was a classic *Railroad Track* Dilemma.

Choice: Confront Mr. Johnson directly	Choice: Pussyfoot around
Advantages:	**Advantages:**
have more respect for myself	avoid being stared at while I'm talking

gain suggestions on better ways of doing the job

clears the air

actually could get some things changed

avoid having to justify my position

can get back at him in other ways

he might eventually get the message

Disadvantages:

(afraid of getting fired)

fear of rejection

(takes a lot of gearing up—energy, planning, thought)

probably be a waste of time

(have to justify myself)

Disadvantages:

don't feel good about the job

(continue to feel resentful)

takes much longer

(nothing may ever change)

(feel guilty that I'm not standing up for myself)

doesn't take my concerns seriously

feel cut off, isolated

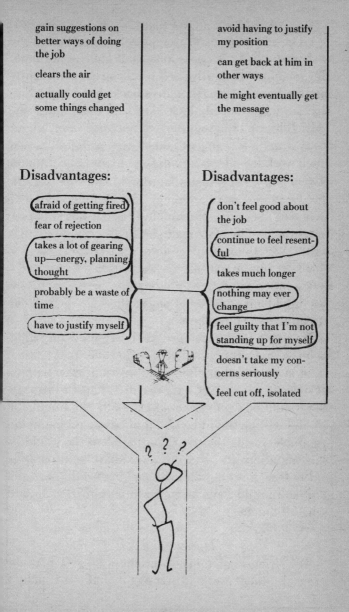

Vicki did not have faith that a confrontation would do any good. And she certainly did not feel confident of being able to carry it out without breaking down and crying. The item about "gearing up," which seems to say "It takes too much energy and time" really means, "I don't think I can do it," "I'm afraid," or "I don't know how."

The group role-played some "confrontation" scenes with Vicki, and she practiced using assertiveness skills. They suggested that she isolate one specific grievance and put her energy into dealing only with that. She chose the *amount* of work that was supposed to be done. The statement she finally came out with was, "Mr. Johnson, once in a while I find that I'm short of time in getting the work back to you, and I was wondering whether you or someone else in the office could give me some suggestions on how I can streamline the procedure."

We don't know whether Vicki ever used this statement, or any other. Chances are that she did not use it right away, but that after some weeks or even months of distress, she might have decided that a confrontation would be worth the risks after all. She would still be afraid! She would be afraid in advance. She would be afraid during the confrontation. And she would be shaking afterward. But she would have acted *in spite of* the fear, knowing that the shaking *would* pass and that she would have taken an important step toward self-fulfillment.

Marlene and Jeff

Two friends of mine, Marlene and Jeff had the same argument over and over again. Jeff was usually a confident and assertive person, but he consistently found himself on the *Tracks* in certain specific situations. This would happen whenever he and Marlene attended a large social gathering that included both family and friends.

Recently, they had been invited to an anniversary celebration for one of Marlene's closest childhood friends. After the meal, Marlene insisted (through clenched teeth) that Jeff remain at the table with her and her parents. But Jeff was more interested in socializing with his own friends. Marlene felt that Jeff neglected and ignored her on many social occasions and that this was simply one more example of the same treatment. Jeff's internal conversation, which took only about three seconds, went something like this: "There she goes again, trying to manipulate me into doing what she wants. I wouldn't mind sitting with her, but we just had the entire meal together, and I think that's plenty. I know she's going to be p——d off for the rest of the evening and probably won't get over it until tomorrow, and *I'll have to live with that face!* But if I sit here just to get her off my back I'll resent it, and I know I'll be looking for some way to get back at her sooner or later."

Jeff was between a rock and a hard place. He wanted to be able to make a comfortable, easy, rational decision about the whole thing, but under the kind of pressure he was experiencing, comfort was unattainable. If you're being badly squeezed, the best you can hope for is to keep from getting your ribs broken. No matter which alternative you choose, *there is going to be a bruise!* Bruises take time to heal. And sometimes wounded people feel like wounding back.

Jeff's dilemma looked like this:

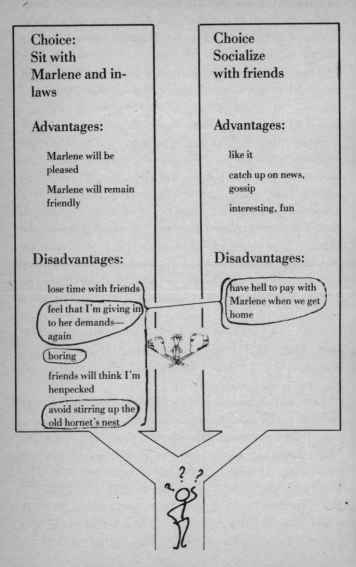

Choice:
Sit with
Marlene and in-
laws

Advantages:

Marlene will be
pleased

Marlene will remain
friendly

Disadvantages:

lose time with friends

feel that I'm giving in
to her demands—
again

boring

friends will think I'm
henpecked

avoid stirring up the
old hornet's nest

Choice
Socialize
with friends

Advantages:

like it

catch up on news,
gossip

interesting, fun

Disadvantages:

have hell to pay with
Marlene when we get
home

The thoughts going through Jeff's mind were painfully famililar. He usually gave in to Marlene to avoid having to deal with her anger, and as on other occasions, he decided to stay at the table. Interestingly, a couple of weeks later, Marlene was furious because Jeff had promised to trim the hedges before their guests arrived for a party and he had "forgotten."

Dilemma Three

In this *Value Pattern*, you will find one line connecting *Advantages* and *Disadvantages* on the *same* side of the diagram. Such a pattern shows that your STRONGEST WISHES are connected with your STRONGEST WORRIES. It is a painful pattern, which causes people a lot of stress, and it looks like this:

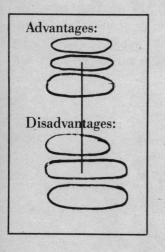

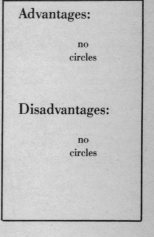

OR

123

Advantages:	Advantages:
no circles	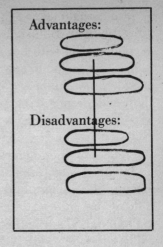
Disadvantages:	Disadvantages:
no circles	

It is as if you were up in a tree wanting to eat a delicious coconut, but a fierce tiger at the bottom keeps you from relaxing and enjoying what you have. Or, maybe you're terrified of even *going after* the coconut, because you have to slip by the dangerous tiger to get it. This pattern is appropriately called, *Tiger 'Neath the Tree*.

It takes determination, strong desire, and a strong tolerance for discomfort to live in the Tiger Tree (but it *is* exciting). If you do not feel that brave or that strong, you might choose the alternative that has no circles in it, even if it is a little dull. Yes, you would like what is on the other side, but not at that price! Not with all that tension and conflict!

Jason and Andrew, both eleven years old, had dilemmas that were similar, although they had never met each other. In fact, their dilemmas, in simplest form were close to being universal: How can I *get* what I want or *do* what I want *without* getting into trouble for it? For adults, trouble can come in many ways, but for children trouble usually means having an important adult mad at you.

Jason had problems mostly at school, while Andy had them at home. Here is Jason's diagram:

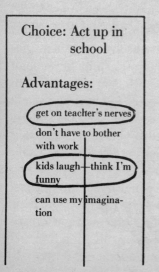

Choice: Act up in school	Choice: Not act up in school
Advantages:	Advantages:
get on teacher's nerves	don't get into trouble
don't have to bother with work	teacher doesn't get mad
kids laugh—think I'm funny	not embarrassed
can use my imagination	better grades
	get respect from other kids

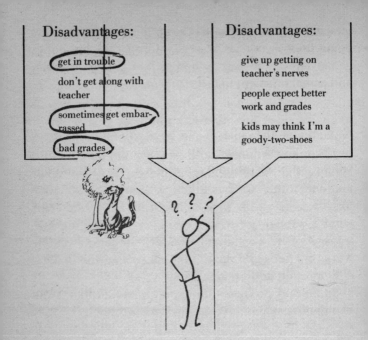

Disadvantages:

- (get in trouble)
- don't get along with teacher
- (sometimes get embarrassed)
- (bad grades)

Disadvantages:

- give up getting on teacher's nerves
- people expect better work and grades
- kids may think I'm a goody-two-shoes

Jason and his *mother* had been in a power struggle for years. He had become an absolute expert at getting on her nerves without ever going quite far enough for her to get genuinely angry. He put up a fight on every point, argued with her every request, and made negative comments about everything she did to please him. In school, he was constantly being reprimanded and sent out of the room. Teachers consistently said he was likeable but exasperating.

Jason had learned that he could make himself *feel powerful* by defeating adults—by "getting on their nerves." Because he was smart, he could get on his teacher's nerves in clever ways—ways that got him recognition and admiration from the other children. He *was* ambitious and wanted the grades, but for the time being he was not at all ready to give up his power game. He was *willing to accept* bad grades, trouble, and embarrassment *in order to win*.

Andy

Andy was the older of two boys. He had a younger brother, Michael, age eight. Michael was good at provoking Andy in subtle ways—by looking at him bug-eyed, poking at him with his foot while they were watching TV, or insisting on playing with his blocks while Andy was trying to do constructions. Andy would resist and resist until the pressure got too great. Then he would let Michael have it. Michael invariably let out a mighty yell, which brought Mom or Dad running. I taught Andy one of the most helpful techniques I know for handling aggressive provocation. It is called the "Bathroom Tecnique."* It doesn't solve the problem, but it gets you out of the immediate conflict and teaches you not to be upset by the behavior.

"Andy," I said, "this is what you need to do. Whenever you find yourself getting angry at Michael, you can be pretty sure that he is 'trying to get you.' Stop what you're doing, go into the bathroom, and lock the

---

* Credit for this technique goes to the late Dr. Rudolf Dreikurs, a student and colleague of Alfred Adler. Dreikurs recommended it particularly as a way in which parents can respond to fighting amongst their children. Most children fight so that a parent will come and pass judgment on who was right (good) and who was wrong (bad). You can test whether or not a fight is strictly for *your* benefit. Next time there is a squabble, try the Bathroom Technique exactly as I have described it. If you have more than one bathroom, choose the one farthest away from the fight. Then count the seconds until the fight travels through the house and ends up right outside the bathroom door. *(Don't try this if you believe one child will seriously try to hurt another).*

door. Be sure there is a lock on the door. You will also need a radio and a special book or magazine. The radio will soothe you and block out the noise Michael makes by pounding on the door or shouting. And the book will give you something useful to do. If you definitely want this to work, you will read that book *only* in the bathroom. That way, you will be *looking forward* to a disturbance, and Michael won't have the pleasure of "getting you."

We looked at the Bathroom Technique as a possible choice that Andy could use whenever he wished. His *Road of Life* Diagram was clear and simple:

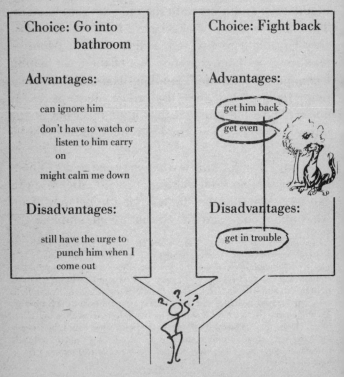

Choice: Go into
bathroom

Advantages:

can ignore him

don't have to watch or
listen to him carry
on

might calm me down

Disadvantages:

still have the urge to
punch him when I
come out

Choice: Fight back

Advantages:

get him back

get even

Disadvantages:

get in trouble

Andy wasn't sure about the Bathroom Technique, but he said he was willing to give it a try. Meanwhile, he usually chose to "get back" and continued to get into trouble. He was successful with the technique only when the real issues of competition and of what looked to him like favoritism were dealt with in family therapy.

Richard

The issue of freedom to speak one's mind came up in an interesting way in the course of marital counseling. Diane and Richard had been married for seven years. Diane had always admired Richard's quick wit and spontaneity. He would do anything on a moment's notice. He never pulled any punches, and you always knew where you stood with him. Richard was also quite capable. Everything he did, he did well.

In the past year or so, however, Diane was finding that the very things that had attracted her to him in the first place were exactly the things that were now driving her nuts (this is very common): he was critical, he was sarcastic, he would say whatever came to his mind without thinking of how it might hurt her feelings; and he was always "coming behind her," pointing out her mistakes, and telling her how she should do things better.

Richard's *Road of Life* Diagram showed that one of his most important desires was the *freedom to speak his mind*:

**Choice:
Think before
I speak**

Advantages:

    less harm would be
    done

    be thought of as con-
    siderate, kind

    potential for closeness

    potential for trust

Disadvantages

    finding it inhibiting

    unable to express
    myself the way I want

**Choice:
Say what I
am thinking**

         *

Advantages:

    less complicated

    simpler

    more honest

    easier

    less confining

    less restricting

Disadvantages:

    does a lot of harm

    very insensitive

    damages people I'm
    close to

    risking my marriage

    creates fear and dis-
    tance

*Richard took his pen & drew
a circle around the whole
thing.

Richard was shaken up when he saw that one of the things he valued most, freedom of speech, was on the verge of destroying his marriage. He wanted above all to save his marriage, but he simply didn't know how to go about it. In the past, whenever he had "forced himself" to keep his mouth shut, he'd become tense and irritable, and sooner or later the words he'd been holding in came out anyway. As in Andy's case, we took a two-part approach. First, we came up with a way to deal with the behavior as it happened. Second, we looked for the underlying purpose of the criticisms and sarcastic remarks.

Diane had been responding to Richard's comments by trying to *absorb* or ignore them. Sometimes she cried. Usually, she withdrew in silence. Richard was mystified by her behavior. From his point of view, he was either helpful or funny. He often apologized but only because it was expected. He sincerely did *not* know what all the fuss was about.

In order to help Richard *feel* something of what Diane was feeling, I gave her very specific instructions. Instead of being a *sponge* to his comments, she was to be a *mirror*. Each time a cutting "remark" was made, I asked her instantly to stop what she was doing, turn to him, look at him, and *repeat* the comment with the *same* wording, the *same* tone of voice, and the *same* inflection. There was to be no anger or hesitation (as far as possible of course) just an instant replay, as accurate and matter-of-fact as a tape recorder. She should then calmly return to what she had been doing. We did some role-playing until Diane got the hang of it. She reported that the first time she did it at home, Richard was stunned into absolute silence.

After the fourth time, he suddenly said, "Hey, that hurts!" Diane *wisely* said nothing. But she continued to repeat any critical or sarcastic remark. By the end of the week, there was an amazing drop in the number of those remarks.

In the course of counseling, it turned out that Richard, the only child of a divorced mother, had taken on the "man of the house" role at an early age. He had been pushed hard to succeed, to make something of himself, and to be "the best." Issues of right and wrong were strong in his family, and he recalled being told often, "I'm telling you this for your own good." A critical point in the therapy was reached when Richard had the insight to say "I feel it is my duty and obligation to point out people's mistakes." In other words, Richard had concluded that in order to belong and to be a *good* person, he not only had to be perfect himself but he had to "improve" others as well.

You now know that Richard was driven by a Troublemaker—*Prestige Seeking*. His corrections and criticisms were giving people this message: "You are not good enough as you are; I have superior knowledge and understanding; I will use this knowledge to make you better (whether you want to be or not!); and of course it goes without saying that *I* will decide what 'better' means."

With these insights, Richard was much more capable of understanding his behavior. He was able gradually to change the way he dealt with people because he *wanted to*. He no longer had to restrain or inhibit what he wanted to say, because what he *wanted to say* was now more positive and respectful.

Carolee

There is a type of *Tiger 'Neath the Tree* dilemma which comes up in some of the most difficult and challenging decisions. The situation is different each time, but the dilemma is the same: I am staying with someone or something that is often very good and often terrible, but I am afraid that if I leave this I will have either nothing at all or something even worse. Typically, the decision involves staying with—or leaving—an intimate relationship, a job, or friends.

Carolee had been dating Severn since their third year in high school. She was a pretty and sociable girl, who was considered "a catch." Sev, intelligent and ambitious, was working on a college degree in business. Theirs had been an intense courtship, and the relationship stayed strong for about two years. Then, Carolee noticed that Sev was occasionally withdrawn and neglectful. He would fail to call and make plans for the weekend, and he seemed preoccupied when they were together. All he said was that he "didn't know" why he felt that way. Then his mood would change, and things would be great for months. After close to a year of this vacillation, Carolee had had enough . . . almost. Should she leave or not? Her dilemma:

Choice: Stay with Sev	Choice: Leave
Advantages:	**Advantages:**
familiar	free to find another relationship
know what I've got	release from tension

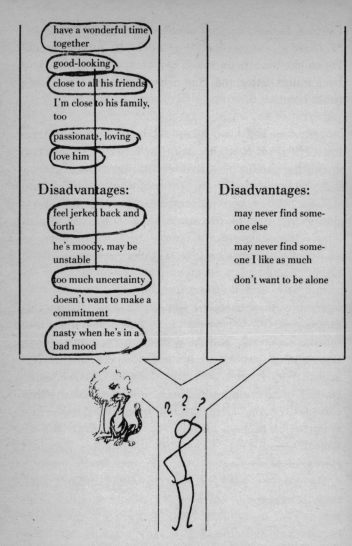

have a wonderful time together

good-looking

close to all his friends

I'm close to his family, too

passionate, loving

love him

Disadvantages:

feel jerked back and forth

he's moody, may be unstable

too much uncertainty

doesn't want to make a commitment

nasty when he's in a bad mood

Disadvantages:

may never find some-one else

may never find some-one I like as much

don't want to be alone

There is an old folk saying, "The devil you know is better than the devil you don't know." Some people who stay in the Tiger Tree are living by this principle.

Carolee decided to stay where she was and "take it." She was afraid to meet "the devil she didn't know." He might have been much worse; but he might have been much better, too. She never gave herself a chance to find out.

There are only two other possible Decision Dilemmas: *Ricochet Romance* and *Cat's Cradle*. These two are different combinations of the three basic dilemmas. They are complex, and sometimes painful; and we will need to explore strategies for resolving Decision Dilemmas before we can tackle them in detail. For now, let me simply call them to your attention, in case they showed up in your diagram.

Dilemma Four

In the fifties, ricochet romance meant disappointment in love—bouncing out of one person's arms into the arms of another who, in the end, proved to be just as disappointing. You are engaged in a *Ricochet Romance* whenever your lines form ONE TRIANGLE. In making decisions, *Ricochet Romance* means that you are bouncing around the alternatives: from WISH-to-WISH-to-WORRY, or from WORRY-to-WORRY-to-WISH. There are four possible *Ricochet Romance* patterns:

As you can see, *Ricochet Romance* already contains a Leaning Ladder, the diagonal line! This means that it contains the *potential* for a reasonably comfortable decision, *but* it also contains *two other dilemmas*. Look at the top two patterns. You see that they each contain a WISH balanced by another WISH. This is the *Monkey Bottles* Dilemma: there is

135

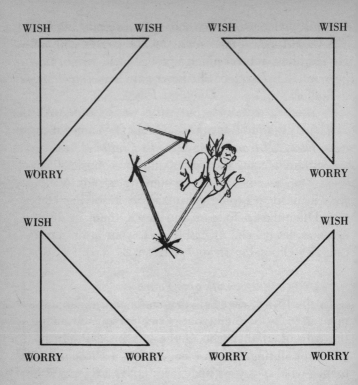

something important you are not yet willing to give up. Now look at the bottom two patterns. They show a WORRY balanced by another WORRY. This the *Railroad Tracks* Dilemma: there is something you are not yet willing to accept. Now look at all four *Ricochet Romance* patterns at the same time. You will notice that every single one has a *Tiger 'Neath the Tree!* One of the sides has *both* something you want very much (an important WISH) *and* something you are afraid of (an important WORRY). *Ricochet Romance* is uncomfortable mostly because it is *unstable.* Bounce around all you want, every time you try to climb that Leaning Ladder, some important WISH or WORRY will jump around in the corner and shout, "Hey, how about me!"

Dilemma Five

The last remaining pattern is *Cat's Cradle*. All the WISHES and all the WORRIES are connected to one another.

WISHES   WISHES

WORRIES   WORRIES

Full of stretches and pulls and lines of tension, this is the most tangled you can get. *Cat's Cradle* is not an *unstable* Pattern, like *Ricochet Romance*. It is a *paralyzing* one! There you are with two potential decisions on paper—the two diagonal Leaning Ladders—and yet no decision at all! The Leaning Ladders are overwhelmed by *all* the other dilemmas: *Monkey Bottles*, *Railroad Tracks*, and *Tiger 'Neath the Tree*.

> No wonder you have trouble making up
> your mind!

Cat's Cradle requires the most careful attention to the Seven Strategies of Decision Making. You may have to use all of them.

Chapter VII. The *Shadow Road* and a Six-Pack of Strategies for Resolving Your Decision Dilemma

If you have ever been lost in a large building, on a school campus, or in a subway system, you were probably grateful and relieved to see one of the world's most welcome signs: **YOU ARE HERE**

Making a decision is not so different. You are "lost" in a maze of conflicting values and unknown dangers. But before you can get out, you have to know where you *are*. And that may not be where you think!

Choice: ———
Advantages:
———
———
———

Disadvantages:
———
———
———

Choice: ———
Advantages:
———
———
———

Disadvantages:
———
———
———

Where am I?

You Are NOT Here.

Strategy One: Find Out Where You Are

Remember Francine? She was the one who could not buy a blouse or order lunch (or do almost anything, actually) without getting herself into a Decision Dilemma. Sometimes it was *Monkey Bottles*: "They both look so good. I just can't make up my mind." Sometimes it was *Railroad Tracks*: "I can't do that because (put something terrible here). But if I do the other, then (put something else terrible here). I just can't make up my mind." Francine usually played it safe by avoiding the issue. Francine took the Shadow Road.

The Shadow Road

In some kinds of decisions, a special third alternative is possible. It is called the *Shadow Road*. Its *Choice*—and it is a genuine choice—is always *do neither*. You have already learned that almost every decision alternative has *both* important Advantages and important Disadvantages. The *Shadow Road* is no exception. But, unlike other alternatives, its Advantages and Disadvantages are the same *in all cases*.

The Advantages of the *Shadow Road* can be attractive indeed. Who wants to be blamed for a "bad" decision? Who wants to feel sorry afterward? Who wants to make mistakes? No one! Of course, in order to avoid these unpleasant outcomes, there is a price to pay. You have to *give up* all the Advantages—all the WISHES—of *both* alternatives.

If you are dealing with an emotionally tense situation, you could use the *Shadow Road* as a time-out place, a temporary refuge where you can gain time and space to get your thoughts together and let your

Your Road of Life Diagram

Choice A

Advantages:

———
———
———

Disadvantages:

———
———
———

Choice B:

Advantages:

———
———
———

Disadvantages:

———
———
———

The Shadow Road

Choice: Do neither

Advantages:

no being held responsible or accountable
no being criticized
no feeling wrong or to blame
no being pinned down
no having to commit yourself
no feeling sorry afterward
no feeling guilty

Disadvantages:

give up all the *Advantages* of Choice A
give up all the *Advantages* of Choice B

feelings settle down. The danger is allowing the *Shadow Road* to become a *permanent hideaway*, forever preventing you from taking action and moving forward. If you choose the *Shadow Road* in order to be *safe*, you lose the right to complain that you never get anywhere.

How to Tell Whether a Shadow Road Is Possible

To tell whether *your* decision is a *Shadow Road* type, ask yourself, *"Must* I take one alternative or the other?" If the answer is YES, then IT IS NOT POSSIBLE to use the *Shadow Road.* You *must* take, or already be acting on, one of the alternatives. If the answer is NO—if it is at all possible to DO NEITHER—then you may use the *Shadow Road* if you wish. Here are some examples:

The Shadow Road is not possible for these decisions:

- have a baby or not have a baby

- get married or stay single

- live in Chicago or not live in Chicago

- work outside the home or not work outside the home

- stay married or get a divorce

- smoke or not smoke

- accept a change in work schedule or not accept a change in work schedule

The Shadow Road *is possible for these decisions:*

- marry Robin or marry Louise (or do neither)

- buy a new car or buy a used car (or do neither)

- paint the kitchen or paint the family room (or do neither)

- buy a sofa or buy a VCR (or do neither)

- vacation at the beach or vacation at the mountains (or do neither)

- say yes or say no (or do neither—"I don't know yet")

- move to La Jolla or move to San Diego (or do neither)

- go to school or get a job (or do neither)

How to Find Out Where You Are

When you are in the state of mind called "trying to decide," you may *feel* as though you are at a fork in the road, or out in space somewhere, or in a foreign country, looking at your decision from six thousand miles away. These feelings are fantasies. There are four, and only four, places you can be:

Place One: You are already, at this very moment, smack in the middle of one of the alternatives.

Place Two: You are in the *Shadow Road*. (Remember that the *Shadow Road* is NOT always available.)

Place Three: You are waiting for some outside event to happen—a telephone call, a graduation, a job offer, receipt of money, etc.—before you need to decide. THE VERY MOMENT THAT EVENT TAKES PLACE, YOU WILL HAVE TO COMMIT YOURSELF TO ONE OF THE ALTERNATIVES.

Place Four: You are waiting for some outside event to happen—a telephone call, a graduation, a job offer, receipt of money, etc.—before you "need" to decide. THE VERY MOMENT THAT EVENT TAKES PLACE, HOWEVER, YOU WOULD *STILL* HAVE THE OPTION OF *DOING NEITHER*.

Suppose you have been trying to decide whether or not to work outside the home. This is an example of Place One: You are already *living in* one of the alternatives. People either work outside their home, or they don't.* Since it *feels* like an unsettled issue, we can assume that you are not presently working outside the home. Here is where you are:

---

* Some people don't work at all. That equals, "not working outside the home." Some people work *in* their homes. That also equals, "not working outside the home."

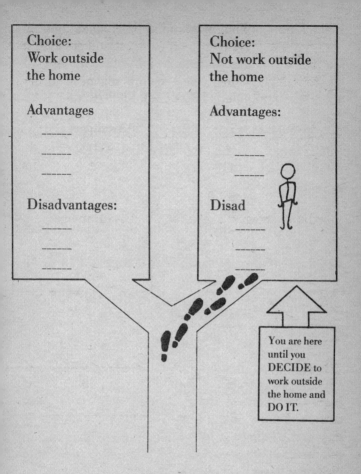

Choice: Work outside the home	Choice: Not work outside the home
Advantages ——— ——— ———	Advantages: ——— ——— ———
Disadvantages: ——— ——— ———	Disad

You are here until you DECIDE to work outside the home and DO IT.

Suppose you can't make up your mind whether to paint the living room white or blue. Could you do neither? Yes. You are in Place Two: the *Shadow Road*. (You may be there for only a few minutes or for years. Until you *decide* to paint the room blue or white, or some other color, you are in the *Shadow Road*.) Your *Road of Life* Diagram looks like this:

Your Road of Life Diagram

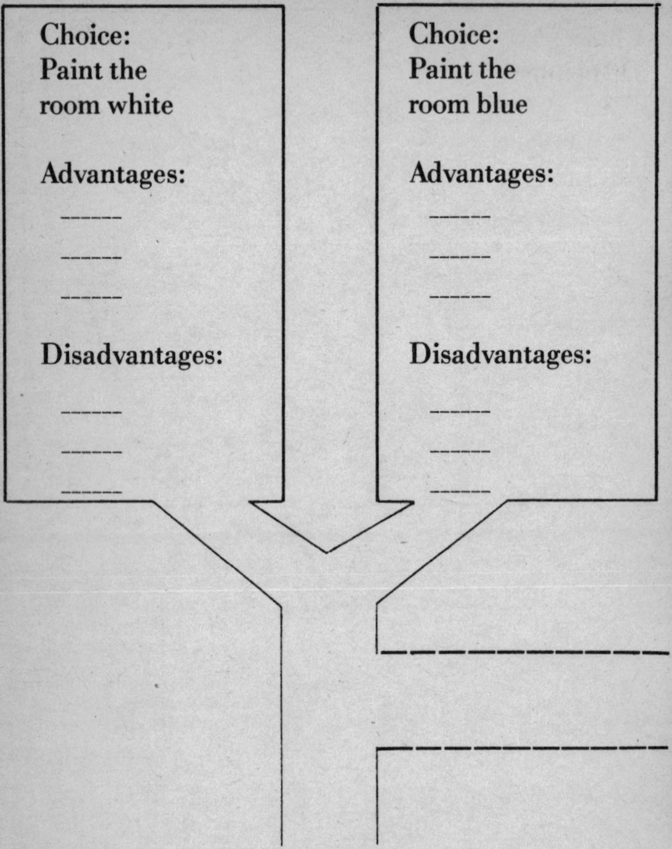

Choice:
Paint the
room white

Advantages:

Disadvantages:

Choice:
Paint the
room blue

Advantages:

Disadvantages:

The Fantasy about Place (2): "I can't make up my mind."
The Truth about Place (2): "I don't want to be pinned down."

Choice:
Do neither

Advantages:

no being disappointed
no feeling wrong or dumb
no feeling embarrassed
no feeling responsible

You are here
as long as you
continue to do
NOTHING.

Disadvantages:

give up all the *Advantages* of painting the
room white

give up all the *Advantages* of painting the
room blue

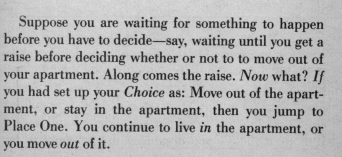

Suppose you are waiting for something to happen
before you have to decide—say, waiting until you get a
raise before deciding whether or not to to move out of
your apartment. Along comes the raise. *Now* what? *If*
you had set up your *Choice* as: Move out of the apartment, or stay in the apartment, then you jump to
Place One. You continue to live *in* the apartment, or
you move *out* of it.

If you had set up your *Choice* as: Buy a house, or buy a condominium, you *could* do neither. You *could* stay in the apartment. Until you actually *buy* the house or *buy* the condominium, you are "doing neither." You are in Place Four. The event (the raise) came and went, but somehow it never seemed possible, or the "right time," to take an action. Place Four is a special type of *Shadow Road*. This is where you go when you want it to look like someone or something else (a circumstance) has decided for you. One example is waiting for a class to be offered near your home, then somehow missing the deadline to register. Or, you get a call which you know is an invitation to a party, and you lose the telephone number. Life is saying to you, "O.K., you said as soon as (X happened), you would (do Y). How about it?" If you are in Place Four, you are saying back to life, "Yes, I wanted it to *appear* that I would make up my mind, but in fact I do not want to (or I am afraid to). I am letting circumstances say "No" for me."

The Fantasy about Place Four: "I'll decide as soon as . . ."
The Truth about Place Four: "I don't want to be held responsible."

Strategy Two: Look for Mirror Images

When you started to think about your decision, you probably discovered that there was *too much* information for you to handle comfortably. When you wrote down your "Yes-But" List, at least you were able to stop that information from whirling around inside your head. Then, you *organized* the information by using the *Road of Life* Diagram. But it wasn't until you relaxed and allowed some of the items to pop out that you were able to *reduce the amount* of information you had to deal with. Instead of twenty-seven items, maybe you discovered seven or eight circles, which showed you your *most important values*. In a way, that step was like panning for gold. You took in a lot of rocks and pebbles and sifted through them systematically until the golden nuggets shone clear. Now, with *Strategy Two*, we will *reduce* the information even further. *Strategy Two* is helpful in another way too. Sometimes it will help you untangle one of the complex Decision Dilemmas (*Ricochet Romance* or *Cat's Cradle*) by simplifying and making more manageable the factors in your decision.

Mirror Images are *pairs* of items which basically say the same thing or express the same idea in opposite ways. *Mirrors* happen when you state one form of the idea as an Advantage and another form of the same idea as a Disadvantage. The Advantage will be at the top of your diagram on one side, and its *Mirror Image* will be at the bottom of your diagram ON THE OTHER SIDE. If you connected them, you would have a diagonal line. Here are several examples of *Mirror Images*:

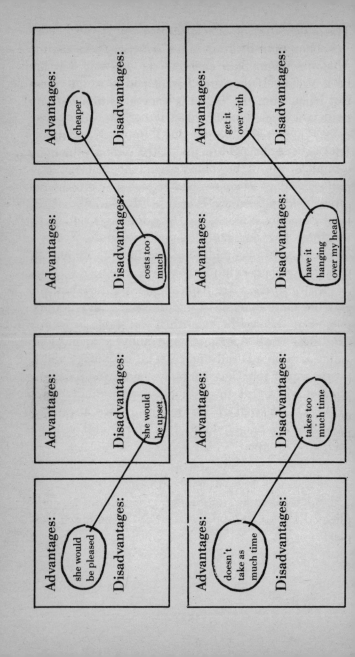

The possibilities are almost endless.

Look at your diagram to see whether there are any *Mirror Images*. Now check to see whether they are both circled. If they are, I want you to *isolate* these two items from the rest. Fix your attention *only* on these two items. Now . . . slowly . . . let your eyes go to one . . . then the other. Look up . . . look down. Look up . . . look down. In a little while, your body will begin to talk to you. You will *feel* a little more pull, a little more energy toward one than toward the other. One will feel heavier or more powerful. Keep loose and relaxed, because the difference between them may be small and delicate.

The less tense you are right now, the more you will be able to sense or "feel" that one *Image* is pulling you just a tiny bit more. When the feeling is definite, *erase* the circle around the weaker item. THIS MAY CHANGE YOUR LINES! Sometimes the circle you erase will be the *only* item you circled in that item's group. This will automatically remove any line or lines that were connected to that group. You can simply erase the line(s), *or* you can draw the diagram over again, using *only* the items that are still circled. Most people prefer to draw it again. It is simpler and cleaner.

Sandy

Sandy's dilemma, for example, looked like the complicated *Cat's Cradle* but turned out to be much simpler:

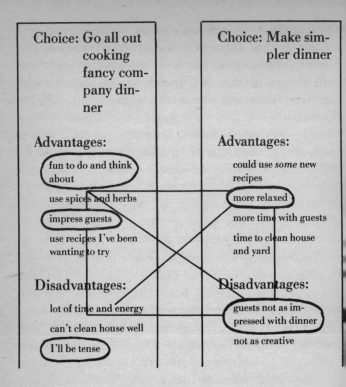

Choice: Go all out cooking fancy company dinner	Choice: Make simpler dinner
Advantages:	**Advantages:**
fun to do and think about	could use *some* new recipes
use spices and herbs	more relaxed
impress guests	more time with guests
use recipes I've been wanting to try	time to clean house and yard
Disadvantages:	**Disadvantages:**
lot of time and energy	guests not as impressed with dinner
can't clean house well	not as creative
I'll be tense	

First, Sandy isolated one of the *Mirror Images:*

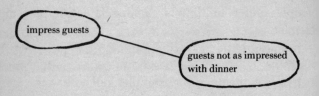

impress guests

guests not as impressed with dinner

Slowly, she let her eyes go back and forth between *only* these two items. (If you let yourself be distracted by looking at the other items now, you will drive yourself crazy. Trust me. You may even want to cover the

rest of the items with your hands.) Back and forth ᴤ
went. It didn't take long. Sandy wanted *very much* to
impress her guests! She loved it when they exclaimed,
"This is fantastic! Where did you get this marvelous
recipe? This is the most delicious _____ I've ever
tasted!"

Once Sandy selected, "impress guests," it eliminated the circle around "guests not as impressed with
dinner" *and* the lines that touched it:

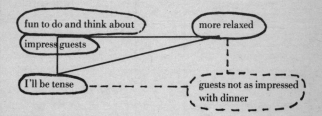

Next, she looked at the other two items which
formed a *Mirror Image:*

Back and forth, back and forth. This one took longer,
but eventually "I'll be tense" felt more powerful. This
eliminated "more relaxed" *and* the lines that touched
it:

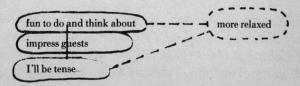

ended up with the much simpler *Tiger in the Tree*—important Advantages and an important Disadvantage on the same side. (I didn't say it was comfortable. I only said it was simpler.) Here, then, was the essence, the *Golden Nugget* in Sandy's decision: "Is it worth being tense in order to impress my guests?"

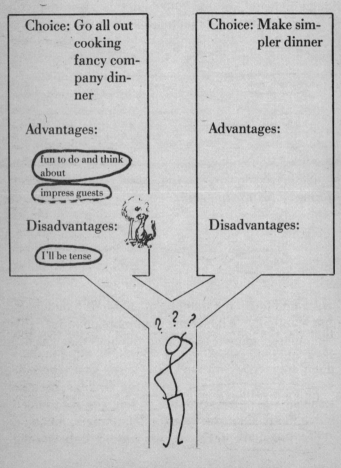

Choice: Go all out cooking fancy company dinner

Advantages:

fun to do and think about

impress guests

Disadvantages:

I'll be tense

Choice: Make simpler dinner

Advantages:

Disadvantages:

? ? ?

Since Sandy did not want to give up "impress guests," she focused on what she could do to minimize her tension. She decided to prepare one plain dish—the vegetable. This relieved *some* of the tension, but that was as far as she could go. Sandy knew she would feel tense and overworked, but she was *willing to pay the price*.

Strategy Three: Quick Rating

The *Quick Rating* Strategy will help to reduce the amount of information you have to deal with even further. And it helps you to find those Golden Nuggets. One of the problems those who work with decision makers face has always been to find or develop some kind of *enjoyable* procedure that people can use to *rate* their values. When you sat back, closed your eyes, and allowed your eyes to wander around the diagram, you discovered automatically and effortlessly which items were important. But in comparison to one another, you still may not know which are of *greater importance* and which are of *lesser importance*. The *Quick Rating* Strategy is a very easy way to find out what YOU can and cannot *do without* or what YOU can and cannot *tolerate*.

Ratings are intensely personal. No one, no one at all, can do them for you. People may have told you that you *should* feel this way or that way, or that you *should not* or "have no right to" feel the way you do. I don't even know you, and yet I *know* that whenever you have acted against your true feelings because someone was putting pressure on you, you got yourself into emotional trouble (tension, fear, anger, anxiety). When you make decisions, you are not only moving

155

forward and getting things done, *you are learning about yourself.* You are discovering (if you keep your eyes open) what pleases YOU, what makes YOU uncomfortable, what makes YOU feel like a good person, and what makes YOU feel like a bad person.

How to Do a Quick Rating

To start with, look at each *Advantage* you have circled. Taking just one at a time, say each of the following statements to yourself:

1 – I could not survive without this.

2 – I could live without this, but it would hurt a lot or be extremely uncomfortable.

3 – I could live without this, but I wouldn't like it.

4 – I guess I could continue to live without this if I have to.

If you are *already living* with one of the alternatives, change the phrasing as follows:

1 – I cannot continue to survive without this.

2 – I could continue to live without this, but it would hurt a lot or be extremely uncomfortable.

3 – I could continue to live without this, but I wouldn't like it.

4 – I guess I can continue to live without this if I have to.

> - *Whenever you rated the item a* $\boxed{1}$, leave it in, and put *another* circle around it.
>
> - *Whenever you rated the item a* $\boxed{2}$, leave the circle as it is.
>
> - *Whenever you rated the item a* $\boxed{3}$, see whether you would be willing to erase the circle.
>
> - *Whenever you rated the item a* $\boxed{4}$, erase the circle.

Now, look at the *Disadvantages* you have circled. Taking just one at a time, say each of the following statements to yourself:

$\boxed{1}$ –I would find this absolutely intolerable.

$\boxed{2}$ –I could live with this, but it would hurt a lot or be extremely uncomfortable.

$\boxed{3}$ –I could live with this, but I wouldn't like it.

$\boxed{4}$ –I guess I could live with this if I had to.

If you are *already living* with one of the alternatives, change the phrasing as follows:

$\boxed{1}$ –I can no longer continue to tolerate this.

$\boxed{2}$ –I could continue to live with this, but it would hurt a lot or be extremely uncomfortable.

$\boxed{3}$ –I could continue to live with this, but I wouldn't like it.

④ –I guess I can continue to live with this if I have to.

> - *Whenever you rated the item a* ① , leave it in, and put *another* circle around it.
>
> - *Whenever you rated the item a* ② , leave the circle as it is.
>
> - *Whenever you rated the item a* ③ , see whether you would be willing to erase the circle.
>
> - *Whenever you rated the item a* ④ , erase the circle.

As an experiment, try *Quick Rating* the items below; then ask a few friends, including one or two of the other sex, to do the ratings without looking at yours. (You probably know what you want more than you think you do.)

A sampling of what some people might want in an intimate partner:

☐ good-looking   ☐ religious

☐ outgoing   ☐ honest

☐ gentle   ☐ playful, fun-loving

☐ financially responsible   ☐ high-achieving

☐ a good parent   ☐ sensitive

☐ a good lover   ☐ aggressive

☐ smart   ☐ kind

☐ athletic   ☐ generous

Ratings

1 –I could not survive without this.

2 –I could live without this, but it would hurt a lot or be extremely uncomfortable.

3 –I could live without this, but I wouldn't like it.

4 –I guess I could live without this if I had to.

A sampling of what some people might dislike about a job:

- ☐ far from home
- ☐ low pay
- ☐ can't use my abilities
- ☐ no benefits
- ☐ too big (too small) of a company
- ☐ no independence
- ☐ no decision-making power
- ☐ no privacy
- ☐ no parking
- ☐ no place to eat lunch
- ☐ ugly office (building/area)
- ☐ noisy
- ☐ no chance of promotion
- ☐ don't like boss
- ☐ don't like co-workers
- ☐ boring

Ratings

1 – I would find this absolutely intolerable.

2 – I could live with this, but it would hurt a lot or be extremely uncomfortable.

3 – I could live with this, but I wouldn't like it.

4 – I guess I could live with this if I had to.

Larry

During a period of intense cold in the winter of 1983, a pipe broke in my neighbor's house and flooded the downstairs level. The pipe served only an outside faucet at the back of the house, so it was more of a convenience than a necessity. Larry had the rugs and draperies cleaned (homeowner's insurance) but he never got around to calling a plumber. Finally, in July, Larry was willing to go through the diagram with me and try some Strategies.

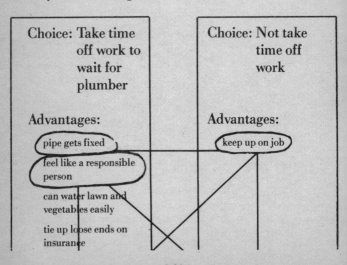

Choice: Take time off work to wait for plumber

Advantages:

- pipe gets fixed
- feel like a responsible person
- can water lawn and vegetables easily
- tie up loose ends on insurance

Choice: Not take time off work

Advantages:

- keep up on job

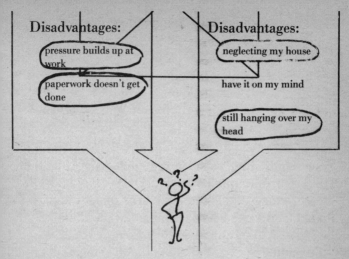

First, we looked for *Mirror Images*. There were three:

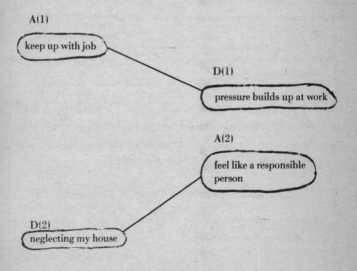

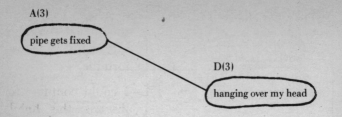

After comparing each *Image*, one pair at a time, Larry felt more pulled toward D(1), D(2) and D(3). These items remained; their *Mirror Images* were eliminated, and Larry's items shrank down to these:

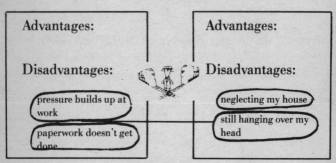

Larry was on the *Railroad Tracks*. His dilemma balanced one set of Disadvantages (neglect the job) against another set of Disadvantages (neglect the house). It was time for a *Quick Rating*.

The Item		*The Rating*
pressure builds up at work	→	②—I could live with this, but it would be extremely uncomfortable.

paperwork doesn't get done	→	2 —I could live with this, but it would be extremely uncomfortable.
neglecting my house	→	3 —I could continue to live with this, but I wouldn't like it. (Larry used "continue to," because he was *already* living in this alternative.)
still hanging over my head	→	3 —I could continue to live with this, but I wouldn't like it.

The *Quick Rating* showed Larry that:

| 2 —pressure builds up at work and | were *more important* than | 3 —neglecting my house and |
| 2 —paperwork doesn't get done | | 3 —still hanging over my head |

He was willing to erase the items rating a 3 , and his decision became clear.

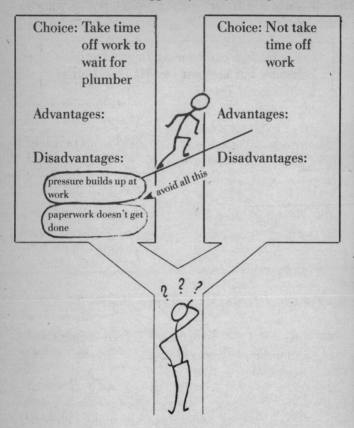

Larry chose *not to take time off work* in order to *avoid* his major WORRY: having pressure build up at work. He wasn't really surprised. After all, this was exactly what he had been doing for seven months. But he was pleased to understand the dilemma. And he was delighted to see that he was *not* neglecting his house because he was a lazy, irresponsible homeowner but because a different *responsibility* had a higher *value* for him.

> *Quick Ratings* can be used for any Decision Dilemma but are best for *Monkey Bottles* and *Railroad Tracks*

Strategy Four: Do Research

Decision making is a way of *gathering information.* This is the First Cardinal Rule. You will get the best possible information by actually making the decision and there is no possible way to get all the information *without* making it, to do so might put you in a risky situation. You don't know exactly what might happen, and you're not sure you want to find out; or you *know* what will happen, but you *don't know* whether you'll be able to live with it, or you suspect that you don't know enough yet even to be thinking about making a decision. You need to *Do Research.* You need to get as much information as you possibly can *before* making a definite commitment one way or another.

Sometimes, there is simply no way to *Do Research* in advance, for instance, having a baby, or undergoing experimental medical treatment. But many deicisons *do* lend themselves to various kinds of research. Getting advance information takes times, and it may take money. Only *you* know whether you can afford to *Do Research* before you make a commitment . . . or whether you can afford not to.

There are two kinds of research: Real-Time Research and Talk-Time Research. By far, the best, the most complete, is Real-Time Research. The name says it. Real-Time means *doing* the thing, but when you do it, you think of it as a *trial*—a *temporary* course of action which you use strictly to *gather information*. (It could become permanent later, of course.)

Look at your alternatives. Would it be at all possible to: (1) go back and forth fairly equally between them; (2) stay in one most of the time, while you experiment a bit with the other; or (3) do one completely for a period of time, then do the other completely for a period of time?

Real-Time Research (1): Go back and forth equally between the alternatives. Going back and forth between two alternatives is rarely possible, but when it is, you have a golden opportunity to learn a great deal about yourself and to discover what you want most. Some of the most important decisions of all—those involving intimate relationships—often lend themselves well to Real-Time Research.

Eddie practiced it when he dated Jody and Kate simultaneously. It worked because he did it *right*. Research is *research*. Research means to look around, to investigate thoroughly. It means that you go into one of the alternatives with the intention of experiencing it one hundred percent. When Eddie was with Jody, he paid attention to her, *and* he paid attention to his own thoughts, feelings, and sensations. "What am I enjoying about Jody *right now*," he asked, "and what am I finding uncomfortable? How does this *feel* inside of me? Is my body tense somewhere (a pretty sure sign of trouble)? Is there information coming at me that I don't want to look at? Would I rather be with Kate?" Then, when he was with Kate, he studied *her*, and he studied *himself* while he was with her.

Does this sound too clinical and serious? Remember that Eddie wanted these relationships to be spontaneous and loose, and that's why he got into the dilemma in the first place! He had never taken the time to *find out* exactly what he wanted and exactly how he might get what he really wanted out of life.

There is a place for spontaneity and a place for serious study. Good decisions require that you be *both* an artist (creative, intuitive, sensing) *and* a scientist (systematic, observant, thinking). You are an artist when you allow the information—good and bad, positive and negative—to come right on in and flow through you. You are a scientist when you step back somewhat from the information and say, "O.K., now what do we have here?"

Here are some other possibilities for using Real-Time Research (1):

- You can't decide between Copier A and Copier B for your office. *Rent them both* for a few months.

- You can't decide whether to walk for exercise or do a TV workout. Try doing one. Live it, breathe it, feel it. Then do the other. Live it, breathe it, feel it.

- You can't decide whether to speak up when someone does something that annoys you or whether to let it go by and keep the peace. Try one approach. How does it feel before? How does it feel during? How does it feel after? Now try the other. How does *it* feel before, during, and after?

- You can't decide whether to paint the kitchen beige or gold. Buy a quart of each and paint some of each in a small area. Live with them both, side by side, for several weeks. Which one do you enjoy seeing more day after day? Which one looks better with your table and cabinets? What do your friends think? (You have told them, of course, that you're doing research—which you are—and that you want to be sure before investing in a gallon of paint.)

Real-Time Research (2): Stay in one alternative most of the time while you experiment a bit with the other. Decisions having to do with jobs, school, and recreation lend themselves well to Real-Time Research (2). Naturally, you will get the most extensive and the most accurate information by actually selecting one alternative and seeing how it turns out. But you can sometimes do pretty well in your research by doing things part-time. That's like putting a toe in the water before jumping into the pool.

A friend of mine was considering leaving her job as a salesperson and setting up a word-processing business in her home. She was taking a training course and enjoyed learning the material, but something bothered her, and she couldn't quite put her finger on it. She said she *felt* bored and restless even though the course was quite interesting. I asked her to pay very close attention to the feelings of restlessness she experienced during the course and to pay close attention to any similar feelings while at the store. The feeling never arose at the store. After a day or two, the solution came to her: "I need to get up and move around!

I hate to be stuck in one place, especially sitting down!" Well, that was the end of the word-processing business. Wasn't she lucky to have discovered that fact before investing in equipment?

Other possibilities for Real-Time Research (2):

- You can't decide whether or not to work outside the home. Try working part-time outside the home. (Yes, the pay will probably be less, and it may not be as challenging a job, and there is a delay involved, but consider all that you can learn by doing this.)

- You can't decide whether to change your college major. Take two or three courses in the field you are considering. In the long run, it may prove to have been well worth the time and money.

- You can't decide whether to move to Charlottesville. "Dip a toe in the water" and visit Charlottesville for five days before deciding to make the transfer.

Real-Time Research (3): Do one completely for a period of time, then do the other completely for a period of time. This is truly an ideal way to do Real-Time Research, since it is probably the closest you can get to the real thing—making a permanent commitment. When the consequences of a decision are very important or costly, and when a permanent decision would be hard to reverse, this can sometimes be an excellent way to try things out. Trial separations, for example, can provide couples with an opportunity to see whether living apart is, on the whole, more fulfilling than living together. (There is often a period of excitement and relief immediately after separating, but those feelings wear off after a few months, and then some of the realities of being single can be genuinely experienced.)

Before leaving where you are and trying something else out, however, *take stock* of where you are. Do a careful and complete *Road of Life* Diagram on the decision, and don't throw away your "Yes-But" List. Get a good feeling for what you want most and are most worried about *right now*. If you do leave, after you have lived for a while in the other alternative, your memory of the worries and hurts will probably fade, and you will miss the Advantages you once had. You will need your list and diagram to remind you of what things were like then.

Other possibilities for Real-Time Research (3):

- You can't decide which part of the country to settle down in. If you are willing to sacrifice some stability and possibly some pay for a while, what better way to find out what you like than to move around? Of course you must balance the gains against the possible negative consequences to others or to your own future.

- You can't decide whether to sell your house and move to Florida. Could you *rent* your house and spend a year in Florida on a temporary basis?

- You can't decide which model car to buy. This can be an expensive proposition. Could you *rent* one model for three or four months, then rent the other for several months before you purchase.

170

Whether or not to do Real-Time Research before making a commitment is also a decision! You already know that it is a way of gathering information, but like any other decision, it has important Advantages *and* important Disadvantages, for example, Real-Time Research is incomplete and doesn't have the feeling of certainty that you would get by doing the real thing; Real-Time Research takes time and energy (sometimes a lot); and Real-Time Research often requires money—money which you might prefer to put into one of the alternatives. Only *you* can tell how much more information you need, how long you can afford to wait, how long it will take to get it, and how much it will cost (in money, effort, or a negative reaction from others). When will you *know* whether it was worth taking the time to do Real-Time Research instead of just selecting an alternative? Afterward. Just like any other decision.

Most of the time, however, you will not have the luxury of being able to do Real-Time Research. When you are pressed to make a decision, you may not have (or be willing to put) as much time, energy, or money into it as it would take. Possibly, the means for doing Real-Time Research—taking a job or buying a house—are simply not available. You certainly *need* advance information, but you cannot get it by *living* in one of the alternatives for a period of time. You need Talk-Time Research.

After direct personal experience, the second-best way of getting information is from other people. I am careful to say *information*. People are wonderful, wonderful sources of information. They are terrible, terrible sources of advice. When you ask people for

171

information, they will probably try to give you *advice*. Remember, when you were making up your "Yes-But" List, how they tried to tell you what to do and criticized your items? If you were *persistent* in making them begin with, "Have you considered . . ." or "Have you thought of . . . ," then you probably got information, not judgment or advice.

Getting good, honest, valuable information through Talk-Time Research is a snap, because people *love* to talk about themselves. But *first*, you have to be clear about what you want from them, and *second*, you have to ask in the right way.

First, be prepared to receive a lot of information you may not need. Have clearly in your mind, though, the few items that you circled in your *Road of Life* Diagram. Hopefully, there were no more than seven or eight circles, with only one or two in each box. That should make them fairly easy to remember. Or, just write them down.

Second, if you ask the wrong question, you will get information that doesn't help! The question "Do you like working here?" will provoke a response of "Yes" or "No," whereas asking, "How do you feel about working here?" will get a personal evaluation, like "It stinks" or "It's great." On the other hand the question "Could you tell me about working here?" will probably be answered by another question—"Huh?"

What is it you really want to know? You want to know what some job is *like*, what actually happens there, what the pros and the cons are. To find out what anything is like, *ask what it's like*!

- *What is it like* being a . . . mother, a student

172

here, a lawyer, having a nose job, playing tennis, etc.?

- *What is it like* doing . . . needlework, construction, working on a political campaign, living in Seattle, etc.?

- *What do (did) you like/enjoy about (what don't (didn't) you like/enjoy about)* . . . this job, Annabelle, that tool, the neighborhood, being married, that store, taking that responsibility, etc.

Next to talking to real live people, statistics, articles, and books may provide helpful information. There is a truly incredible source of information almost in your back yard—the public library. Librarians are information specialists. If they don't have the information, they can usually tell you where to get it.

Research can be used for any type of Decision Dilemma

Strategy Five: Take the Tiger to Tea

All the Strategies you have learned so far—*Find Out Where You Are*, *Mirror Images*, *Quick Rating*, and *Research*—are usable in any of the basic Decision Dilemmas. Strategy Five, *Take the Tiger to Tea*, is particularly helpful in resolving the *Tiger 'Neath the Tree Dilemma* (where an important Advantage is linked with an important Disadvantage on the same side of the diagram).

If your Dilemma is a *Tiger 'Neath the Tree*, there are three possible ways of resolving it:

(1) Stay on the other side, where there is less tension and conflict.

(2) Accept the Disadvantages as a fact of life—something that you have to put up with if you want the Advantages on that side.

(3) Win over the *Tiger*.

The most common worry in all decision making is the fear of bringing about consequences that will have a negative effect on someone else. Who do you think might be hurt, or upset, or angry if you take the action on the *Tiger* side? Your children? Your parents? Your friends? Your husband or wife? Your boss? What do you imagine will happen if you ask for what you want? Have you carried on an endless series of fearful scenes—complete with music, dialogue, and changes of scenery—which take place from beginning to end *entirely inside your own head*? Are you trying to base your decision on information received from the terrors of your imagination?

Take the Tiger to Tea is a way of getting free of this terror. It is a way of getting unstuck and moving again. But it *is* risky. It involves some degree of confrontation with others, and as we know, confrontation can send chills down the spine of many a mature and otherwise self-confident individual. Furthermore, if you are in a Decision Dilemma, you are in a state of *uncertainty*, and uncertainty makes many people even more nervous and afraid than confrontation. These feelings are normal. Expect them.

There are four keys to the success of the *Take the Tiger to Tea* Strategy: (1) *Acknowledge Your Fear*, (2)

Come Prepared, (3) *Set the Stage*, and (4) *Tell the Truth*.

(1) *Acknowledge Your Fear.* You are in a tough situation. How can you possibly expect not to be afraid when you *are* afraid? You can't. If your decision is going to upset or anger a person who is important to you, your feelings will range from reluctance to terror. Acknowledge the fear. Say to yourself, "I'm afraid. I wish I didn't have to deal with this." Then say, "I'm afraid *and* I'm going to deal with it anyway." In spite of, in the presence of, your fear and reluctance, you will be *going to* the people who might be affected negatively by the Tiger alternative. You will be informing them of your coming decision, and you will be asking for their information and help, *openly revealing and describing the negative effects you think your decision is going to have on them.*

(2) *Come Prepared.* Bring your *Road of Life* Diagram to the discussion. It will already be complete, with important considerations circled and your Decision Dilemma identified (probably *Tiger 'Neath the Tree*, although it could be *Ricochet Romance* or *Cat's Cradle*). Nothing will give you greater strength and confidence than being totally clear about your own state of mind. Also, you can use the written diagram both as a starting point and as a help in organizing the discussion.

(3) *Set the Stage.* Prepare the other person or the others by stating *in advance* that you are trying to make up your mind about something, and that you are concerned about how the decision might affect them. Tell them you are interested in having their ideas and opinions on the matter. Arrange a time

when all concerned will be free for about an hour. If possible, try to have this discussion in the evening, after a meal, in a clean and orderly setting.

(4) *Tell the Truth*. At this point in using *Take the Tiger to Tea*, you need to be absolutely truthful about how close you are to actually making a move. Few things are more disrespectful and irritating to others than being told they have a genuine say in the matter when in fact the decision has already been made.

You can ask yourself:

"Am I in the early stage of this decision, where what I want most is *information*?

"Am I in the middle stage, where what I want most is to know whether I can have his/her/their *understanding and support?*"

"Am I in the last stage, where what I want most is for others to *know why* I am very close to taking (or have already taken) an action that affects them?"

As with doing *Research*, you will get responses based on the kinds of questions you ask. If you ask, "Should I do this?" you will get a "Yes" or a "No." If you ask, "Why should I?" or "Why shouldn't I?" *you will be launched into an argument, where they attack and you defend*. Unlike *Research*, however, you will need to allow people to express *their* feelings about what you intend to do or are considering doing.

Sometimes, you will discover that your listeners are rather indifferent. They don't particularly care one way or the other. ("I don't care; whatever you want to do is fine.") In that case, your imagination was creating a problem where none existed.

Sometimes, you will find them more understanding, cooperative, and resourceful than you thought. ("I'm all for it." "I understand." "How can I help?") In that case, your imagination underestimated your social resources. You will have gained moral support and strengthened the relationship, and you may receive actual, physical help.

Sometimes, the responses are as angry or judgmental as you were afraid they'd be. Then, more than ever, you owe it to those expressing these feelings to hear them out. The idea behind this Strategy is to *win over* the Tiger—the negative reactions—by approaching other people with a sense of confidence, friendliness, and a willingness to make peace. Still, in the end, you will have to make a judgment on which weighs more heavily: your needs or theirs. As with all decisions, this is a personal and private judgment which no one else can make for you.

The variety of situations in which you might want to *Take the Tiger to Tea* is very wide, but you might find some of the phrases below helpful in opening discussion, getting the kind of information you want, or asking for support:

- "I've been thinking about making a decision, but I'd like to have a chance to talk to you about it first. When do you think we can do that?"

- "I have made a decision that will have some effect on you, and I'd like a chance to tell you why I decided to do it. When do you think we could talk?"

- "This isn't going to be easy for either of us, and I appreciate your willingness to hear me out."

- How do you think this decision might affect you?"

- "What would it be like for you if I did this?"

- Is there anything I can do to help so that _____ won't be so bad for you?" (This question can be *very* helpful in soothing hurt feelings.)

- "Do you have any ideas about how we can make this more comfortable for each other?"

- Would you be willing to help me?"

- I know this is painful for you, and I wish it didn't have to be this way." (STOP HERE! No "But.")

- "I know this is hard for you to understand, but I hope I can have your support."

And, regardless of the response you got:

- "Thank you for letting me talk this over with you. I appreciate your being honest with me."

Take the Tiger to Tea is best used for *Tiger 'Neath the Tree*, *Ricochet Romance*, and *Cat's Cradle*.

Strategy Six: The One-Year Plan
People usually don't enjoy making trouble. When things are going well at work, in your love relation-

ship, with your friends, with your children, with your parents, the last thing you want to do is rock the boat. Some people make keeping the peace a way of life. They seek tranquillity at any cost. We have already seen how seeking *Protection* can become a Trouble-maker. But *almost everyone* prefers keeping things smooth rather than stirring them up. This universal desire to maintain friendly relationships with others may be leading you into *maintaining* the kinds of interactions that cause you to have trouble making up your mind. For example, you have a dilemma: "Should I say (or do) this, or not?" "Should I give in, or should I push for what I want?" "Should I bring up this thing that has been bothering me, or should I just keep my mouth shut?" And you conclude: "No, it's not worth the hassle. It's not worth disturbing the peace."

You end up with a *short-term gain*: You keep the peace . . . for a while.

You end up with a *LONG-TERM LOSS:* Nothing changes. The problem continues.

The next time you find yourself sacrificing your *needs in a situation* in order to *keep the peace*, ask yourself these very important questions:

DO I WANT THIS EXACT SITUATION TO BE TAKING PLACE *ONE YEAR* FROM NOW?

DO I WANT THAT PERSON TO BE FEEL-
ING EXACTLY THIS WAY AND SAY-
ING EXACTLY THESE THINGS TO
ME *ONE YEAR* FROM NOW?

DO I WANT PEOPLE TO BE TREATING
ME IN EXACTLY THIS WAY *ONE
YEAR* FROM NOW?

If your answer is "Yes," continue to behave as you are behaving right now.

If your answer is "No," the time to make a change is RIGHT NOW!

Once you have determined that you are *unwilling* to continue playing your part in a pattern which is uncomfortable for you, you are faced with the problem of *how* to go about changing your part. The *Tiger 'Neath the Tree* Dilemma is the one which lends itself well to the *One-Year Plan*. Getting something you *want*—and resolving this recurring problem—involves dealing with something you are *worried about*—upsetting someone or rocking the boat. In many such cases, you can use the questions and procedures for *Take the Tiger to Tea*. But sometimes the decision is not that complex or difficult. Sometimes, all it takes is courage, a willingness to be uncomfortable for a while (maybe quite a while), a firm conviction that what you are doing will work out best *in the long run*, and some assertiveness techniques.

A great deal has been written about assertiveness and assertiveness techniques, and I encourage my clients to read as much as they can in this area. I believe it is important, however, not to follow a particular structure mechanically and blindly but to bend it to your own style, using the words and phrases that are natural for *you*.

Usually, an assertive statement will contain one or more of these four components:

(1) information about how you are feeling

(2) information about what circumstances are bringing about that feeling or those feelings

(3) a statement that shows you understand the other person's point of view

(4) information about what *needs to happen* now, what you *would like* to happen now, or what you *have decided* to do.

There are many varieties of assertive statements. Here are a few:

- "Barbara, while you're at the shopping center, would you do me a favor and pick up a few bags of mulch?" (4)

- "Ken, it embarrasses me (1)
  when you talk about my housekeeping to your mother, (2)
  and I wish you wouldn't do it anymore." (4)

- "Jenny, I know you want to be with your friends this afternoon, (3)
  but your room has to be cleaned before you can go out." (4)

- "I know you're upset about it, (3)

and I'm sorry you feel that way, (1)
but that's what I have decided to do." (4)

- "Bill, I'm responsible (1)
  for getting this report out on time. (2)
  I know you've been under pressure the last couple of weeks, (3)
  but I've got to have those figures by the day after tomorrow." (4)

- "I get really angry, Donna, (1)
  when you start putting pressure on me." (2)

- "It makes me feel good (1)
  to get things worked out between us. (2)
  I hope we can always do it." (4)

- "I find that I'm not really looking forward (1)
  to going to the beach. (2)
  I don't want to spoil (1)
  the whole vacation, (2)
  but would you be willing to consider going to the mountains this year?" (4)

- I know you would like me to go along with what you want, (3)
  and I usually give in to you, (2)
  but I'm getting more and more uncomfortable (1)
  about it. (2)
  I'm not willing to give in just to keep the peace. (4)

- "I know you're concerned, (3)
  but I don't want to hear about my weight anymore." (4)

It takes a *long time* for deeply rooted behavior patterns to change. Even when you want to change *your* behavior, it may take others considerably longer to react differently to you. It's like a long, long line of cars at a traffic light that has just turned green. The first car moves right away, but it could be a good, long while before the twentieth car budges an inch.

If you characteristically avoid speaking up when something is bothering you, or if you routinely give in against your true wishes, you must practice assertive statements and assertive behaviors *day in and day out* if you want things to be different one year from now.

> The *One-Year Plan* is suitable for any Decision Dilemma but is best for *Tiger 'Neath the Tree*, *Ricochet Romance*, and *Cat's Cradle*.

Strategy Seven: The All-Time, Sure-Fire, Never-Fail Strategy—Settling

You have excellent reasons for having a hard time making decisions. You have a *natural tendency* to avoid pain. You have a *natural tendency* to want to please other people, or at least not to hurt them. You have a *natural tendency* to want to avoid making mistakes. You have a *natural tendency* to want to know what to expect before you commit yourself. And you have a *natural tendency* to want the most and the best

---

* Notice the difference between what is called an "I"-message and a "You"-message. A "You"-message tries to tell the other person *what to do*. An "I"-message tells how *you* are feeling or what *you want*. In this example, a "You"-message might be, "Please don't tell me about my weight anymore." Most of the time, "I"-messages are received in a better spirit and do not stimulate the other person to resist, defend, or argue.

you can get out of life. Efficient, successful decision making requires that you sometimes go against these natural tendencies.

How many people do you know who can consistently and happily make these statements:

"I don't mind a bit giving up the things I want."

"So it'll cause everyone to hate me. Big deal!"

"Actually, I get a kick out of knowing I made a great big mistake."

"It gives me a real thrill to find out I've gotten second best."

Ridiculous, aren't they? Of course you don't WANT these things! The most *effective* strategy for decision making—the one that will free you from Decision Dilemma more than any other—requires that you make this important distinction: WHAT I *WANT* IS NOT NECESSARILY RELATED TO WHAT I *AM WILLING TO DO*. Take the simple example of doing dishes. You can *feel* however you wish about doing dishes. The dishes don't care how you *feel* about them. They just need to be washed. You could be in any one of these situations:

How You FEEL		What You Are Willing to DO
I enjoy doing dishes,	and	I am going to do them.
I hate doing dishes,	but	I am going to do them anyway.
I enjoy doing dishes,	but	I am not going to do them.

I hate doing dishes, and I am not going to do them.

When Eddie had difficulty giving up what he wanted from both Jody and Kate, he was in a very common type of dilemma. There is a whole stack of Advantages on one side and a whole stack on the other. You want them *all* very, very much. IT IS PAINFUL TO GIVE UP WHAT YOU WANT. Only one thing can make you comfortable about giving up what you want, WANTING SOMETHING ELSE MORE. Then, resolving the dilemma becomes *more important* than "having it all." Eddie did eventually leave Jody and marry Kate. Did he *WANT* to give up Jody? Absolutely not. Was he *forced* to give up Jody? Absolutely not. He chose WILLINGLY to give up Jody in order to resolve his Decision Dilemma and get on with life.

One of the most difficult things to accept is having made a serious mistake. You feel stupid and embarrassed, as if you should have known better. You think that you will be ridiculed and criticized, that someone will say, "I told you so, you idiot!" What is a mistake really? It is a decision whose outcome you *could not possibly have known in advance*. It turned out *after* you took action that there were negative effects you had not anticipated, or that the negative effects were more powerful than you thought they would be. There is no such thing as a bad decision! There *are* actions whose effects you had NO WAY OF KNOWING in advance.

If the consequences of an action do not benefit you, and someone asks, "Why did you *do* it?" (in that cer-

, accusing, you-should-have-known-better tone of e), you might answer, with an attempt at humor, "It seemed like a good idea at the time." I happen to take this statement very seriously. "It seemed like a good idea at the time" says to me that you did what you thought was best and most favorable based on the information you had available to you at the time. Decisions *produce* information. If you knew *then* what you know *now*, you wouldn't have selected that alternative. But you *didn't* know, did you? You *COULDN'T* know! That's what decisions are for. To find things out. Instead of dumping on yourself ("What a dumb thing to do." "I should have known better.") or justifying and explaining *why* you made that decision, you can say—which is the truth—"I gave it plenty of thought, but it didn't turn out as I expected (as I wanted, as I had hoped)."

You are probably not comfortable settling for less than the best. But you may be so caught up in finding The Best that you are paralyzed by even the most trivial decisions. You are acting as if: there *is* a best; you will find it if you look hard enough; and you will recognize it when you see it. You don't want to compromise your standards, and so you are constantly searching—for the Best item on the menu, the Best chair for the living room, the Best car, the Best investment, the Best mate. You look and look and look, while the waitress waits, while cars go out of style, while interest rates go up, while partners get fed up and leave . . . tired of waiting for you to make up your mind.

It could be that you are asking the wrong question. If you are asking, "Is this item (object, course of

186

action) ABSOLUTELY *THE BEST* AVAILABLE ANYWHERE?", common sense has to tell you, "No." *Somewhere* in the world—the United States, China, perhaps Australia—there is, *I Guarantee*, a better gift, dress, pork roast, sofa, or piece of land than the one(s) you are considering right now. What would happen if you asked, "Is this item (object, course of action) *suitable for the purpose*? Will it do very nicely? Does it *meet the needs* of the situation, given the amount of time, effort, and money I have available to put into it?" If your answer is, "Yes, I guess it does," maybe you ought to consider taking it, because that *might* be as good as it's ever going to get.

It is *understood* that you do not WANT to give up what you desire or feel you need. Who would? But would you be WILLING to give up some things in order to resolve your Decision Dilemma and move on?

It is *understood* that you do not WANT to risk making a mistake or being wrong. Who would? But would you be WILLING to take a chance in order to resolve your Decision Dilemma and move on?

It is *understood* that you do not WANT to settle for less than the best. Who would? But would you be WILLING to accept something that adequately meets the needs of the situation in order to resolve your Decision Dilemma and move on?

It is *understood* that you do not WANT to accept discomfort or pain in order to fulfill your desires. Who would? But would you be WILLING to accept some discomfort as a fact of life in order to resolve your Decision Dilemma and move on?

It is *understood* that you don't WANT to look unsure of yourself, doubtful, or weak. Who would? But would you be WILLING to risk some embarrassment (even guilt) for a while in order to resolve your Decision Dilemma and move on?

Settling means: *Accepting What Is*. You take a deep breath and SETTLE for less than all of what you want (but more than nothing) and more discomfort than you feel you deserve (but it could be worse). Settling means accepting the fact that:

> You can't get a custom fit in an "off-the-rack" world.

Let's look at it this way. When you started thinking about your decision, you probably said to yourself, "What should I do, this or that, one or the other, *Choice A* or *Choice B*? And every time you thought of a good reason to make one of the choices, you very quickly thought of another good reason not to. The reasons why you wanted to do it were the "Yes'es," and the reasons not to were the "Buts." In fact, these items went to make up the "Yes-But" List. When you made up your *Road of Life* Diagram, the Yes'es and the Buts became the four sections.

By now, though, you have learned that in order to have the Advantages of Choice A, you will probably have to accept some of the *Disadvantages* of Choice A. Or, in order to receive the Advantages of Choice B, you will have to accept some of its Disadvantages. So, instead of "Yes-But," a decision *really means*, "Yes-*AND*!"

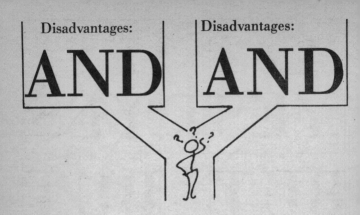

And how about the *Advantages* you may need to give up? Do you think for one moment that as soon as you make a choice, these other WISHES will simply fly off into space, vanish into thin air? Of course not! They will continue to occupy your thoughts for a while. You will have some regrets. But the clearer you are about what a decision is—it is giving up *some* of what you want and accepting *some* of what you don't want—and the more WILLING you are to make one, the more quickly your regrets, and the pain that goes with them, will fade away.

The Panic Afterwards

Sometime soon after *making your decision*, usually within fifteen minutes or less, you will be sorry you did it. A little voice will shout in your ear: "You jerk! What did you go and do that for!" You are undergoing one of life's most common experiences: *Post-Decision Regret*. As the Advantages of the alternative you

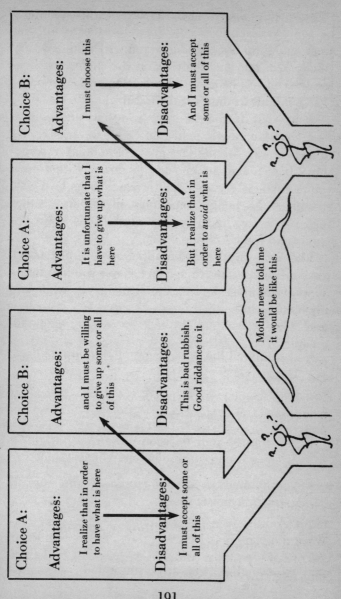

Choice A:

Advantages:

I realize that in order to have what is here

Disadvantages:

I must accept some or all of this

Choice B:

Advantages:

and I must be willing to give up some or all of this

Disadvantages:

This is bad rubbish. Good riddance to it

Choice A:

Advantages:

It is unfortunate that I have to give up what is here

Disadvantages:

But I realize that in order to *avoid* what is here

Choice B:

Advantages:

I must choose this

Disadvantages:

And I must accept some or all of this

Mother never told me it would be like this.

did not choose begin to fly off into the distance, and as the *Dis*advantages you are now stuck with rear their ugly little heads and give you a sly grin, you may panic. You may suddenly regret the choice you have made. You will be tempted to scream out, "Hold on! Wait a minute! I didn't really mean it!"

Well, what do you do now? You wait, that's what. Post-Decision Regret is like an ocean wave. It comes in its own way—sometimes just a little breaker, sometimes big enough to knock you down. Either way, you're going to get wet. And it leaves in its own way, sometimes gradually, sometimes all at once. Either way, *you are going to get dry again.* It is a wave of panic, and you CAN ride it out.

The panic you feel is because you have just LOST some very important things. Whenever you lose something, there must be a period of mourning while you adjust to the loss.

- You wanted the Advantages of *both* alternatives. You lost them.

- You wanted to feel *comfortable* and *certain* about your decision. You lost that.

- You wanted your decision to be *clearly* right or wrong, with no contradictions. You lost that.

- You wanted to appear *confident* and *sure of yourself.* You lost tha†.

- You wanted to avoid *hurting* or *upsetting* someone. You lost that.

- Once you finally made up your mind, you wanted

no more doubt, no more torment. And now you find that you lost that wish too.

Post-Decision Regret is a state of mourning, and mourning takes its own sweet time.

Certain kinds of situations are more likely than others to produce Post-Decision Regret. You will probably feel more panic:

- if your decision had a *Monkey Bottles* Dilemma in it (that is, if there were important Advantages on *both* sides of the diagram)

- if the Advantages on both sides were about *equal* in attractiveness. (You discovered this in the *Quick Rating.*)

- if the decision is going to inconvenience, upset, or hurt other people

- if the decision is irreversible

You are probably afraid of Post-Decision Regret. You have experienced it before, and you know in your bones that it is coming. (It almost always does.) You have been doing everything you could to avoid it—mostly by not making a decision in the first place. But now you know what to expect. You know that it will come; *and then it will go.* Knowing what to expect is your first line of defense.

There are two other important ways you can strengthen yourself so that the wave of Post-Decision Regret will not drown you. The first is to get a good footing. You have already done this by organizing your decision information in the *Road of Life* Diagram, by learning to discover and rate your values, and by applying the Strategies you have just learned.

The second is to turn and look in the right direction. After the wave comes, there is no point looking out to sea, waiting to get hit again. Enough is enough. It's time to head for shore.

At this point in the decision-making process, it is very, very important to be *selective* about the kind of information you will take in. To agonize over what you have given up and to wish you could take it all back is like waiting to be hit by the next wave. This is the time to focus almost exclusively on the ADVANTAGES of the alternative *you have chosen*. As you might guess, your eyes will have a certain perverse tendency to look where they shouldn't. If you genuinely want to ride out this wave, especially if you are the type of person who tries to avoid making decisions, I strongly suggest that you follow these procedures in order: (1) take your *Road of Life* Diagram and fold it as shown below to *isolate the Advantages* of the alternative you have just selected.

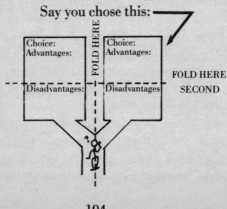

(2) Hold the diagram in front of you and look at it as you sit quietly, or pace back and forth, for five or ten minutes, (3) Put this folded diagram in a conspicuous place for at least twenty-four hours, if you possibly can, with the Advantages showing; (4) *When you feel more settled and comfortable inside* (you may still have *doubts* but no real *panic*), *then* open up the diagram to expose the complete half you have selected.

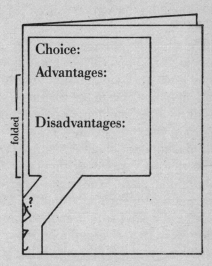

Now that your head is clearer, you are in position to focus once more on the Disadvantages of the alternative you selected and to *plan* how you are going to go about dealing with them (such as: *Take the Tiger to Tea* or *Settle*).

How can you distinguish Post-Decision Regret from being genuinely sorry? Post-Decision Regret happens within a *very short time* after making the decision—from a minute or two, up to about three days.

It usually happens *before* any of the Disadvantages have started to take place. If you change your mind right now and select the other alternative, it is probably *not* because you have received new information and are calmly reevaluating your decision. It may be because you are more afraid to take a risk than you thought, because you want to go back into the *Shadow Road*, or because you realize that you did not in fact have enough information to have made a commitment.

Genuinely negative outcomes usually take some time to unfold. And you will not know how you feel about them until they *do* unfold. (Third Cardinal Rule: You will not be able to tell whether a decision is beneficial until *after* you have made it and had a chance to *experience* the outcomes.)

In times of emotional or physical stress, your attention may be sharply focused on the unfavorable outcomes now taking place. You may criticize yourself for putting yourself in such a "stupid" position. You may feel that you "can't take it another minute" and start looking for ways to reverse the decision.

Please hold on for a few minutes. What you need is balance, and a person under stress is *out of balance*. Promise yourself that you will look at the whole original decision again when you have *time*, when you are physically *rested*, and when you are in a *quiet place*. You then take out your diagram (you kept it in a drawer) and give the whole thing a careful review—all the parts, circles, and dilemmas. Having acted on your decision in the first place, you have now received a great deal of new information. Relaxed and in a balanced state of mind, you are in the best position to reconsider your original decision. It may well be that things are not working out as well as you thought or hoped. It may be that THE TIME IS RIGHT TO CHANGE YOUR MIND. Simply let it be a *thoughtful* change, not an *impulsive* one.

Chapter VIII. Real Decisions by Real People

Tough Decisions 1: Work and School

You have learned how to organize your thoughts so that they stop spinning around inside your head. You have learned to identify the three basic Decision Dilemmas: *Monkey Bottles*, *Railroad Tracks*, and *Tiger 'Neath the Tree*. And you have learned Strategies: for gaining perspective (the *Shadow Road*), for boiling the information down to reveal its golden nuggets (*Mirror Images* and *Quick Rating*), for trying out the alternatives in advance (*Research*), for reducing your fear of causing pain to others (*Take the Tiger to Tea*), for bringing about the kind of future that will make you happy (The *One-Year Plan*), and for handling the wave of panic and sadness known as Post-Decision Regret. You are now ready to pull it all together and apply the skills you have learned to make real, complex decisions.

There are areas in people's lives where complex decision situations seem to come up over and over again: *occupation* (such as, school versus work; which school or which job), *money* (whether to spend it, how to spend it), *changes* (whether to stay where you are or move in another direction), *Troublemakers* (how your hidden desires affect what you do and what you want people to think of you), and the biggie, *intimate relationships* (whether to get involved with someone, whether to stay involved with someone, whether to leave someone).

Often, one complex decision simply leads to another: "Now that I have decided to work, *where* should I work?" or, "Now that I have broken up with Sam, who *should* I go out with?" (I know. I have no mercy.) But then, that *does* seem to be the way things are, doesn't it? Once you learned how to do addition and subtraction, did you think you would never have to do arithmetic again? Decision making is the same way. Decision dilemmas will come up every single day of your life. The idea is not to eliminate decisions but to become as knowledgeable and skilled at resolving them as you can.

We will move through each of the Dilemmas in this chapter in a systematic way, showing which Strategies were most helpful and how each person resolved a dilemma. Each person made the decision he or she *hoped* and *expected* would turn out best. Some were able to continue in the same direction. Others learned afterward that they needed to change their minds and to select the alternative they had first rejected or to find a brand new alternative. In every case—and I want to emphasize this—the decision was *personal*, based on each person's *unique set* of WISHES and WORRIES, and each person's *unique rating* of those values. If your values are different or are in a different *order*, your diagram will be different, your dilemma will be different, and your *decision* will be different.

199

Kevin

A common dilemma for some young people is whether to get an advanced education or to enter the workplace. Kevin was a bright and talented student who had just completed his freshman year in college. He was considering dropping out permanently in order to get started on a career although he had not yet identified the kind of work he would find most attractive. His was a *Cat's Cradle* Dilemma:

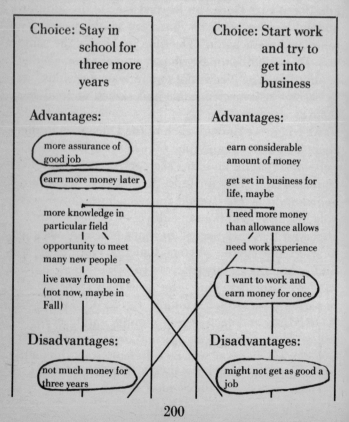

Choice: Stay in school for three more years

Advantages:

- more assurance of good job
- earn more money later
- more knowledge in particular field
- opportunity to meet many new people
- live away from home (not now, maybe in Fall)

Disadvantages:

- not much money for three years

Choice: Start work and try to get into business

Advantages:

- earn considerable amount of money
- get set in business for life, maybe
- I need more money than allowance allows
- need work experience
- I want to work and earn money for once

Disadvantages:

- might not get as good a job

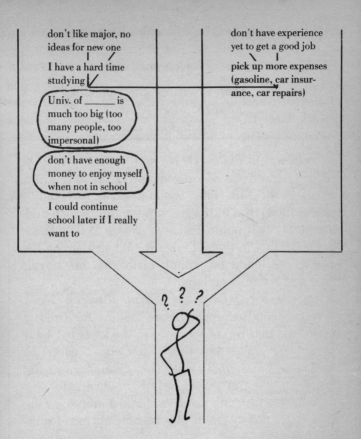

don't like major, no ideas for new one

I have a hard time studying

Univ. of _____ is much too big (too many people, too impersonal)

don't have enough money to enjoy myself when not in school

I could continue school later if I really want to

don't have experience yet to get a good job

pick up more expenses (gasoline, car insurance, car repairs)

Strategy One: Find Out Where You Are. The first question Kevin had to answer was "Where am I?" Here are the possibilities:

Place (1):	*Must* I be in one of the alternatives? If yes, which one am I in right now?
Place (2):	Is it possible to do neither? Am I in the *Shadow Road*?

Place (3):	Am I waiting for something to happen, after which I *must* be in one of the alternatives?
Place (4):	Am I waiting for something to happen, after which I could go into the *Shadow Road*?

Kevin was in Place (4). He had just completed the school year and was now deciding whether to return to college in the Fall. The "something" he was waiting for was the arrival of the registration deadline in mid-August. At that point, he *could* choose to do neither. (Realistically, however, he knew that neither he nor his parents would be willing to tolerate his staying home and bumming around.)

Strategy Two: Look for Mirror Images. Kevin made two small changes before looking for *Images.* He noticed that two of the items in the lower left-hand corner were almost identical—"*not much money for three years*" and "*don't have enough money to enjoy myself when not in school.*" He went ahead and condensed these into one item: "*not much money for enjoyment for three years.*" This became his item for the rest of the procedure.

Next, he noticed that two of the items in the upper left-hand corner were also quite similar. He condensed "*more assurance of a good job*" and "*earn more money later*" into "*more assurance of a high-paying job later.*" When Kevin redrew his diagram, using *only* the circled items, the *Mirror Images* popped right out:

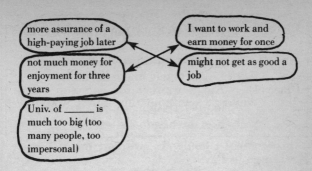

Kevin moved along the diagonals to check them out. He let his eyes go back and forth, one pair at a time, until one of each pair seemed heavier, more solid, had more "pull." The items that had more "pull" for him were, "*more assurance of a high-paying job later*," and "*I want to work and earn money for once*." He could now eliminate the other part of each pair ("not much money for enjoyment for three years," and, "might not get as good of a job") from his diagram.

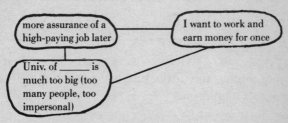

He had reduced his dilemma from *Cat's Cradle* to *Ricochet Romance*, but there was more work to do. We turned to the *Quick Rating*.

Strategy Three: Do a Quick Rating. Kevin looked at each of his remaining three items separately. For each Advantage, he repeated the *Quick Rating* statements to himself in the following order:

> 1 – I could not survive without this.
>
> 2 – I could live without this, but it would hurt a lot or be extremely uncomfortable.
>
> 3 – I could live without this, but I wouldn't like it.
>
> 4 – I guess I could live without this if I had to.

And for the one remaining *Disadvantage*, he said to himself:

> 1 – I would find this absolutely intolerable.
>
> 2 – I could live with this, but it would hurt a lot or be extremely uncomfortable.
>
> 3 – I could live with this, but I wouldn't like it.
>
> 4 – I guess I could live with this if I had do.

I advised Kevin to stop as soon as he felt, "Yes, that's it," and to put the little number beside the item. Here's what happened:

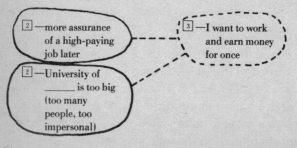

2 —more assurance of a high-paying job later

3 —I want to work and earn money for once

2 —University of _____ is too big (too many people, too impersonal)

In this simple way, Kevin discovered that his desire for a future high-paying job was indeed *slightly stronger* than his desire to earn money right now. And he agreed to erase the circle around, "I want to work and earn money for once." Thus, his diagram was reduced as much as possible.

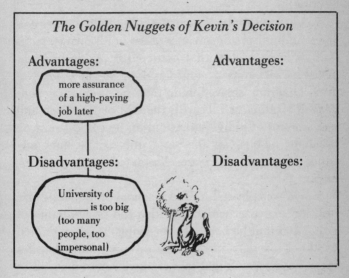

The Golden Nuggets of Kevin's Decision

Advantages:

more assurance of a high-paying job later

Advantages:

Disadvantages:

University of _____ is too big (too many people, too impersonal)

Disadvantages:

At this point, Kevin was clear about what he wanted most (not *comfortable*, mind you, just *clear*) and he realized that in order to *get what he wanted most*, he would need to continue his education. But the question about the University remained. He had a decision and a direction, but there was a *Tiger* in it. Time for *Research*.

Strategy Four: Do Research. Kevin had chosen that University because "everyone around here goes to the University of _____." Also, at the time he made that decision, he was unsure about which field he wanted to enter. That university provided an easy, inexpensive way to go to school and he was certain that he would know a lot of the people there. *Afterward*, he discovered things about the university that he did not like, but he had no qualms about the education he was getting.

Kevin went to the library to find out what other colleges and universities were situated in his own state, as well as in each state that bordered it. Aside from expense, which was a consideration, Kevin's *Road of Life* Diagram showed him that he was *quite concerned* (Rating of ②) with the size of the place and the amount of individual attention he could count on receiving. Thus, all the state universities, and any other large schools, were eliminated from consideration.

Kevin was pleased to find a school of moderate size and low expense, which provided the same quality of education that he had been receiving. It was a branch of the University of _____ several hundred miles away, in a scenic mountain setting. Kevin decided to attend a summer session there in order to do *Real-Time Research*, and he enjoyed it a great deal. By the end of the summer session, his dilemmas were resolved and his mind made up.

Strategy Five: Take the Tiger to Tea. Not necessary. This was accomplished by *Doing Research*.

Strategy Six: The One-Year Plan. Not necessary. This was contained in the original decision.

Strategy Seven: Settle. Kevin had to do some settling. The difference between *having money now* and *having money later* was very small. In other words, both were rated as having almost equal value. It *hurt* to give one up. It *hurt* to think of enduring three more years without enough money to have fun. These were his genuine, honest feelings. Nevertheless, Kevin was WILLING to give up having money now in order to get something he wanted MORE: a better, high-paying job in the future.

Mary

Mary had two part-time jobs, one as a waitress, the other as a tutor in a small, private elementary school. The situation at the school was so bad that she was considering quitting her tutoring job. There were only a few items in Mary's *Road of Life* Diagram, but the dilemma—a *Ricochet Romance*—was causing a lot of distress.

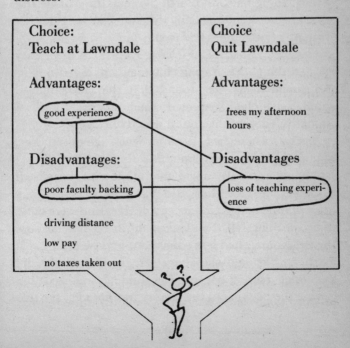

Choice:
Teach at Lawndale

Advantages:

good experience

Disadvantages:

poor faculty backing

driving distance

low pay

no taxes taken out

Choice
Quit Lawndale

Advantages:

frees my afternoon hours

Disadvantages

loss of teaching experience

Strategy One: Find Out Where You Are. Mary was in Place (1)—already living in one of the alternatives.

Strategy Two: Look for Mirror Images. There was a *Mirror Image* at either end of the one diagonal line:

Mary hoped eventually to get a full-time job in the public school system, working with children who needed special education, so gaining teaching experience (which was hard to come by) was very important to her. Going back and forth between the *Mirror Images*, she could not feel any difference in weight, consequently both circles had to stay in.

Strategy Three: Do a Quick Rating. When Mary applied the *Quick Rating* statements to the two *Mirror Image* items, she found that they were indeed equal, as she had suspected. Each one rated a ☐2: I could live without this, but it would hurt a lot.

She was astonished, however, when she got a "Yes, that's it" feeling on "poor faculty backing," for it rated only a ☐4. We talked about that a bit, because it surprised me, too. Mary said that most of the teachers at Lawndale had their master's degrees and were older than she. She felt they looked down on her because she was young, had less education, and wasn't a "real teacher." She said she almost laughed when she did the *Quick Rating* because she suddenly realized that having the backing of the faculty was *not why she was there*. Of course it would have been preferable to have it, and of course it would have felt good, but it was not important to her at *this* time, on *this* job. Mary was a temporary employee, and that was the way she wanted it. She was there for the experience, and she was getting it. Faculty backing on her permanent, full-time, career job would have been quite a different story. But she would have to cross that bridge when she came to it.

It took only these three moves for Mary to get "unstuck." When she removed "poor faculty backing," she had a *Leaning Ladder* and thus a clear, comfortable decision.

Strategy Four: Do Research. Not necessary.

Strategy Five: Take the Tiger to Tea. Mary toyed with this for a while, thinking about whether it was worth the time and effort to try to win the faculty over. She decided it was not, that she would just let nature take its course. Then another surprising thing happened. As she "let go" of the pain of feeling one-down, she was able to relax. She must have projected a subtle message to the other teachers: "I'm not tense and afraid of you anymore." And, without a word about the subject having been spoken, they gradually began to warm up to her, asking her questions about what she was doing with her students and giving advice about how to work with them in the classroom.

Mary had been anxious and defensive with the regular teachers. Once *she* was no longer afraid, *she* opened up the possibility of friendship, and they responded.

Strategy Six: The One-Year Plan. Not necessary. This was contained in the original decision.

Strategy Seven: Settle. Only a minor degree of settling was necessary, and Mary settled for that easily. It was easy, because her rating of "good experience" was so high ($\boxed{2}$) and "poor faculty backing" so low ($\boxed{4}$). It's easy to Settle for something that you discover doesn't bother you very much.

Frank

The last example in this category deals with the issue of retirement, with its many conflicts regarding money, self-identity, enjoyment, and obligation.

At age fifty-four, Frank was approaching the time when, if he wished, he could retire early. At fifty-five, he would be entitled to receive sixty percent of his average salary for the last three years of his employment. If he chose to wait until he was sixty, he would receive seventy-eight percent.

Frank and his wife, Meredith, had a seventeen-year-old daughter, still at home, who planned to attend college. Two sons had already graduated: one had been supported partially by an academic scholarship, the other had worked two years and then had taken out student loans. Nancy was a good, though not gifted, student who worked hard to get good grades. Frank did not think she would be able to make it if she had to work part-time. The need to finance his daughter's education was one of his most important considerations, but by no means the only one. Here is his complete diagram—a *Cat's Cradle* Dilemma:

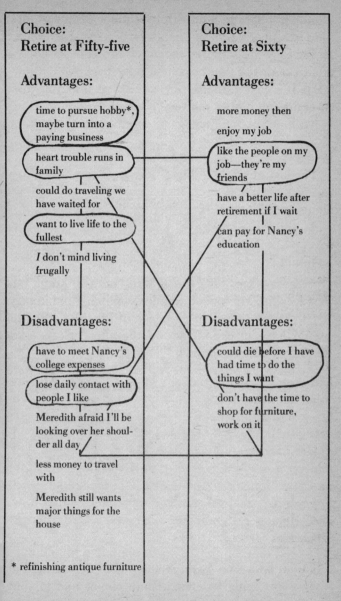

Choice: Retire at Fifty-five

Advantages:

time to pursue hobby*, maybe turn into a paying business

heart trouble runs in family

could do traveling we have waited for

want to live life to the fullest

I don't mind living frugally

Disadvantages:

have to meet Nancy's college expenses

lose daily contact with people I like

Meredith afraid I'll be looking over her shoulder all day

less money to travel with

Meredith still wants major things for the house

Choice: Retire at Sixty

Advantages:

more money then

enjoy my job

like the people on my job—they're my friends

have a better life after retirement if I wait

can pay for Nancy's education

Disadvantages:

could die before I have had time to do the things I want

don't have the time to shop for furniture, work on it

* refinishing antique furniture

211

Strategy One: Find Out Where You Are. Frank was in Place (3). He was waiting for something to happen. By the time he reached the age of fifty-five, then he would have to choose one of the alternatives: leave work, or continue to work.

Strategy Two: Look for Mirror Images. There were three *Mirror Images* in Frank's diagram. One was:

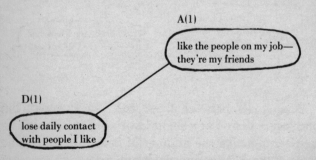

He went back and forth, feeling for the "weight," but they were evenly balanced. Both circles had to stay.

The second *Mirror Image* was:

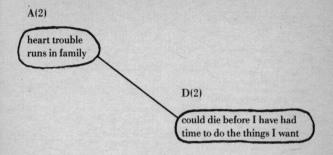

This time there was no contest. His eyes were pulled dramatically to the possibility of dying. The third *Mirror Image* uses one of the above items again:

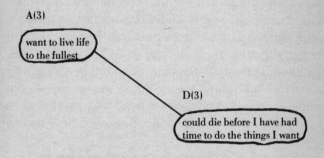

The "pull" between these was almost equal, but once again there was a slight favoring of the second.

After reducing the number of items by eliminating some of the *Mirror Images*, Frank's diagram was simplified somewhat but still full of conflict:

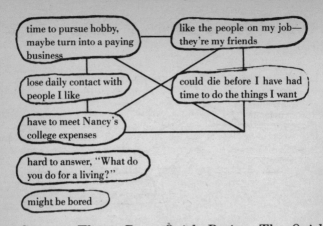

Strategy Three: Do a Quick Rating. The *Quick Rating* Strategy proved helpful in reducing the *information* but not in reducing the *conflict.* Frank realized that with a little creativity he could come up with a good answer when asked about his job. Furthermore, if he did go into furniture refinishing, this question would provide a splendid opportunity to promote the business. His hobby, as well as the possibility of travel, also took care of "might be bored." (In fact, the more he thought about it, the more he thought he would probably find plenty—even too much—to do, unlike a retired Army officer who was overheard to say, "I don't know what to do, because I have no one to report to.")

Frank was fortunate to have these interests and the health and expertise to carry them out. He was a person who wanted to and who *could* keep himself well occupied. If *you* do not presently have a compelling interest in a hobby or activity, then boredom or lack of work identity could be powerful Disadvantages to early retirement.

Using the *Quick Rating* Strategy, Frank was able to eliminate two more items:

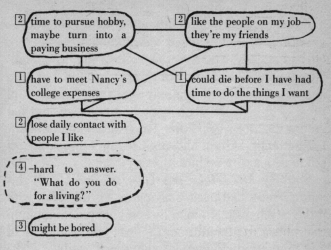

[2] time to pursue hobby, maybe turn into a paying business

[2] like the people on my job—they're my friends

[1] have to meet Nancy's college expenses

[1] could die before I have had time to do the things I want

[2] lose daily contact with people I like

[4] –hard to answer. "What do you do for a living?"

[3] might be bored

And the Golden Nugget emerged.

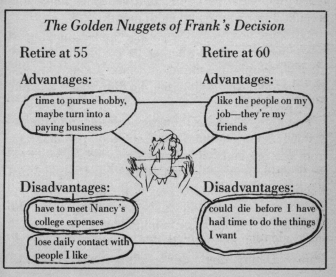

The Golden Nuggets of Frank's Decision

Retire at 55

Advantages:

time to pursue hobby, maybe turn into a paying business

Retire at 60

Advantages:

like the people on my job—they're my friends

Disadvantages:

have to meet Nancy's college expenses

lose daily contact with people I like

Disadvantages:

could die before I have had time to do the things I want

It was clear that Frank's highest priority for his own happiness was balanced equally against his obligation to his daughter.

Strategy Four: Do Research. Not applicable. Frank felt he had as much information as he needed. He had already explored other ways of financing Nancy's education. Student loans were available, but for a limited amount, covering only about thirty percent of the expenses at the school she had selected; and her grades did not qualify her for an academic scholarship. Nancy herself had applied for other kinds of scholarships with no luck.

Strategy Five: Take the Tiger to Tea. Up to this point, Frank had been working on his dilemma with little outside help. In fact, he had not even brought up the subject to Meredith and Nancy (although he had had some terrific fantasies, where each would cry—he hated that—and carry on, and generally make him feel like a worm for opening his mouth).

With his heart pounding (yes—grown man, heart pounding), he asked whether he could talk to them after dinner about a decision he was trying to make, and they agreed. (Believe me, he didn't taste one bite of his dinner.)

Frank described his thought processes from the beginning, showing them each stage of the diagram, from the original, with items uncircled, to the final draft with circles boiled down and rated. He pointed out that the *most* painful part of the decision was trying to meet his responsibility to Nancy while also meeting his responsibility to himself.

Nancy did *not* fall all over him and say, "Oh, Daddy, Daddy, don't worry. I'll manage somehow."

No, indeed. She was upset. But she was *also* sympathetic, quite sympathetic, to his needs. Meredith was upset also, not for herself but because she felt that since Frank had managed to put the boys through school, he had some obligation to do the same for Nancy.

It was not an easy scene. There were tears. Nancy cried for herself *and* for her father. She loved him dearly and didn't want to see *him* suffer any more than he did her. They decided to table the issue until the next night, hoping that with three heads put together instead of one, they would be able to come up with some kind of compromise.

It was Nancy who suggested it. She asked whether her father would be willing to support her completely for two years, after which if she had not done well enough to qualify for financial assistance, she would leave school to work for a year or two and then return to get her degree. For Frank, it would mean delaying his retirement two more years. He agreed.

For this family, given *all* the unique characteristics of their particular situation, this was an excellent compromise. Frank was relieved, pleased to have been able to share the responsibility of making this decision, and gratified by the knowledge that the family members were moving toward the same goal: the optimum welfare of *all* concerned, under the specific circumstances that existed.

Strategy Six: The One-Year Plan. In Frank's case, of course, this became the *Two-Year Plan*—an arranged time period *at the end of which* things would be different based on actions taken RIGHT NOW. True, on a day-to-day basis, his activities and behavior would be pretty much the same, at least as far as work duties were concerned. But knowing for certain that a change was coming, he could begin to prepare for it. His *attitude* changed from, "I am a person who works at _____," to "I am a person who will be retiring in two years, and I'd better get in gear to prepare for it."

Strategy Seven: Settle. Frank settled for a lot. He *accepted* the fact that once he retired he would lose close contact with people he liked very much. He took measures to reduce the pain of that loss by becoming a more active member of his church and by joining a local association of collectors and sellers of antiques. He *accepted* the fact that early retirement would place a financial burden on him, particularly as it affected Nancy's education. And in order to minimize this burden, as well as to minimize the discomfort of what could be called "selfishness" and "irresponsibility," he agreed to work for two more years. Finally, Frank accepted a *postponement* of the time when *he* felt he could begin to live life to the fullest. But he did NOT settle for a lifetime (or even five more years) of doing without what *he* needed most.

Choosing between Two Jobs, Schools, or Activities

Once you have decided that, yes, you want to work or go to school, get physically fit or join a bird-watching club, the question then remains, "Which one?" In my experience, this question has produced some of the greatest decision agonies of all time. Other decisions may be painful because you don't want to hurt someone or suffer pain, but the kinds of decisions in this section seem to paralyze people—

usually because the Advantages are so *evenly balanced*. Sometimes, it hardly matters a whit which one you choose, such as a dish on a menu, but that doesn't matter. The necessity to choose still paralyzes you. Nevertheless, as you use the Strategies, especially when the decision has important consequences for the future, you will find that they help, even in these often troublesome situations.

Bruce / Dawn / Amy / Jonathan

The four examples that follow came up in a workshop I did for a group of young people. Each pits one specific set of desires against another specific set of desires. Each uses the Seven Strategies somewhat differently, but to arrive at a true and comfortable resolution, one of the Strategies turned out to be highly important. (Can you guess which one?)

Bruce

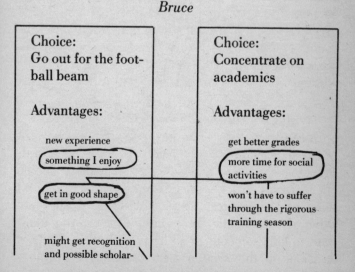

Choice:
Go out for the football beam

Advantages:

new experience
something I enjoy
get in good shape
might get recognition and possible scholar-

Choice:
Concentrate on academics

Advantages:

get better grades
more time for social activities
won't have to suffer through the rigorous training season

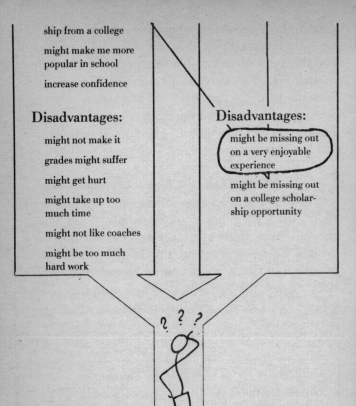

ship from a college

might make me more
popular in school

increase confidence

Disadvantages:

might not make it

grades might suffer

might get hurt

might take up too
much time

might not like coaches

might be too much
hard work

Disadvantages:

might be missing out
on a very enjoyable
experience

might be missing out
on a college scholar-
ship opportunity

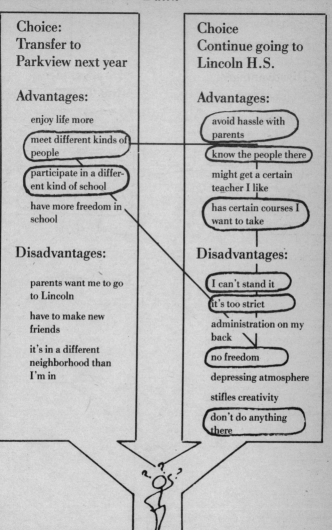

Choice:
Transfer to
Parkview next year

Advantages:

enjoy life more

meet different kinds of
people

participate in a differ-
ent kind of school

have more freedom in
school

Disadvantages:

parents want me to go
to Lincoln

have to make new
friends

it's in a different
neighborhood than
I'm in

Choice
Continue going to
Lincoln H.S.

Advantages:

avoid hassle with
parents

know the people there

might get a certain
teacher I like

has certain courses I
want to take

Disadvantages:

I can't stand it

it's too strict

administration on my
back

no freedom

depressing atmosphere

stifles creativity

don't do anything
there

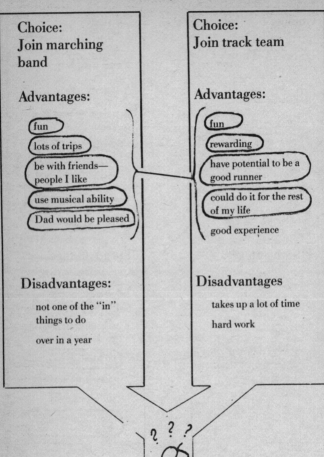

Choice:
Join marching band

Advantages:

- fun
- lots of trips
- be with friends—people I like
- use musical ability
- Dad would be pleased

Disadvantages:

not one of the "in" things to do

over in a year

Choice:
Join track team

Advantages:

- fun
- rewarding
- have potential to be a good runner
- could do it for the rest of my life
- good experience

Disadvantages

takes up a lot of time

hard work

**Choice:
Participate in the
Dance-A-Thon***

Advantages:

gain Shelton's (news-
paper's faculty advi-
sor) support

make Sue happy
(editor of school
newspaper and
girlfirend

raise money for *The
Front Page*

have a good time

Disadvantages:

can't dance

won't be able to go to
the AFS orientation

have the hassle of
getting and collecting
money from sponsors

**Choice:
Attend the AFS****
orientation**

Advantages:

able to do work at
Lenny's (part-time
busboy)

find out what I'll have
to do for the AFS
fundraiser

counting on me to be
there

need to plan the AFS
event

Disadvantages:

won't help raise money
for *The Front Page*

Shelton will be p——d

Sue will be mad

* fundraiser for the
school newspaper,
The Front Page

* *American
Field Service, an
organization which
places foreign students
in American high schools

Strategy One: Find Out Where You Are. All four students were in Place (4); when an opportunity or deadline came up, they could choose to take one of the alternatives, or they could choose neither. Amy's is the clearest case of a potential *Shadow Road.* You can see that it would be easy for her to join neither the marching band nor the track team. *Technically*, the other three could also *do neither*—Bruce and Dawn could conceivably drop out of school, and Jonathan could conceivably choose to attend neither event—but that possibility is so unlikely that it is probably not worth considering.

Strategy Two: Look for Mirror Images and *Strategy Three: Quick Rating.* For ease of comparison, I have combined these two Strategies to show the similarity among these Decision Dilemmas.

Bruce

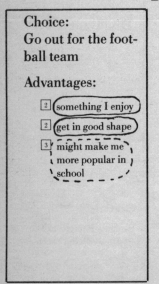

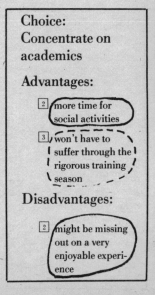

The Golden Nuggets of Bruce's Decision

Go out for the football team

Advantages:

- something I enjoy
- get in good shape

Disadvantages:

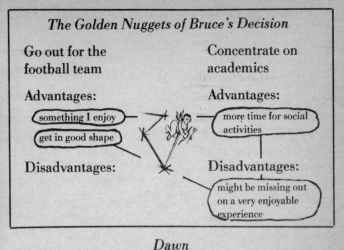

Concentrate on academics

Advantages:

- more time for social activities

Disadvantages:

- might be missing out on a very enjoyable experience

Dawn

**Choice:
Transfer to
Parkview next year**

Advantages:

- 3 meet different kinds of people
- 2 participate in a different kind of school

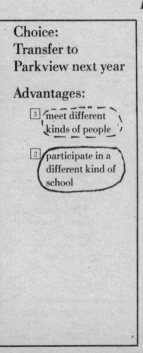

**Choice:
Continue going to
Lincoln H.S.**

Advantages:

- 2 avoid hassle with my parents
- 3 know the people there
- 4 has certain courses I want to take

Disadvantages:

- 2 no freedom
  (Dawn realized that all the Disadvantages she listed were really variations of "no freedom")

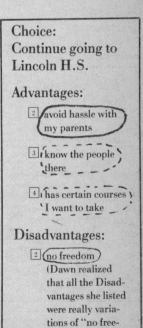

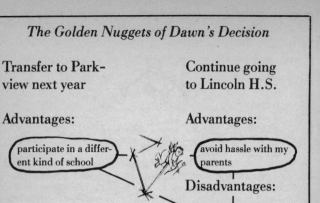

The Golden Nuggets of Dawn's Decision

Transfer to Park-
view next year

Continue going
to Lincoln H.S.

Advantages:

Advantages:

participate in a differ-
ent kind of school

avoid hassle with my
parents

Disadvantages:

no freedom

Amy

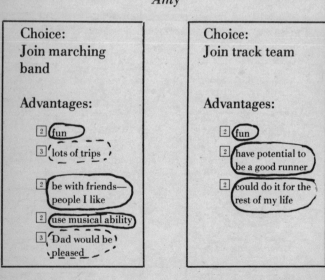

Choice:
Join marching
band

Advantages:

2 fun

3 lots of trips

2 be with friends—
people I like

2 use musical ability

3 Dad would be
pleased

Choice:
Join track team

Advantages:

2 fun

2 have potential to
be a good runner

2 could do it for the
rest of my life

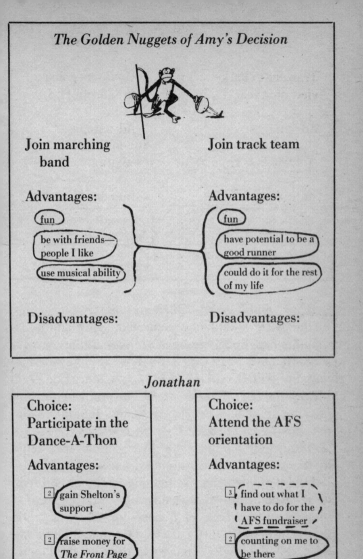

The Golden Nuggets of Amy's Decision

Join marching band

Advantages:

- fun
- be with friends— people I like
- use musical ability

Disadvantages:

Join track team

Advantages:

- fun
- have potential to be a good runner
- could do it for the rest of my life

Disadvantages:

Jonathan

Choice: Participate in the Dance-A-Thon

Advantages:

- [2] gain Shelton's support
- [2] raise money for *The Front Page*
- [3] have a good time

Choice: Attend the AFS orientation

Advantages:

- [3] find out what I have to do for the AFS fundraiser
- [2] counting on me to be there
- [2] need to help plan the AFS event

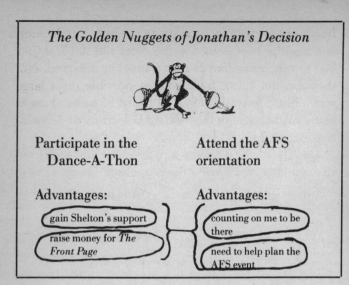

The Golden Nuggets of Jonathan's Decision

Participate in the Dance-A-Thon	Attend the AFS orientation
Advantages:	**Advantages:**
gain Shelton's support	counting on me to be there
raise money for *The Front Page*	need to help plan the AFS event

Bruce and Dawn's Dilemmas are *Ricochet Romance* with Advantages connected. Amy and Jonathan are caught between two *Monkey Bottles*. All the students have STRONG DESIRES on one side balanced by STRONG DESIRES on the other side.

Strategy Four: Do Research. The problem for three of these students—Bruce, Amy, and Jonathan—was not lack of knowledge. They each knew what to expect and were familiar with the nature of each activity. For them, *Research* was not necessary.

Dawn, though, had something genuinely difficult to contend with—the feeling of "no freedom." I brought up the issue of freedom to the group. Did they want it? Did they have it? Did they think it was possible? The twelve students in the workshop represented two different high schools. The consensus was this: Yes, they all wanted more flexibility and more freedom to make choices about courses, curriculum, and standards of behavior. No, they did not feel they had as much freedom as they wanted or deserved. No, they did not think freedom was possible on a large scale, but a few said they had heard of some changes being made through the Student Government Association.

Dawn had been feeling so pressured and restricted that she was sure some other school would just *have* to be better. She found out that "It ain't necessarily so." In fact, after this discussion, she realized that a "desire to escape from restriction" was the real reason the choice had come up in the first place. Once she saw that she might be jumping out of the frying pan into the fire, she decided to stay where she was, and her Decision Dilemma was resolved (more or less).

Strategy Five: Take the Tiger to Tea. Not applicable.

Strategy Six: The One-Year Plan. The One-Year Plan does not lend itself well to the *Monkey Bottle* type of Dilemma. It seems to help most when important *Disadvantages* are in the picture, especially when they are happening right now.

These four young people did not believe that the decision they made right now would greatly affect their futures one year from now. Yes, they might look back and say, "Gee, I wish I had chosen the other way," but that would not be an earth-shattering realization. The one who came closest to needing the One-Year Plan was Bruce. If he chose to go out for the football team, he would risk lowering his grades. But as you can see from his original diagram, fun was more important to *him* than grades.

Dawn's dilemma was resolved, but Amy and Jonathan still had *Monkey Bottles*, while Bruce had a *Ricochet Romance* with Advantages connected. There is only one Strategy that always works with Advantages connected, and that is to Settle—but only if you want to end up with *something*. If you simply *cannot Settle*, if you *cannot* give up what you feel you *must* have, if you allow yourself to be tormented by the thought that you are not getting all of what you need and deserve, then you may be more comfortable in the *Shadow Road*. From there, you can say to people, "I'm trying to make up my mind" (. . . while you're busy *not* making up your mind).

Strategy Seven: Settle. Bruce decided to go out for the football team. He was WILLING TO ACCEPT the rigorous training and loss of time for socializing. Though these considerations were not quite *as* important, he was also WILLING TO ACCEPT that he might get hurt and that his grades might suffer.

Dawn did *not* Settle. Oh, she stayed where she was all right—the other school seemed just as restrictive—but she chafed and complained and continued to be irritable about the "unfair" rules and restrictions. She took no part in the student government: "What can *they* do to change things?" she grumbled. Just being in one of the alternatives doesn't mean you have settled. Settling means ACCEPTING that, given all the circumstances, the total situation is about the best it can be *right now*.

Amy settled. She decided to join the track team. In order to get its Advantages, she was WILLING TO GIVE UP going on the trips, being with her friends in the band, using her musical ability, and pleasing her father in that particular way. She ACCEPTED the fact that track is hard work and would take a lot of time.

Jonathan settled, although his decision was more difficult than those of the others because either way he went, he was going to upset someone. Jonathan felt, however, that his greater responsibility was to the AFS Club, and that is what he chose. He liked to please others, but once his mind was made up, that was it. He is one of those fortunate few who do not torment themselves with visions of what might have been. He didn't want to upset Sue and Mr. Shelton, but he didn't feel *responsible* for their being upset either. That was *their* choice.

Alan

Alan had just graduated college and was in the beginning stages of thinking about a career. One strong alternative was to join the Coast Guard, to which both his father and grandfather had belonged. And from time to time, he entertained the idea of becoming a pilot. These were the alternatives he selected as a way of exploring his choices.

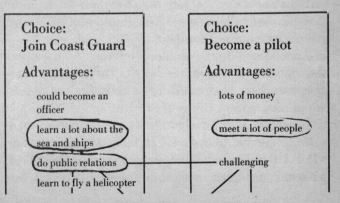

Choice:
Join Coast Guard

Advantages:

could become an officer

learn a lot about the sea and ships

do public relations

learn to fly a helicopter

Choice:
Become a pilot

Advantages:

lots of money

meet a lot of people

challenging

231

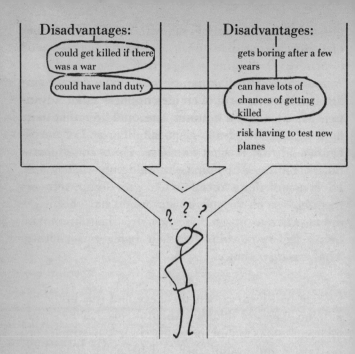

Strategy One: Find Out Where You Are. Alan was in Place (2), the *Shadow Road.* He did not *have* to join the Coast Guard, nor did he *have* to become a pilot. He was *doing neither,* and there was no deadline or other event which would have forced him to commit himself one way or the other.

Like many other people, however, Alan *felt* as though the world were in a state of suspended animation (an idea often used in science fiction stories, where the subject continues to live and move, while time stands still for the world), a "timeless" state called, "Trying to decide." In fact, he was spending *time* in the *Shadow Road,* gaining perspective (Yes), gaining relief from a sense of responsibility (Yes), but also using up *time* and living without the Advantages of either alternative.

Strategy Two: Mirror Images. There are no *Mirror Images* in Alan's diagram. Specifically, a *Mirror Image* is when one form of an idea appears as an Advantage at one end of a *diagonal* line, and the other form appears as a Disadvantage at the other end of the diagonal. *Mirror Images* do not go across the diagram horizontally, nor do they go up and down. They only go diagonally. Therefore, the desires that Alan expresses—"public relations"/"meet a lot of people"— are not Mirror Images. However, they *are* related, and this relationship turned out to be one of the keys to resolving his dilemma.

Strategy Three: Quick Rating. Alan's specific Decision Dilemma was resolved with this step. However, it did not end his need to make a major decision. It just didn't turn out to be the particular decision he was thinking about! Alan's *Quick Rating* turned out as shown below:

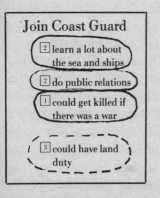

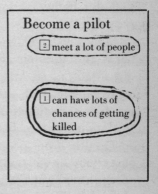

Both sides of the Diagram contained an item that Alan would have found *absolutely intolerable*: living with the possibility of getting killed! He looked hard at why he had even chosen these particular alternatives in the first place.

After some discussion, Alan revealed that he had never seriously considered any career other than the Coast Guard. It was more or less "expected" that he would follow in his father's footsteps. When an opportunity came along to practice this new decision-making technique, he selected the idea of being a pilot, something he had always thought a glamorous and exciting thing to do. The *Quick Rating* proved to be a shock, as he suddenly realized, "Hey, what am I letting myself in for here!"

As both of Alan's Choices evaporated before his eyes, he landed back on Square One. But this time, he was on Square One with *awareness*. He knew a little bit about what he wanted and a lot about what he didn't want. Now, he was closer to thinking about a career that would be satisfying to *him* as a unique individual, whether or not it was "what everyone in his family did."

Strategy Four: Do Research. Let's look closely at what Alan found out about himself. With only a few items to go on, we know that Alan likes people. He likes to interact with them, and he likes to meet new ones. It was meaningful that this important value got into the diagram on both sides, was circled on both sides, and had no specific connection with either the Coast Guard or with aviation.

Then, there was the idea of learning about the sea and ships and being disappointed at having land duty.

Alan learned that he loved being *out on the water* and that he was eager to learn about ships and navigation.

I assigned Alan a very specific Research task: Find out everything you can about careers in navigation which are nonmilitary, which enable you to meet a lot of people, and which keep you out on the water. Alan returned in a week, almost walking on air. He had decided that he would work toward establishing a career as a sailing instructor, perhaps adding boat sales and rentals at some point. While this might eventually involve moving to a warmer climate, such as Florida or Hawaii, Alan planned to spend the next several years developing his knowledge and skills and saving money before making a major move.

Strategy Five: Take the Tiger to Tea. Not applicable to the decision as such, but Alan did have to *Take the Tiger to Tea* after all. He had to explain to his parents, especially his father, why he had decided against the Coast Guard. His father's argument that the risk of getting killed in the Coast Guard is extremely small was a powerful one, and Alan was affected by it.

He asked for a few more days to think it over. During these few days, he "turned the job over to his brain" to work on. "O.K., brain," he said, "you know what the facts are now. Would you please work on it and let me know how it comes out?" At the end of three days, Alan said to himself, "I go into the Coast Guard," and he felt how it felt. He described the feeling as, "tight and heavy." Then he said to himself, "I become a sailing instructor." This time he felt distinctly light and excited. This was his choice.

At first, his parents were upset. They were less upset, however, when they saw how confident he was about his decision. And their upset diminished greatly as Alan began to take instruction, and they could see the full extent of his enthusiasm, dedication, and hard work.

Strategy Six: The One-Year Plan. This was a vital element in the decision; it automatically enters into most decisions involving a career choice.

Strategy Seven: Settle. Alan did not have to Settle. He was most fortunate in being able to combine *all* the important things he wanted in a career into a third alternative. If he had to Settle for anything at all, it was for having disappointed his family, particularly his father.

Rebecca

Rebecca's job dilemma was a good deal more complicated than Alan's, because she was already established in a job—until she learned that she would be let go in ninety days because of financial cutbacks at her institution. Rebecca was a social worker with ten years experience, divorced, with custody of two children, a boy twelve, and a girl seven. Rebecca had worked with families as well as individual adults, specializing in cases complicated by drug or alcohol abuse. The agency job paid only moderately well but had excellent benefits, and until the cutback she considered her job secure. The agency had offered to keep her there on a part-time basis, but she would have to switch to working exclusively with emotionally disturbed adolescents.

Rebecca had been toying with the idea of going into private practice in her home and she saw this transition period as a possible opportunity to try that out.

At the same time, her income was moderate at best, and she did not know whether she could survive a pay cut without something substantial and reliable to supplement it. This is how she set up the alternatives:

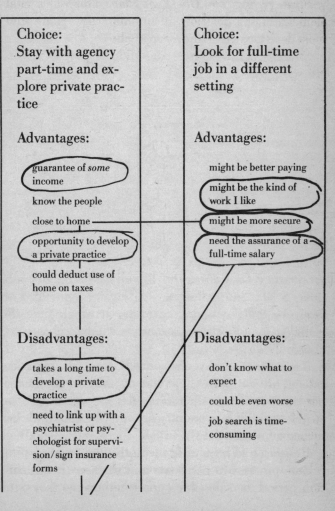

Choice:
Stay with agency part-time and explore private practice

Advantages:

guarantee of *some* income

know the people

close to home

opportunity to develop a private practice

could deduct use of home on taxes

Disadvantages:

takes a long time to develop a private practice

need to link up with a psychiatrist or psychologist for supervision/sign insurance forms

Choice:
Look for full-time job in a different setting

Advantages:

might be better paying

might be the kind of work I like

might be more secure

need the assurance of a full-time salary

Disadvantages:

don't know what to expect

could be even worse

job search is time-consuming

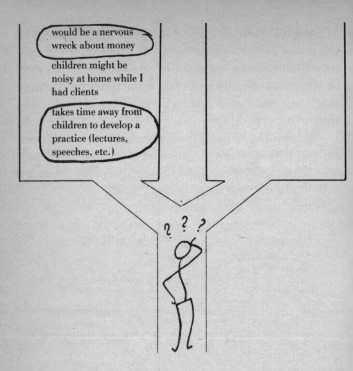

Strategy One: Find Out Where You Are. Rebecca was in Place (4). She was waiting for something to happen, the ninety-day deadline, at which time she could take one of the alternatives she had chosen, or she could *do neither*.

Do neither? Are you surprised? Here are just a few of the other things she could do: She could borrow money to take courses in computer programming. She could work for a temporary agency. She could ask her ex-husband or relatives to take temporary custody of the children while she devoted full-time to developing a private practice. And so on. The point is not that she *should* or *should not* (or whether *you* would or would not) do any of those things. The point is that when you are not compelled by the nature of circumstances to be *in* one alternative or the other, a number of other options may open up. Sometimes, a *"do neither"* can unleash a whole flood of creative alternatives.

Strategy Two: Look for Mirror Images. The *Mirror Images* in Rebecca's diagram have to do with money and financial security. Each *Image* matches the same item against another:

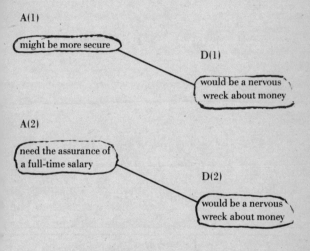

A(1)

might be more secure

D(1)

would be a nervous wreck about money

A(2)

need the assurance of a full-time salary

D(2)

would be a nervous wreck about money

Notice that the item on the left is a certainty: *"would* be," while those on the right are possibilities: *"might* be." The reality of the situation was that at this point, without another specific job in mind, Rebecca would have to balance a *known* Disadvantage against a *possible* Advantage. As her eyes went back and forth between the items, she was pulled toward "would be a nervous wreck about money" in both cases. This reduced her diagram as follows:

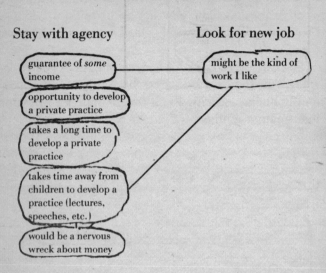

Stay with agency

- guarantee of *some* income
- opportunity to develop a private practice
- takes a long time to develop a private practice
- takes time away from children to develop a practice (lectures, speeches, etc.)
- would be a nervous wreck about money

Look for new job

- might be the kind of work I like

Strategy Three: Do A Quick Rating. Rebecca's Diagram was still a *Ricochet Romance* Dilemma, but was well on its way to becoming a *Tiger 'Neath the Tree.* This Strategy clinched it. Here is how it happened.

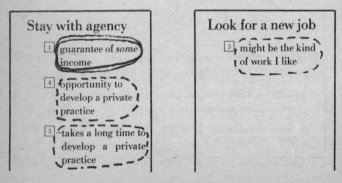

Stay with agency

1. guarantee of *some* income
4. opportunity to develop a private practice
3. takes a long time to develop a private practice

Look for a new job

3. might be the kind of work I like

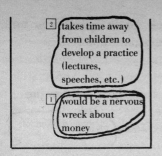

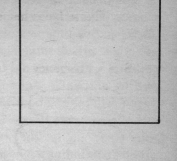

Rebecca would prefer to do the kind of work she really liked. Who wouldn't? But she was *willing* to eliminate that circle and the other low-rated items in order to boil the decision down even further and reveal its Golden Nuggets.

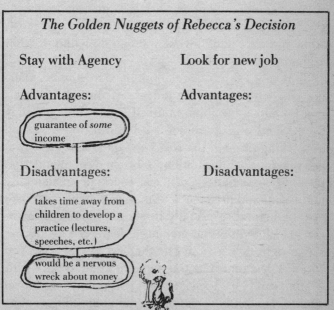

The Golden Nuggets of Rebecca's Decision

Stay with Agency   Look for new job

Advantages: Advantages:

> guarantee of *some* income

Disadvantages: Disadvantages:

> takes time away from children to develop a practice (lectures, speeches, etc.)

> would be a nervous wreck about money

Here, then, was the essence of Rebecca's dilemma: Can I tolerate being a nervous wreck about money and spending time away from my children in order to guarantee myself *some* money coming in? The answer was, "No." Rebecca did not feel that the Advantages of this particular *Tiger 'Neath the Tree* Dilemma were worth putting up with its Disadvantages.

Rebecca made the decision not to accept the part-time position, but she was, of course, left with the problem of finding a new job.

Strategy Four: Do Research. Looking for a job can be one of the most important, and frustrating, pieces of *Research* a person ever has to do. It affects your life deeply—your self-image, your social status, your health, your opportunities. It takes every bit of thought and skill you can bring to it, because essentially it is a search for yourself: what you *need* most, what you *want* most, what you can do without, what scares or worries you.

To do a good job search, you need maximum information—about yourself and about the job. You already know a lot about yourself (more than you may think), and you can discover it in intuitive ways, such as working through the *Road of Life* Diagram. But to get *maximum* information, I often recommend that people take a battery of tests, especially personality and vocational preference tests. (Intelligence tests can also be helpful, especially if you are looking at a career which requires an advanced degree.) The job you are in right now may not be the best job for you. You sort of know that, but you may not know exactly why. Testing can help. I suggest that you contact your local Mental Health Association or the counseling centers at nearby colleges and universities to see where these tests can be obtained. Aside from testing, it will help to talk to people who are already doing the kind of work you are thinking about. This, as you know, is *Talk-Time Research*.

Rebecca was concerned about salary and benefits, and this information was easy to get. But she had also circled "might be the kind of work I like." On this, she knew she needed help. She enjoyed her work but wasn't sure just what it was about doing social work that was so satisfying. She decided to be tested and found out some things she already knew but others that were new to her. These are some of the things she already knew: she liked working with people; she enjoyed challenging, difficult work; she liked coordinating her work with that of other people (a good team player); and she knew that, aside from a certain minimum amount, money was not as important as an interesting job. She was surprised and intrigued, however, by the *new* things she discovered: she liked to develop plans and programs, she was the type of person who could have a lot of influence over others, she had a good mind for detail, and (well, she was not really so proud of this one, but there it was) she liked to tell people what to do! In a nutshell, Rebecca discovered that she had managerial/leadership ability. It was an ability that served her well in psychotherapy, but in addition, it opened up a vocational path that she had not taken seriously—administration.

Rebecca's job search took two months of hard work. She got assistance developing a résumé, which now included the areas of program development, project management, and administration. She contacted colleagues and wrote to organizations, asking for suggestions about whom she might contact regarding a job possibility. This process produced over twenty interviews.

I would like very much to report that Rebecca's dream job materialized before her very eyes. This did not happen. But she *was* offered a job at a hospital, for slightly higher pay, providing ongoing therapy and aftercare for patients being treated for drug or alcohol abuse. She requested, and received, permission to talk at length to the person who was leaving the job and satisfied herself that it would suit her.

With ten years experience in the field, and with her newly discovered self-knowledge, Rebecca was now in a position to be quite precise about the kind of position she would pursue or would try to create for herself in the future. As a by-product, she realized that private practice was not her cup of tea after all. It was too isolated and didn't provide enough in the way of *coordinating* her work with the work of other people.

Strategy Five: Take the Tiger to Tea. Not necessary. Rebecca was so certain she could not tolerate "would be a nervous wreck about money" that there was no point talking to her children about the possibility of having less money available. She *did* talk to them about the effects the job change would have on their lives and how it could be made more agreeable for everyone concerned.

Strategy Six: The One-Year Plan. This Strategy was high on Rebecca's list of important considerations, except that her plan was not for as definite a period as one year. Nevertheless, it was a plan which involved keeping her eyes open, keeping up her contacts in the community by being active in professional organizations, and generally "letting it be known" that she was available for consideration if an administrative position opened up in her field. In other words, Rebecca knew where she was headed (to a different position from where she was now), but she didn't know how long it might take to get there.

Strategy Seven: Settle. More than anything else, Rebecca settled for *accepting some risk*. She gave up the security of the part-time job in the *hope* that something much better would turn up. There was no guarantee. But she did not let herself get caught in a maze, turning here and there, praying that she would find some way out. She *bettered* her chances of finding something by going after a job in an intelligent way and by putting a lot of time and effort into it. For the time being, for the sake of financial security, she was *settling*, both for a salary below what she thought she could receive eventually and for a job that was not precisely what she wanted and could do best. This, then, was a temporary settling, with an open time limit on it.

Tough Decisions 2: Money—Getting It, Spending It

Money, money, money—the sharpest of all the Brass Tacks. How to get it? How to spend it? How to get more? Most decisions about money are not about money. Only criminals use the direct approach: if you want money, take money. The rest of us have to go through some intermediate step to get money—like working.

245

In some decisions, "more money" appears as a critically important value all by itself. If you say, "I am thinking of taking this job because it pays more money," people will simply nod their heads in understanding and say, "Ah, yes." Rarely do they ask, "Well, George, what do you intend to *do* with the money?" It is simply *accepted* that more is better; even though *everyone* you talk to, from a pauper to a millionaire, will say he or she doesn't have enough. Could we all agree on something right here? Could we just go ahead and agree that there really is no such thing as "enough" money, simply because as money increases, *desires* increase step by step. Think of the tension and pressure that would be eliminated. You would *know* for an absolute fact that you do not and never will have enough money. That your next-door neighbor does not and never will have enough money, that no one on the face of the earth has or ever will have enough money . . . *unless* you conclude, "I have enough money for all of the things I really *need* and some of the things I *want*." (Try it. It's very relaxing.)

Other decisions focus more on the idea of what to do with the money you do have. These lead to questions like: "What should I do with the money I save if I don't do *X*?", or "What should I do with the money I get if I sell *Y*?", or "What can I do to get money to buy *Z*?" We have already agreed (haven't we?) that there is never enough money, but questions about what to do with what *is* available probably make up the majority of decisions about money. Let's look at three of them.

Pat's decision involved whether to sell one item in order to get money for a different item. Rob's involved whether to spend money now or spend it later. And Betty's involved spending money for purpose *A* versus spending it for purpose *B*.

Pat

Pat's dilemma was whether or not to sell his motorcycle. His circles produced the *Ricochet Romance* pattern, heavier on the Disadvantages:

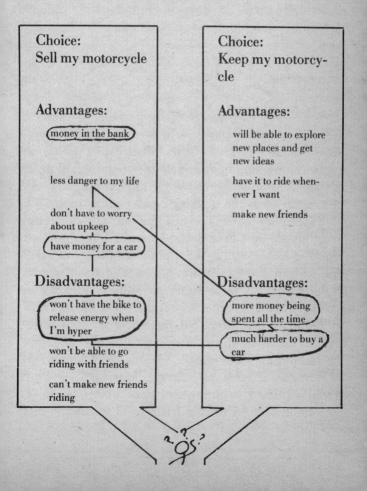

Choice:
Sell my motorcycle

Advantages:

(money in the bank)

less danger to my life

don't have to worry
about upkeep

(have money for a car)

Disadvantages:

(won't have the bike to
release energy when
I'm hyper)

won't be able to go
riding with friends

can't make new friends
riding

Choice:
Keep my motorcycle

Advantages:

will be able to explore
new places and get
new ideas

have it to ride when-
ever I want

make new friends

Disadvantages:

(more money being
spent all the time)

(much harder to buy a
car)

Sometimes (not always), if there are only a few items, and especially if there is only *one item* in the corner of the triangle: a *Ricochet Romance* Dilemma can be resolved in only one step.

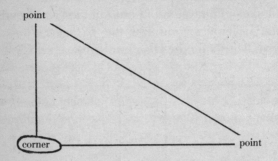

Since every *Ricochet Romance* contains a diagonal, it has the potential in it for a comfortable decision—Leaning Ladder. If the item (or items) in the *corner* can be eliminated by reducing its power, by finding an alternative that will produce the same result, or by *accepting* it—only the *Leaning Ladder* will remain.

I asked Pat to focus on just that one item in the corner, but his eyes kept going around the diagram, reminding him of all the other possibilities. I then asked him to put his hands over the rest of the diagram, leaving exposed *only* "won't have the bike to release energy when I'm hyper." Now, he could prevent himself from getting distracted and could pay close attention to the hang-up in the corner. In a few moments, he started to get unstuck. "I suppose I could find other ways of releasing energy," he said. "I guess I could go down to the school and shoot baskets, or maybe go along with my friends. They usually pick me up."

Pat was closer to deciding to sell the motorcycle, but you can see that he was less than wildly enthusiastic about it. A motorcycle carries a lot of emotional weight, and he needed a couple of months to get used to the idea. The final push came when he needed new tires and would have had to put out over one hundred dollars.

Did Pat WANT to go riding with his friends? Yes! Did he WANT to be able to explore new places? Yes! Would he have *preferred* to use the bike rather than a basketball to get rid of tension? Yes! He chose to sell the bike because he wanted something else *more*. He wanted a *car*.

Terry

A friend of mine, retired but building a business as a private consultant, had a small house right on the Potomac River. He was a fine boatman, and had always had a pleasure boat of one kind or another. At this point in his life, however, he was in a very tight financial position. Undaunted by it, and as if performing some kind of religious ritual, he would dutifully scour the "Boats—Sale" ads every Sunday, circling the ones that caught his fancy. Sure enough, it wasn't long before he located the perfect boat (why do some people *insist* on torturing themselves?), but of course he didn't have the money to pay for it. Now, this was a man who was used to getting what he wanted, through hard work, charm, making sacrifices—whatever it took. It just about killed him not to have this boat, and he was on the verge of going into debt to buy it.

He agreed to work through the decision, using the

***Road of Life* Diagram.** It was a simple, but conflicted decision—a real *Cat's Cradle.*

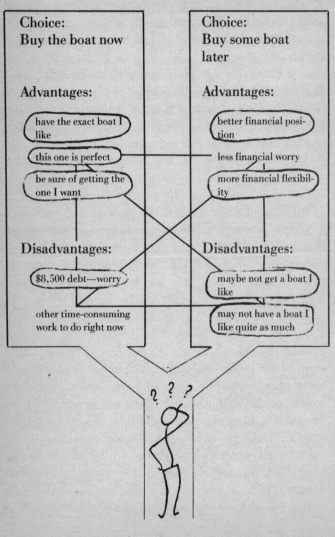

Choice:
Buy the boat now

Advantages:

have the exact boat I like

this one is perfect

be sure of getting the one I want

Disadvantages:

$8,500 debt—worry

other time-consuming work to do right now

Choice:
Buy some boat later

Advantages:

better financial position

less financial worry

more financial flexibility

Disadvantages:

maybe not get a boat I like

may not have a boat I like quite as much

Terry was a creative person, who managed to say pretty much the same thing eight different ways. Let's simplify the diagram right off. All the Advantages of *Buy the boat now* express one central idea: "be sure of getting the perfect boat." All the advantages of *Buy some boat later* could be expressed as: "better financial position." And, instead of three Disadvantages of *Buy some boat later*, we could say: "may not get a boat I like quite as much later." Since the idea of having other work to do right now was not circled, we can express the *essence*—the Golden Nuggets—of Terry's decision like this:

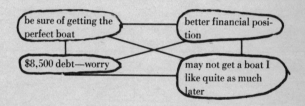

Strategy One: Find Out Where You Are. Terry either bought *that* boat, or he did not buy *that* boat. He was in Place (1): he *had* to be in one or another of the alternatives.

Strategy Two: Look for Mirror Images. The items in Terry's decision were basically two *Mirror Images*:

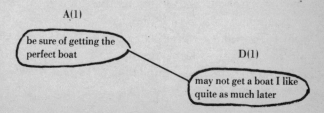

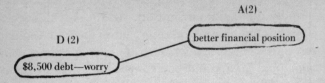

Looking at one pair at a time, Terry let his eyes go back and forth, trying to feel the weight. His "pull" was toward the Disadvantages. He *hated* to have to worry about money. And he *hated* not being able to have what he wanted, so the *Cat's Cradle* diminished to the simpler *Railroad Tracks*:

Strategy Three: Do a Quick Rating. After the *Quick Rating*, it was clear to Terry what the decision would be. The "$8,500 debt worry" scored a ⬜1 (I would find this absolutely intolerable . . . given my total financial position right now), while "may not get a boat I like quite as much later" scored only a ⬜3 (I could live with this, but I wouldn't like it). Not even close. And the one remaining Golden Nugget revealed a clear decision.

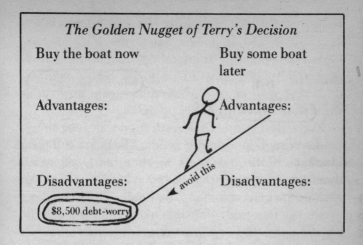

The Golden Nugget of Terry's Decision

Buy the boat now

Buy some boat later

Advantages:

Advantages:

Disadvantages:

Disadvantages:

avoid this

$8,500 debt-worry

Strategy Four: Do Research. Terry's Research consisted of continuing to search the ads. His knowledge about boats and the types available in his area was excellent. All he needed to find out was how often the kind of boat he wanted came up for sale.

Strategy Five: Take the Tiger to Tea. Not applicable.

Strategy Six: The One-Year Plan. Terry had found himself in a very common type of conflict situation: "If I don't grab *it* now, *it* (or something of equal attractiveness) may not be available later. Then, I'll miss out completely." Have *you* ever had this thought? Are you afraid that the future will let you down? Do you believe that the good things of life are in such short supply that deprivation is just around the corner?

We, and our enterprises, pride ourselves on being creative and productive. We *expect* things to get better. We expect better products of all kinds five years from now. In fact, we hardly buy anything unless it says, "New and Improved." It seems ironic that we believe two opposite things: first, that things (products, quality of life) will tend to get better, and second, that we'll never find anything again as good as the one we're looking at right now.

Not only are more interesting and elegant things being created, but durable goods, like boats and cars, circulate. Cars and boats are *constantly* changing hands. It's not likely that the exact kind you want can stay off the market for long, especially if you're *willing* to put the time and effort into looking for it *when the time is right*. To be *willing* to put off having what you want right now (the boat, say) for the sake of having more later (the boat *and* a better financial position), you must have a sense of trust in the future, a sense that life will provide, that good things and good people are everywhere—although they may not fall out of the sky right into your lap.

There is a delightful, true anecdote from the world of opera that describes what I am talking about. Leo Slezak, a noted singer, was engaged in a long aria from Wagner's *Lohengrin*. At the end of this aria, a swan boat was to appear from the wings. He would get in, and the swan would carry him majestically offstage. To his great distress, he saw as he was singing that the swan had arrived too soon. Glancing over his shoulder, he watched helplessly as it glided across the stage and disappeared into the wings. Maintaining his composure, he finished his aria, turned confidently, and called backstage, "What time is the next swan?"

If Slezak had hope that there would be another swan, maybe Terry can have hope that there will be another boat.

Strategy Seven: Settle. You saw from the examples of the four teenagers that *Monkey Bottles* usually required the most settling. *Railroad Tracks* are a close second. Terry wanted *most* to avoid a worrisome $8,500 debt. He *avoided* this worry by choosing to put off buying the boat. Believe me, he did not *WANT* to give up buying that precise boat. He did not WANT to take the risk of never finding a boat he wanted again. But he was WILLING to give up the boat now and WILLING to take the risk in order to *avoid* a major financial worry. This was a classic case of *settling*.

Betty

Since money is usually a means to some other end, not an end in itself ("collecting" money is like "collecting" flower seeds), and since you never have enough to buy all the things you have decided you want and deserve, it is an area ripe for conflict and tension. In fact, money often acts as a smokescreen to disguise personal issues such as, "my needs *versus* theirs," or "who gets to decide." Betty's decision certainly *involved* money, but was money the real issue?

Choice: Send Monica and Greg to private school	Choice: Send Monica and Greg to public school
Advantages:	Advantages:
better scholastic education	friends in neighborhood

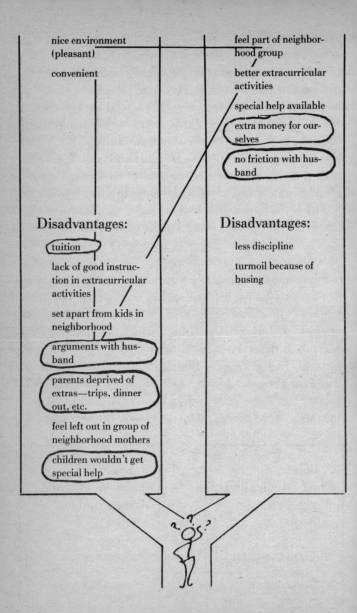

Strategy One: Find Out Where You Are. Again, strictly on technical terms, Betty could choose to *do neither.* She could keep her children out of school, and some people do try to do that. Realistically, however, Betty is in Place (1): she *must* be in one or another of the alternatives given here.

Strategy Two: Look for Mirror Images. Notice that Betty included "special help available" (a mirror image of "children wouldn't get special help") as an Advantage of public school, but she did not circle it. This often happens. You may find that the *Mirror Images* take care of themselves during the relaxation/circling procedure, and you never circle the paired item in the first place. Betty *was*, however, left with two clear *Mirror Images*:

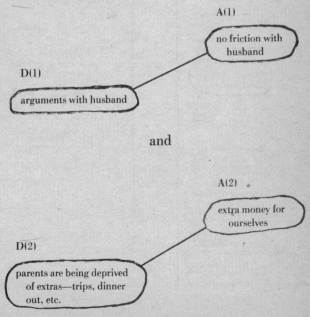

A(1)

no friction with
husband

D(1)

arguments with husband

and

A(2)

extra money for
ourselves

D(2)

parents are being deprived
of extras—trips, dinner
out, etc.

The only *Image* item Betty could eliminate was, "no friction with husband." A good argument might also be made for eliminating "tuition" as a separate item, since its main effects seem to be: depriving parents of extras and causing arguments with husband, and both of these have already been circled.

Strategy Three: Do a Quick Rating. Betty's *Quick Rating* showed her clearly what was *most* important. It simplified and clarified the real issues, but it did not help much to reduce her inner conflict:

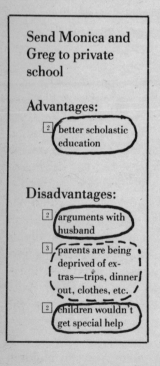

Send Monica and Greg to private school

Advantages:

2 better scholastic education

Disadvantages:

2 arguments with husband

3 parents are being deprived of extras—trips, dinner out, clothes, etc.

2 children wouldn't get special help

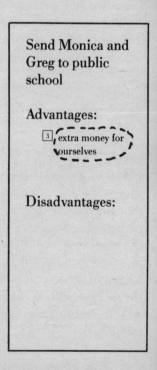

Send Monica and Greg to public school

Advantages:

3 extra money for ourselves

Disadvantages:

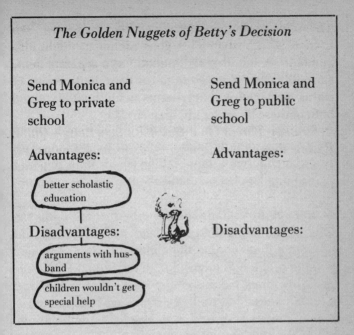

The Golden Nuggets of Betty's Decision

Send Monica and Greg to private school

Advantages:

better scholastic education

Disadvantages:

arguments with husband

children wouldn't get special help

Send Monica and Greg to public school

Advantages:

Disadvantages:

Strategy Four: Do Research. A small amount of Research was needed. Betty already believed, having talked to friends whose children attended either private school or public school—had children in both— that the quality of education in the private school was higher. But she felt she did not know enough about the amount of special help that was actually available in each situation. Classes in both types of schools were large; yet, at least for children who needed assistance, the public schools had many more resources. Betty still needed to know the answers to some very specific questions:

• How much special help were *her* two children

likely to need? (She could talk to her children and their teachers about this.)

- If they did need help, what resources were available within each school setting to provide it? (She could talk to the school principals about this.)
- If resources were insufficient, could special help be provided through a tutor, or by working with the children at home? (She could think this over and talk to her husband about it.)

Strategy Five: Take the Tiger to Tea. Here was the crux of the issue. Betty and her husband, Rex, *did not agree* that sending the children to private school was the best use of money for all concerned. You have probably already guessed that it was Betty's *husband* who felt most deprived of extras and that the arguments centered around *who* would actually decide where the children went to school and how the money would be spent.

Betty felt very torn between wanting to provide a good education for her children and wanting to avoid arguments with Rex. Yet, she had never brought the issue out into the open, with her children *or* her husband, at least in the spirit of seeking mutual cooperation and resolution. (Arguments don't count!)

It was time for this step. Betty brought the original diagram to the discussion, but strictly as a starting point. Essentially, she was willing to start the decision-making process all over again, this time using *everyone's* input from the beginning.

There was little change in the number of items (Betty had touched on all the important considerations), but, not surprisingly, the children *rated* the items very differently. They wanted to remain with their friends, they wanted to feel part of the neighborhood group of children, and they very much wanted the extracurricular activities. From their point of view, the "lack of discipline" and the "turmoil about busing" were virtually nonexistent. They seemed to be things that parents worried a lot about but that children handled quite well.

The children also brought up another interesting point. Not only would the parents be deprived of extras. So would they! Private school tuition meant fewer clothes, less going out to dinner for everyone, and less interesting vacations for everyone.

Strategy Six: The One-Year Plan. This was, of course, the underlying issue of the decision in the first place and did not need to be treated as a separate Strategy.

Strategy Seven: Settle. What about the quality of education—Betty's major worry? Monica (ten) and Greg (eight) were bright children, who had done well in school so far. The family was active—went to museums, concerts, read, and had lively discussions with each other. *These particular children* and *this particular family* seemed to have enough motivation and inner strength to overcome the obstacles even of a poor school setting, which was not the case here. After a lot of discussion and rethinking of the issue, Betty was able to *overcome* (make peace with) *her fear* that she was being irresponsible by not providing *absolutely* the *best* education that she could find. Her fear of being irresponsible was not only exaggerated but was undermining her relationship with both her husband

and her children.

Betty was able to *Settle* because of the positive interaction with her family. She *Took the Tigers to Tea.* They put milk and sugar in it and gave it back to her.

Tough Decisions 3: Making a Major Change

I have heard it said that change can be worse than death; at least after you die you don't realize what you've lost. Research has shown repeatedly that *change*, especially major change, is one of the most stressful experiences you can undergo. In fact, it is actually possible to predict your chances of becoming seriously ill within one year, based on how many major changes you have gone through in the previous year.

As a decision maker, you need to know these things about change:

MANY PEOPLE INTENSELY DISLIKE MAJOR CHANGES.

MANY PEOPLE ARE *AFRAID* OF CHANGE.

MANY PEOPLE WILL CHOOSE TO STAY WHERE THEY ARE BECAUSE THEY FEEL *SAFE*, NOT BECAUSE THEY LIKE WHAT'S HAPPENING THERE.

The problem is that change moves you from *what you know*, to *what you don't know*. FEAR OF CHANGE IS FEAR OF THE UNKNOWN. Yes, you can make some predictions and guesses, and you can talk to people. But you can never KNOW FOR SURE until you make the change a reality.

We will look at four examples dealing with *change*:

- Aggie decided whether to continue living with her boyfriend, Mark, or to move out.

- Vince decided whether to stay in the Washington, D.C., area or to settle out West.

- Janet decided whether to remain a homemaker or get a job.

- Wilhelmina (Willie) decided whether to let her bubbly self out or continue to keep it inside.

Aggie

Aggie, twenty-seven, had been living with her boyfriend, Mark, for a year and a half. They had known each other for years and had a close circle of mutual friends. There were some problems in the relationship—not fatal ones, but Aggie felt she needed space. She had a tendency to lean on people, to get them to take care of her; so moving out of the apartment could be more than just a move. It could be a symbol of her growing desire for independence.

Aggie's Dilemma was a *Cat's Cradle*:

Choice: Move out of the apartment	Choice: Stay in the apartment
Advantages:	Advantages:
become more independent	stable living condition

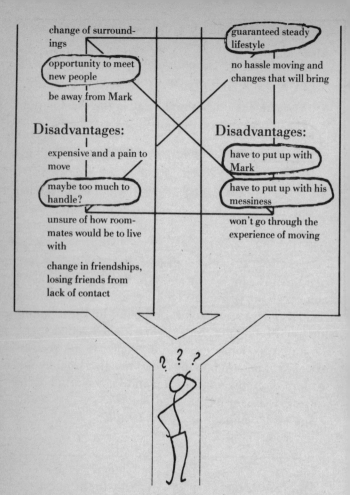

change of surround-
ings

opportunity to meet
new people

be away from Mark

guaranteed steady
lifestyle

no hassle moving and
changes that will bring

Disadvantages:

expensive and a pain to
move

maybe too much to
handle?

unsure of how room-
mates would be to live
with

change in friendships,
losing friends from
lack of contact

Disadvantages:

have to put up with
Mark

have to put up with his
messiness

won't go through the
experience of moving

Strategy One: Find Out Where You Are. Decisions that take the form of *Stay/Change* are always Place (1). You are always *already* inside one of the alternatives! If you wish, you can take the little figure at the bottom and put it *where you are*. This is how Aggie's diagram would look:

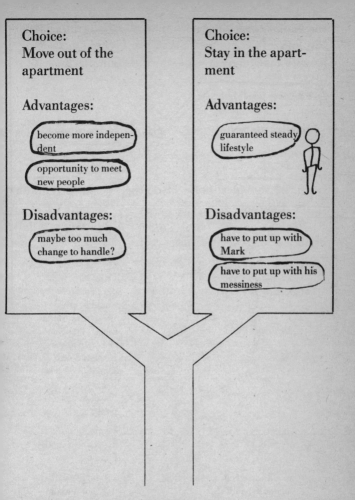

Choice: Move out of the apartment	Choice: Stay in the apartment
Advantages:	**Advantages:**
become more independent	guaranteed steady lifestyle
opportunity to meet new people	
Disadvantages:	**Disadvantages:**
maybe too much change to handle?	have to put up with Mark
	have to put up with his messiness

Strategy Two: Look for Mirror Images. Notice that once again, one of the *Mirror Images* got taken care of in the circling process. Aggie circled, "have to put up with Mark," but not "be away from Mark." The one remaining *Mirror Image* shows very clearly the essential element in almost all Change decisions—the known versus the unknown. Aggie even provides us with a dead giveaway—the question mark:

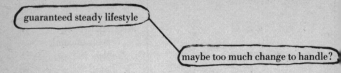

guaranteed steady lifestyle

maybe too much change to handle?

Both seemed equally attractive. So both remained in the diagram.

Strategy Three: Do a Quick Rating. Aggie's items came out with clear differences:

become more independent	[2] I could live without this, but it would be extremely uncomfortable. (This came close to being a [1], but it was something Aggie was *working* on. She didn't have it yet.)
opportunity to meet new people	[4] I suppose I could live without this if I had to.
maybe too much change to handle?	[2] I could live with this, but it would be extremely uncomfortable.
guaranteed steady lifestyle	[2] I could live without this, but it would be extremely uncomfortable.

266

have to put up with Mark	3 I could continue to live with this, but I wouldn't like it.
have to put up with his messiness	2 I could continue to live with this, but it would be extremely uncomfortable.

Aggie was willing to eliminate the 3 and the 4. After *Mirror Images* and *Quick Rating*, then, the essence of her Decision Dilemma was obvious:

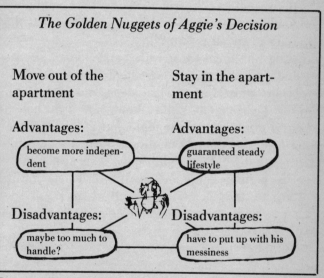

The Golden Nuggets of Aggie's Decision

Move out of the apartment

Stay in the apartment

Advantages:

become more independent

Advantages:

guaranteed steady lifestyle

Disadvantages:

maybe too much to handle?

Disadvantages:

have to put up with his messiness

It was still a dilemma, but a very clear one. Now, Aggie could focus attention on those few elements that she had discovered were of the *highest* importance to her.

Strategy Four: Do Research. Aggie was in a good position, if she chose, to do *Real-Time Research.* She could experiment with, or *try out,* the alternative containing the change. The questions that came up for Aggie, however, were, "How *much* change can I handle right now?" "Can I make a *gradual* change instead of a *complete* change? Can I put a toe in the water first, before jumping in and maybe drowning?"

We looked closely at the items remaining in Aggie's diagram, especially "become more independent." "How," I asked, "does an independent person behave?" Aggie replied, "They don't seem so dependent on what other people think. They just go ahead and do things without worrying about it." I continued, "How do dependent people *let others know* that they are worried and uncertain?"*

Aggie was silent for a while, and I knew she was mentally rehearsing her own interactions with others, especially with Mark. She suddenly looked up with a twinkle in her eye. "Well, I know how *I* do it," she said. "I'm always asking him what to do. And then after I do something, I'm always asking him for reassurance that I did the right thing." I suggested to Aggie that perhaps being independent or dependent had nothing to do with where or with whom she lived—that maybe it was a matter of *how she behaved* no matter *where* she was.

"Wouldn't it be easier," she asked, "if I were on my own and *had* to make my own decisions?" "Yes," it would be easier," I replied. "You might also get lonely and rush back to Mark just for the companionship." Then, Aggie had an insight. "Why don't I do my *Real-Time Research* while I'm still living with Mark.

* The point of this question was to focus Aggie's attention on actual *behaviors*, rather than on some general *idea*. It is *behaviors* which reveal your personality. And it is *behaviors* which let other people know how you are feeling and what you want from them.

I have a feeling that every time I say, 'Mark, do you think I should? . . .' or, 'Mark, what would you think if I? . . .', I'm probably asking for trouble. I want to practice not saying these things, or if that's too hard, at least not saying them so often. I want to see how that feels. And you know, there's another thing. Thinking that maybe I will move out someday, I have a feeling his messiness isn't going to bother me as much. I'm tired of picking up after him and nagging about it. I'm going to keep my side of the bedroom clean, and I'll probably take care of the kitchen and bathroom because I can't stand them being dirty, but he can do as he likes with the other rooms. I'm just going to leave that up to him."

I think you can sense that Aggie had already begun to change. The rest was a matter of working out the details. Aggie was justifiably afraid of too much change. By definition, *too much* means TOO MUCH! She found an ideal way to experience both alternatives more or less at the same time, like Eddie who dated two women at the same time. She kept her eyes and ears open, and she monitored her feelings closely as she began to test out "the waters of independence." She liked it. She felt freer. And gradually her confidence in her own judgment grew.

Mark was another story. He was used to being consulted. He liked giving advice and approval (or withholding it). He liked the original "contract": You lean on me, and I'll take care of you. When Aggie began, subtly, to operate under a different set of rules, he was confused and upset. He wasn't sure he liked, "the new Aggie." Over a period of several months, the relationship deteriorated, as Mark struggled to put Aggie back into a dependent position, and Aggie resisted. Eventually they decided to go their separate ways. Aggie considered moving in with roommates, to ease the transition, but decided against it. She *was* afraid of being on her own, and she *was* afraid of the major change it would require. But she felt better about herself. By practicing "being independent," she had developed enough courage to strike out on her own.

Strategy Five: Take the Tiger to Tea. Aggie's *Tigers* were her fear of too much change and Mark's messiness. She won over the first *Tiger* by changing gradually, by dipping a toe in the water. The second resolved itself. It lost its power over her as soon as she realized she didn't *have* to take it forever.

Strategy Six: The One-Year Plan. This Strategy was important in Aggie's decision. She was already uncomfortable in her present situation. The fact that she was seriously considering a move showed that she was probably not willing to be where she was one year from now. Her *present* independent behaviors were shaped by the question, "One year from now, where do I want to be, how do I want to feel about myself, and how do I want people to be treating me?"

Strategy Seven: Settle. Aggie did not Settle. In fact, she was able to unstick herself from her Decision Dilemma by *not* settling. She was not willing to put up with the fear of change *or* with Max and his messiness. When she said, "I am not willing to settle for this; WHAT DO *I* NEED TO DO TO SEE THAT IT IS DIFFERENT?", the way to a change became clearer.

Aggie needed counseling help in order to get out of her decision dilemma. Sometimes, an objective person, someone who can help you think through the alternatives and who gives you both ideas and emotional support, is necessary. Major changes are hard to accomplish all on your own.

Vince

In most ways, Vince, twenty-two, was undecided about what he wanted out of life (and what he was willing to put into it!). After high school, he had taken odd jobs here and there, mostly in construction. He had a good head on his shoulders but wanted to be "his own man" and found it hard to work under a lot of restrictions. He hadn't ruled out college or a trade school, but he knew he still had some exploring to do. His present Dilemma was whether or not to stay in the Washington, D.C., area.

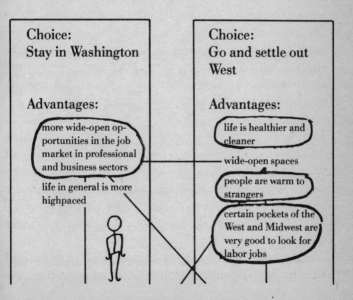

Choice:
Stay in Washington

Advantages:

more wide-open opportunities in the job market in professional and business sectors

life in general is more highpaced

Choice:
Go and settle out West

Advantages:

life is healthier and cleaner

wide-open spaces

people are warm to strangers

certain pockets of the West and Midwest are very good to look for labor jobs

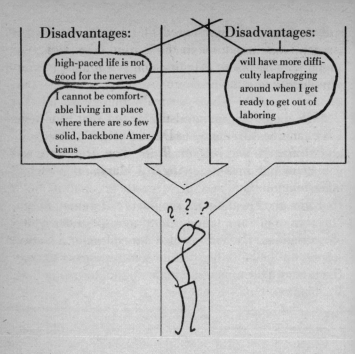

Vince certainly has definite opinions about things, and you can see that he is no fool. He doesn't want to cut off his options. What he wants is to have his ideal geographical setting *now* without risking his job opportunities in the *future*.

Vince's diagram has a couple of interesting features. First, notice the length of the items. I give a standard instruction to keep the items as short as possible, preferably four or five words. Vince, however, has things to say, and he wants to be sure that he says it all. Also, he tends to be a rebel, resisting anyone's "rules" or "suggestions" if he can.

Second, he states an item as an Advantage ("life in general is more high paced") but immediately contradicts it below ("high-paced life is not good for the nerves"). You can be on the lookout for this in your own diagrams. You may find that you are listing *characteristics* of a choice alternative—warm climate, tall, or inexpensive—when you really don't *care* all that much about the characteristic. Be sure that your items are genuine Advantages or Disadvantages to *you*.

Strategy One: Find Out Where You Are. Vince was in Place (1), presently living in a Maryland suburb of Washington, D.C.

Strategy Two: Look for Mirror Images. Often, people with strong, definite opinions can easily feel different "weights" in their *Mirror Images*. This was true for Vince. There were two clear *Mirror Images* and one not so clear:

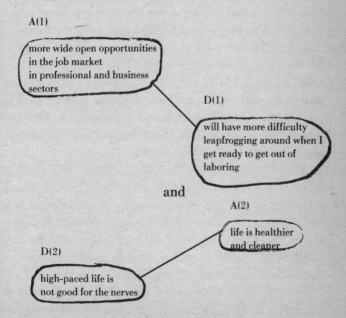

A(1)

more wide open opportunities
in the job market
in professional and business
sectors

D(1)

will have more difficulty
leapfrogging around when I
get ready to get out of
laboring

and

A(2)

life is healthier
and cleaner

D(2)

high-paced life is
not good for the nerves

273

Vince felt more "pull" toward A(1) and A(2).

Vince's dilemma reminds me of a story about three men who move to the same city in another part of the country. When the first man arrives, he asks the first native he meets, "Tell me, how are the people here?" The native asks in return, "How were they where you came from?" "Terrible," says the man. "Well, they're terrible here too," replies the native.

When the second man arrives, he also asks, "How are the people here?" And again the native asks, "How were the people where you came from?" "Well," he says, "some were good, and some were bad." The native says, "Here too, some are good, and some are bad."

The third man also wants to know about the people. When asked about the people back home, he answers, "They were terrific, best people in the world. I hated to leave." And the native says, "They're terrific here too. Best in the world. You'll never want to leave."

Strategy Three: Do a Quick Rating. Vince's decision Dilemma was now reduced to a very few items. After doing a *Quick Rating*, a Leaning Ladder emerged, and his decision was clear:

The Golden Nuggets of Vince's Decision

Stay in Washington

Go and Settle out West

Advantages:

Advantages:

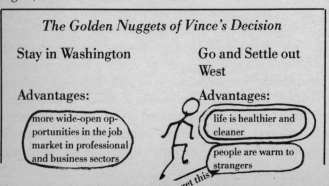

more wide-open opportunities in the job market in professional and business sectors

life is healthier and cleaner

people are warm to strangers

get this

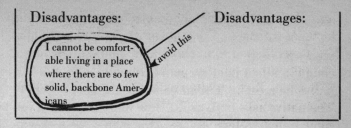

| Disadvantages: | Disadvantages: |

I cannot be comfortable living in a place where there are so few solid, backbone Americans

avoid this

Vince was a person with very strong desires and very little tolerance for living with less than what he wanted. We can suspect that in time his tolerance might soften, that he might discover happiness depends more on *who* you are than *where* you are. But at this stage in his life, Vince was certain about what he wanted and where he would find it.

Strategy Four: Do Research. Not applicable. Information can't get in when the door is shut.

Strategy Five: Take the Tiger to Tea. Not applicable.

Strategy Six: The One-Year Plan. Considerations for the future entered into Vince's decision at first but were quickly eliminated as his desire for Advantages in the *present* time became dominant.

Strategy Seven: Settle. Not necessary when the dilemma resolves into a Leaning Ladder.

Janet

One of the most common Change situations facing women today is whether to remain (or become) a homemaker, or to get a job outside the home. Rising costs of living and rising levels of *desire* make outside work a necessity for some and a very attractive option for others. Aside from an improvement in financial status (which we already know won't be *quite* enough), more and more women want the specific kinds of satisfaction that outside work can provide—especially mental stimulation and knowing that someone values their labor enough to pay for it.

It seems that a woman's desire to work, or to have the satisfactions that work provides, is not directly related to her satisfaction in the home. In fact, many women find home-centered activities extremely pleasant and rewarding. For others, however, they are insufficient.

Before having children, Janet worked as an office manager in a mid-size insurance company. She was a good manager, efficient, competent, and good with people. Her training in bookkeeping was a real asset in handling office expenses, and she was routinely consulted about the company's larger-scale financial planning.

Janet's children were now ten, fourteen, and sixteen. Expenses were rising constantly, and she was seriously considering a return to work:

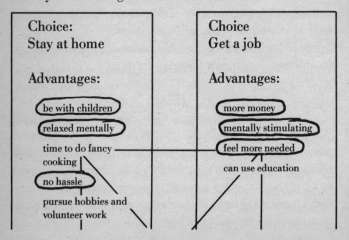

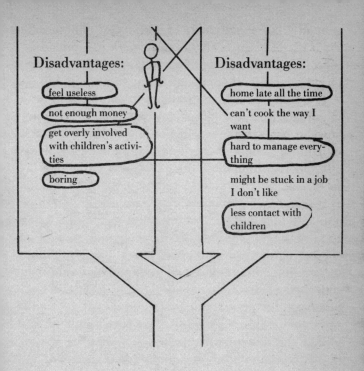

Disadvantages:

- feel useless
- not enough money
- get overly involved with children's activities
- boring

Disadvantages:

- home late all the time
- can't cook the way I want
- hard to manage everything
- might be stuck in a job I don't like
- less contact with children

Janet's diagram contained a lot of circles. A lot of things, then, were important to her, and a lot of items were in conflict with one another. If your diagrams contain many, many circles, take plenty of time with the Strategies which *reduce* information: *Mirror Images* and *Quick Rating*.

Strategy One: Find out Where You Are. As in all Change situations, Janet is in Place (1). She is already living in one of the alternatives—Stay at home.

Strategy Two: Look for Mirror Images. Janet had many *Mirror Images*:

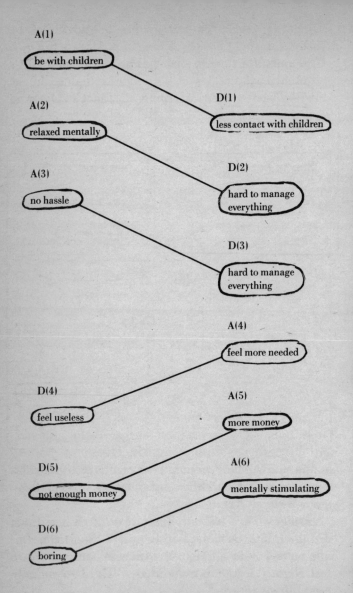

A(1)
be with children

D(1)
less contact with children

A(2)
relaxed mentally

D(2)
hard to manage everything

A(3)
no hassle

D(3)
hard to manage everything

A(4)
feel more needed

D(4)
feel useless

A(5)
more money

D(5)
not enough money

A(6)
mentally stimulating

D(6)
boring

Janet was able to eliminate some, but not all, of the *Mirror Images*. She felt clearly more drawn to *D(2)*, *A(4)*, and *A(6)* than to their pairs. The other *Images* felt evenly balanced, and both sides remained in the diagram. After *Mirror Images*, Janet's Diagram looked like this:

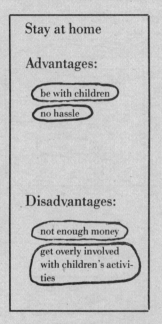
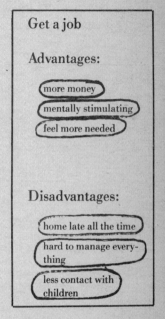

Stay at home

Advantages:

be with children

no hassle

Disadvantages:

not enough money

get overly involved with children's activities

Get a job

Advantages:

more money

mentally stimulating

feel more needed

Disadvantages:

home late all the time

hard to manage everything

less contact with children

It was a little better but not much. It was still complicated, with several important items in each category. We turned to the *Quick Rating*.

Strategy Three: Do a Quick Rating. When Janet did the *Quick Rating*, another one of the *Mirror Image* pairs was eliminated. "No hassle" turned out to feel slightly less important than, "Hard to manage everything."

Janet felt that her tendency to get overly involved with the children's activities was something she could avoid on her own. She had a tendency to take on more responsibility than was her share and had already learned that this *prevented* her children from taking an appropriate responsibility for their own behavior and its consequences. When she Quick Rated it a 4 , it was because she knew she could change it, not because it wasn't important:

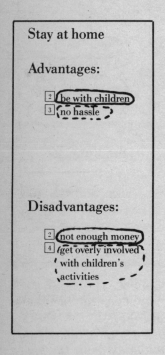

Stay at home

Advantages:

- 2 be with children
- 3 no hassle

Disadvantages:

- 2 not enough money
- 4 get overly involved with children's activities

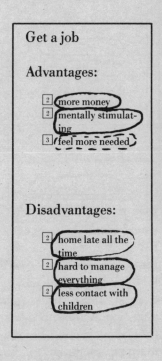

Get a job

Advantages:

- 2 more money
- 2 mentally stimulating
- 3 feel more needed

Disadvantages:

- 2 home late all the time
- 2 hard to manage everything
- 2 less contact with children

Janet's last version, then, of the *Road of Life* Diagram revealed, finally, its Golden Nuggets:

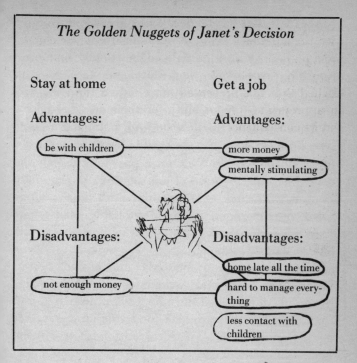

The Golden Nuggets of Janet's Decision

Stay at home

Advantages:

- be with children

Get a job

Advantages:

- more money
- mentally stimulating

Disadvantages:

- not enough money

Disadvantages:

- home late all the time
- hard to manage everything
- less contact with children

Strategy Four: Do Research. This was the *Research* question: "Could Janet make money and receive mental stimulation in some way that did not take her away from the children and that did not make life impossible to manage?" The obvious solution was to look for a part-time job.

First, Janet checked the want ads. She found that part-time bookkeepers were paid very little—a far cry from the nice salary she had received as an office manager. And she got the same story from the employment agencies she contacted.

Next, she considered the possibility of starting a bookkeeping business on her own, working out of her home. This didn't suit her for a number of reasons. She enjoyed being out of the house, she wanted the stimulation of working with other people, and there would be a period of time while she got herself established that might involve more hassle and expense than she was willing to put up with.

After checking the agencies and talking to friends who worked (she could not locate anyone who was doing bookkeeping privately on a part-time basis), she concluded that the *kind* of job she wanted, especially in terms of income, would require a full-time commitment. Furthermore, it would probably take a few years for her to work her way back into the level she had previously attained.

Janet did not want, indeed could not tolerate, a whole lot of hassle and disorganization. At this point in her life, she decided the money wasn't worth it, and that she would have to look for a different source of mental stimulation. Janet decided to stay where she was.

Strategy Five: Take the Tiger to Tea. Janet didn't need this Strategy, but many women in situations similar to hers do. In fact, it is probably the one Strategy they will need more than any other in order to reach resolution. Had Janet needed the money more, or had she found it intolerable to be without that outside mental stimulation, she would have been helped by going to the people who would be affected most—her children—and following the steps outlined in Chapter VI: (1) Acknowledge Your Fear, (2) Come Prepared, (3) Set the Stage, and (4) Tell the Truth.

Children, especially, are often much more cooperative and understanding than you might think, particularly when you show them *both sides* of the situation (so they don't think you're trying to ram something down their throats) and sincerely invite their help. A working mother can benefit the entire family. There is more money available, and the working mother, happier and more fulfilled through her *own* efforts, can avoid putting pressure on her children to behave or achieve in order to reflect well on her. Also, if household routines and chores are negotiated openly, in a spirit of mutual cooperation, the children can acquire a sense of being really needed, of being capable of making quite meaningful contributions to the family's welfare.

Strategy Six: The One-Year Plan. The One-Year Plan was not strictly applicable, though Janet knew that at *some* point in the future, perhaps when her youngest was well into high school, she would definitely want to return to work.

Strategy Seven: Settle. Janet had to Settle all right. It took awhile to get used to the idea that she probably wasn't going to be earning an income in the foreseeable future because, in her mind, she had already spent the money several times over. But Janet had learned that what she wanted more than anything else was a well-ordered, well-organized life.

Janet was a manager by nature and felt terrible when situations became "unmanageable." In order to avoid "unmanageability," she had to *accept* lack of money and mental stimulation through outside work. And in order to avoid "unmanageability," she had to accept the risk of "putting her eggs into the children's basket"—living *her* life through *them*. The task of settling was made more *tolerable* by finding out that a high-paying job in her field was probably not available—or not worth the time it might take to find it—but that did *not* make the settling a whole lot easier.

Janet added one activity to her life that helped her through the settling period. She had always had a flair for the arts, especially design, and so she decided to enroll in a Design/Graphic Arts class at the community college. It cost some money (not too much), but it paid for itself many times over by providing a challenge, an interest, and some self-satisfaction.

Willie

I had been working with Wilhelmina (Willie, as her friends called her) for about three months when she suddenly began sobbing softly during one of our sessions. Periodically, she would flush, and quickly turn away as if I had caught her doing something naughty. I waited until this obviously painful insight or fantasy had run its course. In due time, she relaxed and looked up. "I think I'm dull," she said, "and no one else thinks I'm very interesting either. I'm too quiet. I can never think of anything to say. People think I'm putting on airs, but the truth is I'm afraid of making a fool of myself. So I act reserved and pretend to be 'in control'."

Willie, forty-one, had had a strict religious upbringing. Moral standards in her family were extremely high; and discipline, especially for breaking a religious rule, was based on fear and punishment. As a child, Willie had a quality which she'd found difficult to control, and which had caused her no end of trouble. She couldn't help but see the humor in things. From the age of four or five, some little event would tickle her fancy, and she would burst out in delighted giggles. Later on, she was able to suppress her merriment, but now and then it was perverse enough to break through. Her parents did not approve of laughter in general (life to them was a deadly serious business), and when Willie laughed at things which could *in any way* be taken as an affront to their religious beliefs, she was severely punished.

By the time she was ten, Willie had become quite successful at stifling her sense of humor; in fact, she sometimes wondered how on earth she had ever found funny what she was now beginning to take seriously. She became what people called "a very nice girl," quiet and well behaved. She almost always did the "proper" thing . . . except when she became tired or overstimulated, then she might talk and laugh, and some of her former "sparkly" self would come out for a while.

In early adulthood, Willie gradually drifted out of her formal religion and eventually claimed to follow no particular religious belief. But many of the behavior patterns remained. She could not, except when she had had a good deal to drink, "let down her hair." She was polite, nice, proper, and unobtrusive in her dealings with people, but she suspected that, on the whole, people found her stiff and aloof.

Willie dressed beautifully, in tasteful fashions and colors, always clean, crisp, and well put together. But she never wore anything the slightest bit revealing. Both her behavior and her clothes put on a good show. They did the job of presenting a socially acceptable (from her point of view) *outer shell* to the world, while cleverly hiding the sensitive, spontaneous, parts of herself that lay bubbling beneath the surface.

Willie's shell served a vital function. It protected her. Turtles may not have a lot of fun, but they are certainly *safe*. Willie's shell protected her from exposure, embarrassment, and possibly from being taken advantage of. A laughing person is pretty helpless; Lord knows what someone might try to do! However, Willie was tired of plodding along. Her marriage was dying, her composure was getting shaky, and her anxiety level kept rising. Her vibrant self was trying to get out, and it scared her to death.

Several weeks after the crying episode Willie found the courage to try a *Road of Life* Diagram. (We had used it once or twice to work on problems Willie was having with her children and husband, and she knew that it clarified issues. She had carefully avoided using it for her own personal dilemma, because *she didn't want the issue to be clarified!* As long as she kept it fuzzy, she knew she wouldn't have to do something about it.) But it was time. Her own body wasn't letting her hide comfortably any more.

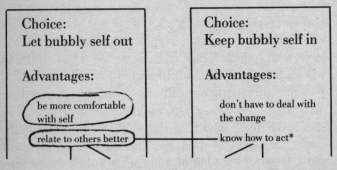

Choice:
Let bubbly self out

Advantages:

be more comfortable with self

relate to others better

Choice:
Keep bubbly self in

Advantages:

don't have to deal with the change

know how to act*

* This characteristic doesn't always *show up*, but it may be an important reason why you choose to stay where you are, even though you are suffering. You don't really *enjoy* suffering, but it feels familiar and secure. You

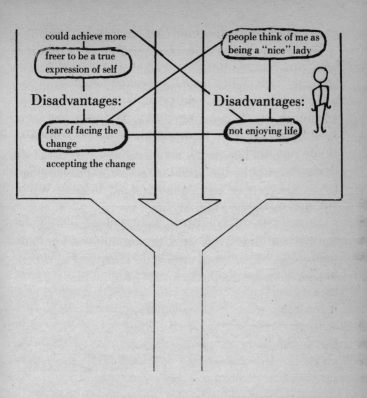

could achieve more

freer to be a true expression of self

people think of me as being a "nice" lady

Disadvantages:

Disadvantages:

fear of facing the change

not enjoying life

accepting the change

Strategy One: Find out Where You Are. Like other people contemplating a *change*, Willie was in Place (1): already living inside one of the alternatives (Keep bubbly self in), experiencing all of its Advantages and all of its Disadvantages.

know *how to do it!* You know what other people's reactions will be. To change this behavior would upset your whole social structure. And that's scary. (This kind of person is different from the *martyr*, who needs to call *attention* to the suffering—in order to be sure that it is noticed and admired. Martyrdom is a form of *Prestige Seeking:* "Look at how much I am suffering. I suffer more than, and better than, anyone else. And I want credit for it.")

Strategy Two: Look for Mirror Images. Willie's *Mirror Images* were fairly clear-cut, but there was one interesting twist. Willie had circled, "fear of facing the change," but she did *not* circle the similar "accepting the change" or its *Mirror Image*, "don't have to deal with the change." What could this mean? Willie gave the answer: "I think I might be able to *handle* the change if I could only get up enough guts to face it in the first place! I'm afraid to *face it!*" (This gave me a clue as to how we might go about helping Willie through the crisis, but that comes later.)

Each of the circled Advantages of "letting her bubbly self out" was a different, important aspect of "enjoying life." Each in its own way, then, was a *Mirror Image* of "not enjoying life."

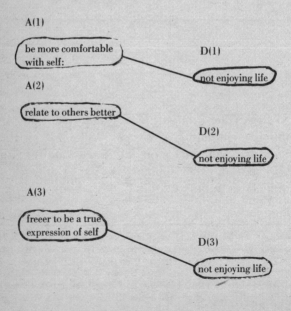

A(1)

be more comfortable with self:

D(1)

not enjoying life

A(2)

relate to others better

D(2)

not enjoying life

A(3)

freeer to be a true expression of self

D(3)

not enjoying life

In each case, Willie was far more drawn to the (D): "not enjoying life." This reduced her diagram to a few critical items:

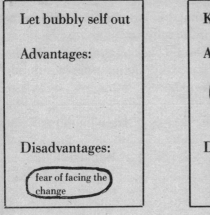

Let bubbly self out

Advantages:

Disadvantages:

fear of facing the change

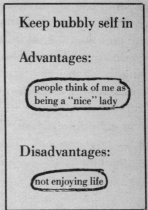

Keep bubbly self in

Advantages:

people think of me as being a "nice" lady

Disadvantages:

not enjoying life

We did some more talking before going on to the *Quick Rating*. I asked Willie to expand a little on the idea of being "nice." What had it meant in the past, and what did it mean to her now? She said that in the past, especially through adolescence and up to her marriage at age twenty-two, she must have heard a zillion times, "Oh, she's such a nice girl," "Isn't she a nice girl?" People would say to her mother "Hazel, you're blessed to have such a nice girl." And on and on. Being *"nice"* had become the *sum total* of Willie's identity. To act "not nice" would have been to commit a form of psychological and social suicide. To be sure, her distress now arose because that part of her self-identity—a part that wasn't working well for her any more—was dying.

I asked Willie what "being nice" meant to her now. She answered, "It means being a stately, conservative lady, who . . . (and here she blurted) . . . who doesn't do 'that'." (I didn't have to ask what "that" was. I knew. And so do you.) "Willie," I asked, "do you want to enjoy doing 'that'?" Her eyes filled with tears. "Yes, I do," she said. "I really do."

Strategy Three: Do a Quick Rating. We did the *Quick Rating* as a formality, both suspecting in advance how it would turn out.

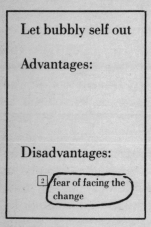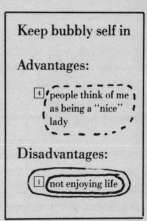

Let bubbly self out	Keep bubbly self in
Advantages:	Advantages: 4 ⌐ people think of me as being a "nice" lady ⌐
Disadvantages: 2 (fear of facing the change)	Disadvantages: 1 (not enjoying life)

Her Dilemma, after *Mirror Images* and *Quick Rating*, was a powerful set of *Railroad Tracks*.

The Golden Nuggets of Willie's Decision	
Let bubbly self out	Keep bubbly self in
Advantages:	Advantages:

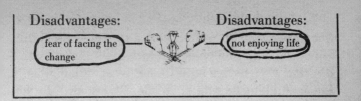

Disadvantages: **Disadvantages:**

fear of facing the change — not enjoying life

Strategy Four: Do Research. Willie knew where she wanted to go, so in that sense her decision was made. But she didn't know *how* to do it, and she was afraid to take those first few steps, to push through the heavy swinging doors that said, "Only Fun-Loving People Allowed Inside."

Now, if you were terrified of dogs, how would you conquer your fear of them? By walking into a pen containing twelve attack-trained Dobermans? If you were terrified of the water, would you let yourself be tossed into a turbulent ocean? And if you were terrified of being exposed or humiliated, would you appear on "60 Minutes" to discuss your personal views on sexual hygiene? Of course not! How *would* you begin to conquer your fear? By taking teensy, weensy little steps in the direction you think will be rewarding. By starting with puppies and shallow water and mental rehearsals.

Willie worked in an organization where staff meetings were held on a weekly basis. While she could easily approach people on a one-to-one basis, especially on business matters, she found it almost impossible to speak up at these staff meetings. I gave Willie three assignments:

(1) For two weeks, she was to carefully observe one or two other people, especially women, whom she con-

sidered "bubbly." She was to take special notice of their facial expressions, where they looked, and how they held their hands and bodies. She was to watch and imitate them *mentally* with her own face and body, in fantasy moving as they moved, saying what they said.

(2) She was to select one behavior each day that she had previously observed and mentally rehearsed, and use it *at least one time.* I told her that the eye contact, body position, and facial expression would be more important than saying any particular words.

(3) She was to make at least one spontaneous comment during every staff meeting, *without* being asked a question or being spoken to first. She was to freely give a piece of information, and the information had to be the true and honest expression of a thought, opinion, or feeling.

Don't think for a minute that these were easy assignments. Willie said they were the hardest things she had ever had to do. She kept wanting to turn away, run and hide, avoid the issue, look somewhere else. But, gradually, she was able to keep her attention focused. At first, she felt like a spy. She could feel herself getting hot as she looked at these people. I reassured her by saying that bubbly, vivacious people who use a lot of gestures and animated expressions *enjoy* being looked at; that's why they do it. At least she could do them a favor and cooperate.

The mental rehearsal was much easier than she had thought. Why? Because she was a natural. All she had to do was to get back in touch with the light-hearted child in her who had found it so easy to laugh and be open.

Carrying out the behavior, though, was another story. Willie was so afraid. It felt foreign to her, unlike her. What would people think? I suggested that she begin with hand gestures, then try facial expressions, then body positions/movement, and lastly, eye contact (since this is the most intimate of behaviors, outside of physical touch).

The changes I asked Willie to make were so small and so gradual that the responses from other people were barely noticeable. Willie was sure that the first time she tried a spontaneous, free movement of her hands, everyone would turn and stare at her in shock and amazement. Of course, no one even noticed. And so it went with the rest of the assignments. No one noticed anything specific, and no one called attention to, or remarked directly about, *any* of the things she was starting to do differently. People *did* ask two questions: "Have you changed your hair?" and "Have you lost weight?" Willie simply looked and felt *better*, and this was what they noticed.

Strategy Five: Take the Tiger to Tea. Whenever a decision Dilemma contains powerful Disadvantages, the *Take the Tiger to Tea Strategy* may be appropriate. The question is, "Is there any possible way I can eliminate, or minimize the effects of, this Disadvantage?"

There is a way of minimizing *fear*, in particular, which most people turn to spontaneously. Suppose you were at the entrance of a path through a dark forest. To get where you want, you have to take that path although you may be afraid of getting lost, and although ferocious animals are lying beside it waiting for you to pass. What would you do?

I know what *I* would do. I would go get a friend and say, "Will you come with me, and can I hold your hand?" Look, we're not built to face danger alone. Don't be ashamed of needing your hand held. That's what friends are for. If your decision involves fear, especially fear of change, find someone you can talk to. And not just at the beginning of the path, but all the way along it, at least until you can see some light shining through the leaves on the other side.

Strategy Six: The One-Year Plan. Willie's *body* felt the need for a change before her *mind* recognized what was happening. The effort of suppressing her spontaneity and good humor had worn her out. She was depressed, confused, and *tired.* Her body had said, "Not one more day." Forget one more year.

Strategy Seven: Settle. Because the changes Willie made were so gradual, she hardly noticed that she was settling, but indeed she was. Was she *settling* for happiness? No, that doesn't make sense. Willie settled for—accepted the need for, was willing to take the risk of—CHANGING, in order to get what she wanted: *enjoyment of life.*

Touch Decisions 4: When You're Caught by a Troublemaker

Every thought you think, every decision you make, every action you take expresses your VALUES: what you think is important, how you feel about yourself and others, and how you expect other people to behave toward you. For example, people who are loud and flamboyant in their behavior are saying to the world, "Hey, everyone, lookie here. This is ME!"

People who *don't* want to reveal themselves and their values try to show as little behavior as possible by "disappearing into the woodwork." (It doesn't work, of course. We all know you're there. Why not come out and enjoy the fun?)

The examples in this section all have to do with self-image—how your *values* affect or influence the decisions you make. If you consider it important to meet the needs of a situation, participate constructively in your social group, and respect your own needs as well as the needs of others, then your decisions are likely to be successful and efficient. *But*, if you are acting in order to enhance your position to the detriment of others (Prestige Seeking), or to be in control (Power Seeking), or to please others at all costs (Pleasing), or to protect yourself from having to take responsibility (Protection), then you are in the grip of a Troublemaker. And you will have *trouble* making decisions.

We will look at three decisions makers here: Lesley, a beginning golfer who was afraid to go out on the golf course; Jules, who was having trouble with Rick, a new employee; and Louise, whose house was full of clutter.

At the end of this section, I have selected four more examples for you to practice on. They will give you a chance to sharpen your skills before tackling decisions *you* may face which involve PLEASING OTHERS.

Lesley*

"Lesley admires people who are more capable than she. This case is very surprising since Lesley comes

---

* I am indebted for this example to Pat Hague, of Wilmington, Delaware, who also provided the background information.

across as being very capable and intelligent. She hides behind that façade. She also comes across as being morally superior and as being someone who knows what should be done. You can see she'd like people to think she's better than she really feels she is."

(Yes, the plague of the *Prestige Seekers:* feeling that they can never quite live up to the standards they have set for themselves, hoping no one will find out The Truth, and putting on one hell of a show.)

Lesley's Troublemaker shows up clearly in her *Road of Life* Diagram, in words such as: dumb, admire, big shot, humiliated, and the telling expression, "better and better and better." Lesley was trying to decide whether to play golf in her back yard or go out to the course.

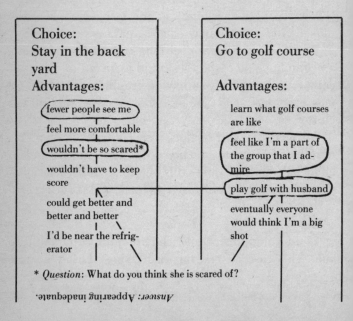

Choice:
Stay in the back yard
Advantages:

- fewer people see me
- feel more comfortable
- wouldn't be so scared*
- wouldn't have to keep score
- could get better and better and better
- I'd be near the refrigerator

Choice:
Go to golf course
Advantages:

- learn what golf courses are like
- feel like I'm a part of the group that I admire
- play golf with husband
- eventually everyone would think I'm a big shot

* *Question*: What do you think she is scared of?

Answer: Appearing inadequate.

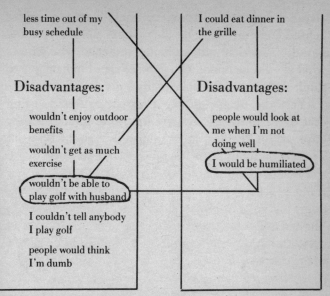

less time out of my busy schedule	I could eat dinner in the grille

Disadvantages:

- wouldn't enjoy outdoor benefits
- wouldn't get as much exercise
- wouldn't be able to play golf with husband
- I couldn't tell anybody I play golf
- people would think I'm dumb

Disadvantages:

- people would look at me when I'm not doing well
- I would be humiliated

Strategy One: Find out Where You Are. At the time of creating the diagram, Lesley was in fact playing in her backyard. Her situation, though, is a *Shadow Road* type because the distress in *both* alternatives could become so great that the person chooses to *do neither.* For Lesley, the *Shadow Road* will continue to be an option, although she is not there at this moment.

Strategy Two: Look for Mirror Images. Lesley has four *Mirror Images* among her circled items:

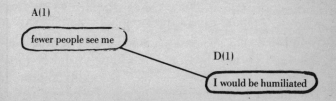

A(1)

(fewer people see me)

D(1)

(I would be humiliated)

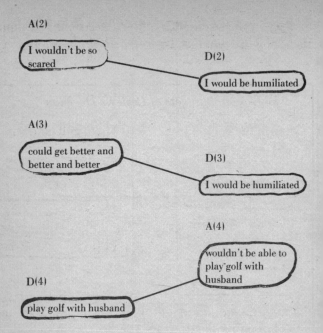

A(2)

I wouldn't be so scared

D(2)

I would be humiliated

A(3)

could get better and better and better

D(3)

I would be humiliated

A(4)

wouldn't be able to play golf with husband

D(4)

play golf with husband

Lesley had a strong fear of being humiliated. The negative forms of this *Mirror Image*—D(1), D(2), and D(3)—far outweighed their positive pairs. Lesley also felt more pulled toward D(4). She very much wanted to join her husband in this activity. In fact, that was the main reason she had started to take lessons, to be with her husband and his friends (a group she admired).

Strategy Three: Do a Quick Rating. Lesley was close to giving, "I would be humiliated" a ☐1 (I would find that absolutely intolerable), but after considering whether she would be willing to endure *some* appearance of inadequacy *until* her skills improved, she allowed that she might lower the rating to a $\boxed{1.5}$, but no further! Her Decision Dilemma, then, boiled down to a *Tiger 'Neath the Tree*.

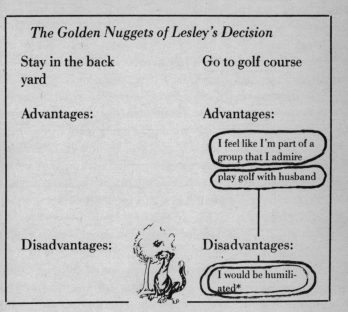

The Golden Nuggets of Lesley's Decision

Stay in the back yard	Go to golf course
Advantages:	Advantages:
	I feel like I'm part of a group that I admire
	play golf with husband
Disadvantages:	Disadvantages:
	I would be humili-ated*

The fear of feeling humiliated was obviously a potent one for Lesley. No sane person *wants* to feel humiliated, but people differ widely in their tolerance of the feeling. Some people already feel inadequate, so the humiliation only confirms their previous opinion of themselves. Some people can (and do) use feelings of inadequacy to gain sympathy or attention from others. Some use inadequacy in a charming, appealing way and are able to chuckle at themselves in a spirit of self-acceptance.

* Any fractional number up to $\boxed{2}$, such as 1.5 or 1.75 , recieves a double circle

But there are two personality types who do *not* handle humiliation very well. These are the *Power Seekers* and *especially* the *Prestige Seekers*. To *Prestige Seekers*, who want more than anything else to feel superior and to be admired, humiliation is almost unbearable. It is a feeling which *they often create in themselves* although it has no bearing whatever on reality. They feel humiliated when no one is trying to humiliate them! They feel embarrassed when no one is trying to embarrass them! On the contrary, other people are usually trying to be as helpful, tolerant, and patient as they know how. Ironically, *Prestige Seekers* can be exceptionally gentle and patient with the inadequacies of others. But not with themselves! Oh, no. Lesley's *Tiger* has sharp teeth indeed.

Strategy Four: Do Research. Lesley was one of those people who would do almost anything to avoid exposing herself to public failure. At this point in her psychological development, Lesley could not afford to practice out on the course in front of her husband's golfing friends. She had to find some alternate location or quit the sport. (If she quit because she was afraid of being humiliated, she lost the right to complain that she couldn't play golf with her husband.)

The lawn was fine for practice putting and short shots, but only the very, very, very rich can practice teeing off in their backyard. Lesley investigated other practice facilities in her area and located a driving range and a municipal golf course. Once or twice a week, she went out to the driving range; and she did something clever on the municipal course. She drove out to the course whenever she could, trying to arrive at a low-use part of the day. She selected only one hole each day, but each day a different hole. And she played it over and over again. If she didn't feel she had mastered "the lesson" of that particular layout, she continued to play it until she felt comfortable and had some sense of mastery.

Lesley was not a talented golfer, and it took several months of practice before she felt she could show up at the club. It was late in the season before she got there. She cringed whenever she made a terrible shot, and she had her share of them, but she made a pretty decent showing overall.

Strategy Five: Take the Tiger to Tea. It may *seem* that Lesley took the tiger to tea, but she didn't. She *avoided* the possibility of being humiliated by practicing her buns off. Golf is *clearly* right or wrong, good or bad, and you have *at least* seventy-two chances of making a perfect fool of yourself. If Lesley had not been able to afford the time or money to practice on her own, she would probably have quit playing.

Strategy Six: The One-Year Plan. This Strategy was the main thing that kept Lesley going. She missed out on a lot of socializing for *one year* in order to prepare herself for a more satisfying experience the *following year*. Since golf has a built-in standard which is impossible for most mortals to meet, Lesley may never have felt "adequate" (to a *Prestige Seeker*, adequate = perfect), but we can expect that her willingness to put a lot of effort into the attempt would eventually pay off in terms of improved skill and greater self-approval.

Strategy Seven: Settle. Lesley did not Settle. It is doubtful that she *could* have settled, unless the possibility of humiliation accompanied something she wanted or needed *desperately*. Otherwise, she would want either to avoid the situation completely, or to develop her skills to the point where humiliation would be almost a nonexistent possibility.

Jules

Jules owned a moving company franchise and employed, depending on the season, from ten to fifteen people. Jules had recently hired Rick, thirty, from another company. Rick was an exceptionally good worker—reliable, courteous to customers, careful, and clever about finding ways to solve unusual technical problems. The fly in the ointment was that he hadn't been able to get along with his previous supervisor.

Rick didn't like to be, as he put it, "pushed around," and would argue at length if told to do something in a way he didn't want to do it. Jules took him on, hoping that he could "do something" with him. Jules suspected that Rick might do better in a supervisory position and offered to make him a foreman. Well, things went from bad to worse. Rick continued arguing with his new supervisor (Jules), but now, in addition, he was causing resentment among the men *he* was supposed to be supervising. Good workers in the moving industry are hard to find so Jules did not want to fire him.

Naturally, Jules had a strong personal interest in the decision, but regardless of his own personality and values, he was also an agent for the company. As a business person making a business decision, part of Jules had to *become* the company because, in effect, he had to decide for the *organization* as well as for himself. Jules's Decision Dilemma was whether to keep Rick on as foreman or to demote him to a mover.

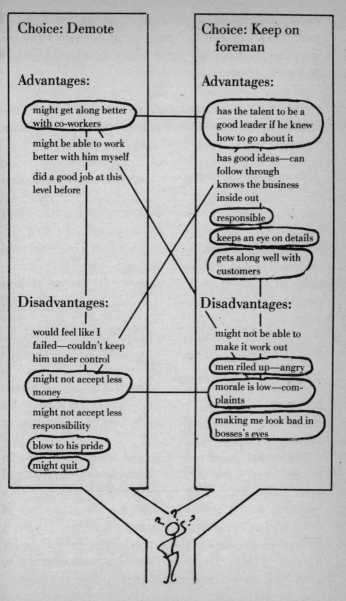

Choice: Demote

Advantages:

might get along better with co-workers

might be able to work better with him myself

did a good job at this level before

Disadvantages:

would feel like I failed—couldn't keep him under control

might not accept less money

might not accept less responsibility

blow to his pride

might quit

Choice: Keep on foreman

Advantages:

has the talent to be a good leader if he knew how to go about it

has good ideas—can follow through knows the business inside out

responsible

keeps an eye on details

gets along well with customers

Disadvantages:

might not be able to make it work out

men riled up—angry

morale is low—complaints

making me look bad in bosses's eyes

Strategy One: Find Out Where You Are. Jules is in Place (1). He is already living in one of the alternatives, now experiencing all of its Advantages and Disadvantages.

Strategy Two: Look for Mirror Images. There are only two *Mirror Images*. Both relate to Rick's ability to get along with the other workers:

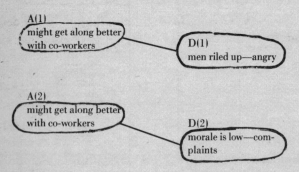

For Jules, the issue was "heavier" in its negative statements: D(1) and D(2). This eliminated the single circle in the upper left and reduced his dilemma to the unstable *Ricochet Romance:*

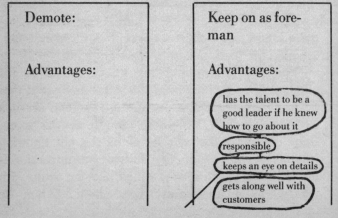

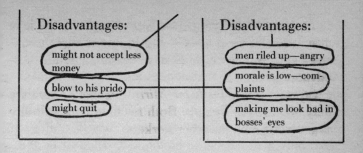

Disadvantages:
- might not accept less money
- blow to his pride
- might quit

Disadvantages:
- men riled up—angry
- morale is low—complaints
- making me look bad in bosses' eyes

Strategy Three: Do A Quick Rating. When doing the *Quick Rating* Jules encountered a position that comes up in many important decisions. How do you rate a risk? How do you make a judgment about something that may never even happen? At this stage in your decision, RATE THE RISK AS IF IT IS A PRETTY GOOD BET. Later on, you will use Research to find out as much as you can about whether the risk really exists. Then, you will use *Take the Tiger to Tea* (if possible) to *minimize* or *eliminate* risks that you find to be genuine.

I asked Jules to look at every "might" and every "might not" among his circled items and to CHANGE them to "probably would" or "probably would not." So, "might not accept less money" became "*probably would not* accept less money," and, "might quit" became "*probably would* quit."

When Jules changed the items as suggested, he discovered a mighty surprising thing. He discovered that he was more worried about a MIGHT than about a PROBABLY WOULD! Somehow, there was something about the *uncertainty* of it, the not knowing whether or not it would happen, that was uncomfortable all by itself. In a way, it had nothing to do with whatever the uncertainty was about. When he changed the uncertainty into a pretty good bet, he found he could get a handle on it: "Now that I *know* what I'm dealing with, I can *do* something about it!"

In this particular decision, Jules discovered that if he had rated "might quit" before the change, it would have gotten a ②, because the possibility scared him. Yet, after the change to "*probably would* quit," it rated only a ③, because he *knew* it wouldn't be the end of the world. He knew he would be able to find someone to replace Rick.

If you are a manager or a supervisor, you may find that you are rating items differently than you would if you were making a personal decision. I think Jules's ratings make this clear:

④ -*probably would not accept less money* (after changing "might not" to "probably would not")

④ -*blow to his pride*

④ -*probably would quit*

② -*has the talent to be a good leader if he knew how to go about it*

② -*responsible*

① -*keeps an eye on details* (This may seem like quite a high rating for the item, but remember that Jules is representing a business, and a business cannot survive without proper attention to detail.)

① -*gets along with customers* (another survival requirement)

2 –*men riled up—angry* (Why didn't this rate a 1 ? Managers would definitely differ on the importance of this item. Some business operations require smooth, harmonious working relationships among the staff. Others do not. Some *managers*, based on their individual personalities, require harmonious working relationships. Others do not. Jules would have preferred smooth relationships, but he also knew that his business has a higher than average potential for conflict, and he was willing to tolerate more than, say, *you* might in *your* business operation.)

2 –*morale is low—complaints*

3 –*making me look bad in bosses' eyes* (This low rating may surprise you. But Jules was his own man. He was an independent manager whose bosses were at a distance. He had been offered, and had accepted, a great deal of responsibility. He knew that problems would arise several times a day! Sure, he wanted the smoothest operation possible, but as he looked at this item, he understood that he would not look bad for *having* the conflict, only by letting it go on and on without getting it resolved. However, the longer he allowed the situation to deteriorate, the higher this item would begin to rate.)

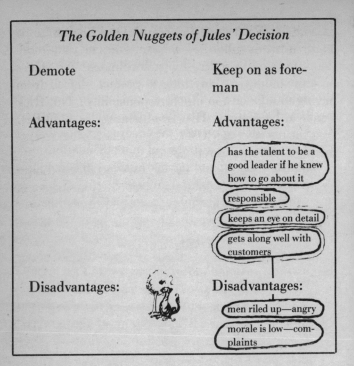

The Golden Nuggets of Jules' Decision

Demote

Keep on as foreman

Advantages:

Advantages:

has the talent to be a good leader if he knew how to go about it

responsible

keeps an eye on detail

gets along well with customers

Disadvantages:

Disadvantages:

men riled up—angry

morale is low—complaints

Strategy Four: Do Research. Not necessary.

Strategy Five: Take the Tiger to Tea. Is Rick worth working on? Is it worth it to the company to resolve this conflict? Jules certainly thought so. Now came the hard part. Early in the game Jules knew he would not be able to make this decision without help—Rick's help. The question was not whether to approach him, but how.

If you, or someone you know, is in a Decision Dilemma which involves people not getting along well with one another, as in Rick's case, you can bet your bottom dollar one of the Troublemakers is at work. Look back at the Classic Conflicts on pages 74, 71,

82, and 93. What does Rick want? Does he want to be *admired* by his subordinates? No. Does he want more than anything to *please* his subordinates? No. Does he want more than anything to *protect* himself from having to take on too much responsibility? No. Rick wants to be *obeyed*. His Troublemaker is POWER. And the response to POWER by others is often resentment, rebellion, and retaliation.

Suppose Rick should want to get out of this power struggle; first of all, because it feels bad, and second, because things don't get done. One thing a *Power Seeker* invariably wants is to get things done and to get them done efficiently. How can Rick, or anyone else who is in a power struggle (you, maybe?), get out of it?

- THE KEY TO GETTING OUT OF A POWER STRUGGLE IS TO REALIZE THAT YOU NEVER HAD THE POWER IN THE FIRST PLACE! YOU HAVE NEVER *MADE* ANYONE DO ANYTHING!

- PEOPLE DO WHAT YOU WANT BECAUSE THEY *CARE FOR YOU* AND WANT TO PLEASE YOU, OR

- PEOPLE DO WHAT YOU WANT BECAUSE THEY ARE *AFRAID OF YOU*. YOU CAN HURT THEM OR TAKE SOMETHING IMPORTANT AWAY FROM THEM.

- PEOPLE ARE OBEYING YOU BECAUSE OF WHAT *THEY* WANT, NOT BECAUSE OF WHAT *YOU* WANT.

Here are several illustrations:

I am *choosing* what he/she wants because:

I don't like to see him/her angry (fear of loss).

I don't want to get a spanking (fear of pain).

I think it is right to obey authority (desire to live up to a moral code).

I don't want to lose my job (fear of loss).

It's part of the system, and I knew it when I signed on (desire to keep an agreement).

I don't want to rock the boat (fear of confrontation/instability).

I love him/her (desire to please).

I'm sure you can think of many other examples from your own experience. I would like you to notice two things: (1) No one in these illustrations is obeying in an attempt to *meet the needs of the situation*. Attention is not on "what needs to be done," but in "How am I doing in this power game?" (2) While they all may *seem* to be obeying, each is in fact *gaining* a desire or *avoiding* a fear. The person "in charge" is simply showing them *how* to do it.

You know this is true because you can totally destroy the illusion of power (and it *is* an illusion) by simply saying one little word: "No." What will happen next? The boss or the authority will begin to apply pressure *in the direction of your fear*: "If you don't (do what I want), then I will (carry out whatever event will cause you pain, loss, or confrontation)." The idea is to raise your level of fear so that you will CHOOSE to obey. But it *is* a choice.

History shows repeatedly that people have been willing to suffer pain, loss, even death in order not to give in. The lesson on power taught by history is that you cannot *make* a person do what you want *if* that person is willing to suffer your worst consequence. Yes, you can yell, you can get angry, you can threaten, you can plead, you can disapprove, you can withdraw affection, but you cannot *make* it happen.

Jules was helped by having a good understanding of how power seems to work—and actually does work—in human relationships. But this is not necessary. Positive changes can be brought about in power-based relationships by using a few simple techniques that almost invariably reduce anger and tension.

First, ask for input in making the decision. This is the hardest step by far. It means you are admitting in advance that you do not have all the answers (horrors!).

Second, *listen* to the input, and take it seriously.

Third, make *requests* instead of demands. Ask rather than tell.

Fourth, say "Thank you."

Rick was very, very sensitive to issues of power. On his previous job, he was always resisting the exercise of it, either directly by refusing to do things as told, or indirectly by complying outwardly while griping and causing dissension behind the foreman's back. When he moved to Jules's company, he found himself on the other side of the power structure, but he hadn't yet learned to deal with people on any basis *other* than that of power, namely, by winning cooperation.

Jules, being a natural cooperation seeker, was in a good position to model (teach by example) successful approaches to supervision that Rick could learn and copy.

First, ask for help. The least threatening, and probably the most effective, approach to a power-sensitive person is the good, old "I" message. Jules said, "Rick, I'm having some problems* with the way the men are reacting to you, and I'd like your help on it." Now, Rick was a dedicated, responsible employee—some would say *too* responsible—and he was more than willing to learn what he could, especially things that would lessen the undercurrent of hostility he sensed and the feeling that he was being sabotaged.

Second, listen. Jules was a naturally good listener, but he didn't know exactly how to translate his own skill into something Rick could take and use on his own. He started by giving Rick what he thought were helpful suggestions. "Take the time to really listen," he said, "and give the guy your full attention. Show some interest. And if you don't like what he's saying, for heaven's sake don't interrupt! Let him have his full say, *then* put in your two cents worth. If you like his ideas, tell him so. If not, tell him why, and come up with a better one."

Listening skills take practice! Rick could not be expected to become a good listener in one easy lesson, but Jules's suggestions gave him something to work toward and a way of measuring his progress. Without fully realizing it, Jules had touched on almost all the qualities of a good listener. Such a person is attentive, interested, does not interrupt, gives recognition, and

* There's the "I" message.

312

uses the other person's ideas, thoughts, and opinions whenever possible.

Third, make requests. Again, making requests was something that came naturally to Jules but not to Rick. Rick did not know *how* to ask instead of tell/demand. All Jules did was ask (ask!) him to try that approach and especially to watch his tone of voice. (Even a "dictionary perfect" request wold be spoiled by an irritated, critical, impatient tone of voice.)

Jules gave Rick some phrases to use when making his requests: "Would you give me a hand with? . . . We need to . . . How about trying? . . . Would you? . . . What would happen if we? . . . What do you think of? . . . I think it would work better if we _____; what do you think?"

Fourth, say thank you. As long as Rick had the notion that he was *making* people do things, he felt he owed them nothing. In his mind, doing the thing, especially doing it *his* way, was their duty or obligation, and when the task was done, the cycle was complete.

As Rick became more aware that their cooperation was a kind of "gift" to him—given by choice, out of their own free will—he began to see the value of saying, "Thank you." He even added a little frosting from time to time by adding, "Good job," or "I like the way you did that."

Do I need to tell you that the men were shocked? I don't think so. They didn't know what to make of it. This is a trick, they thought. What is he up to? (a natural reaction when people have learned not to trust someone). In time, and with Jules's help, the "tightness" began to soften.

Rick and the men never became pals, nor would

this have been appropriate, but gradually they did learn to trust and respect one another. Rick learned that when he asked for help and suggestions, they gave it. And the suggestions were good! The men learned that they could speak up and disagree without fear of anger or retaliation. Jules was helped by intervening when it was necessary to get things back on track, and he managed to save a very valuable employee.

Rick did not find the process easy. Valuable, yes. Necessary, yes. Easy, no. It went against his grain from the very beginning, and it often seemed to him that he was losing more than he was gaining. But he stuck with it and, in the end, made his peace with it.

Strategy Six: The One-Year Plan. This Strategy was uppermost in Jules's mind when he brought up the dilemma in the first place. Like most managers, his eye was on the future of the company and on the steps he had to take right now to insure that he would even *be* in business in one year.

Strategy Seven: Settle. Jules did not have to Settle and would not have settled for unrest and low morale in order to keep Rick on as foreman.

But *Rick* had to Settle. Look back at the Classic Conflict of the Power-Seeker on pages seventy-four and seventy-five. Rick had to Settle for almost *every single one* of the Disadvantages listed under: *Act Mainly to Meet the Needs of the Situation*:

He felt less "on top of things"

There were more mistakes

Some details were overlooked

He was held responsible for his workers' mistakes

At times the work was not done as efficiently as if he had *told* them how to do it

People wanted to—and did—do things differently from the way he would have done them

Why did he Settle for all these things? Because he *wanted* all the Advantages just above. And eventually he got them.

Louise

To Louise, a decision situation was more than a nuisance and more than a difficult dilemma. It was a catastrophe. Louise was no more comfortable making decisions at age 47, than she had been at the age of four. Every decision seemed to present her with an infinite number of possibilities, all of which could be arranged ninety different ways to produce ninety different outcomes. She could not stop looking at the possibilities and the "what if's" long enough ever to come to a conclusion. On those rare occasions when she acted decisively, she tortured herself afterward thinking about the possibilities she had overlooked and what might have happened if she had chosen differently.

When I asked Louise to bring up an example of how indecisiveness was causing difficulty in her life, she gave me one that was simple, yet profound. *Louise could not decide what to do with the mail that came to her house.* Every day, she had to make at least four or five immediate decisions: Keep it? Throw it away?

Give it to someone else? Answer it? Buy from it? Contribute to it? It was impossible for her to decide. So, what she did was put it into a pile, "to be looked at later." Every available surface was covered with toppled-over stacks of letters, flyers, and catalogues. When the clutter became overwhelming, she might steel herself for a session of "going through the mail." She would work at it for about fifteen minutes before her decision-making juices ran out and she had to stop.

Basically, Louise saw the problem as beginning with the delivery of the mail. At that point, she felt she had two alternatives: keep it or throw it out. Her *Road of Life* Diagram came out like this:

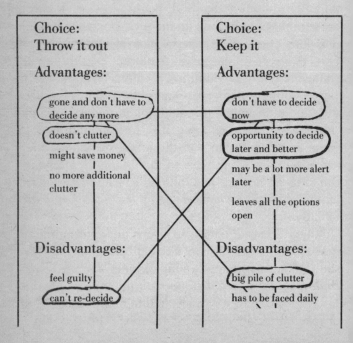

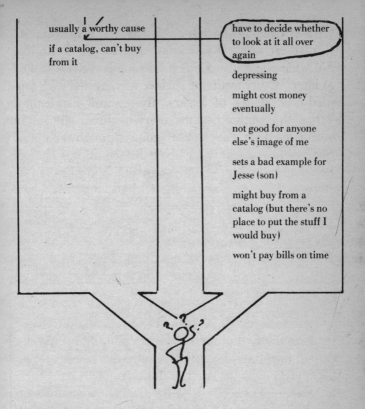

usually a worthy cause

if a catalog, can't buy from it

have to decide whether to look at it all over again

depressing

might cost money eventually

not good for anyone else's image of me

sets a bad example for Jesse (son)

might buy from a catalog (but there's no place to put the stuff I would buy)

won't pay bills on time

Strategy One: Find Out Where You Are. Louise *wanted desperately* to escape to the *Shadow Road*! She was happily tucked away there in many other areas of her life and *thought* she was there in regard to the mail situation. But no. Sure as anything, she was living right there in, "Keep it," feeling the full force of all those Disadvantages, especially the ones she circled.

Strategy Two: Look for Mirror Images. There are three *Mirror Images* here, and they are quite clear:

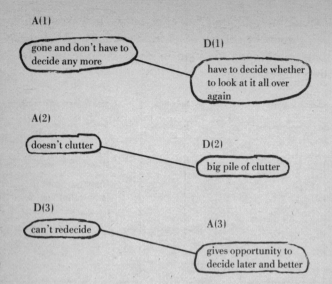

A(1)

gone and don't have to decide any more

D(1)

have to decide whether to look at it all over again

A(2)

doesn't clutter

D(2)

big pile of clutter

D(3)

can't redecide

A(3)

gives opportunity to decide later and better

True to form, Louise could not feel any difference between the first or second of any pair. She could not (would not?) decide. All the circles remained, and no discomfort was alleviated by this step.

Strategy Three: Do a Quick Rating. Sometimes an item will be phrased in such a way that it is hard to apply the *Quick Rating* statements. This may happen when you want to be *rid of* something (a person, a thing, a characteristic, a feeling, a worry, or an obligation), and one of the alternatives helps you get rid of it. For example, if traffic noise keeps you awake at night, an *Advantage* of sleeping in a different room, or on the sofa, might be: no traffic noise. But *Advantages* are things you *get* or *receive*, and the *Quick Rating* statements won't work unless you're talking about something you GET. Therefore, when you find an Advantage in your diagram that talks about something being gone, or getting relief from something, I suggest that you *change* the item to read: "free from." Here are some examples:

no traffic noise	becomes	*free from traffic noise*
don't have to decide anymore	becomes	*free from having to decide*
no more nagging	becomes	*free from nagging*
no hassle	becomes	*free from hassle*
don't have to deal with him/her/them/it	becomes	*free from having to deal with him/her/them/it*
no more worry	becomes	*free from worry*

When Louise changed her items to show the idea of freedom, or relief, it was easier for her to use the *Quick Rating* statements for Advantages:

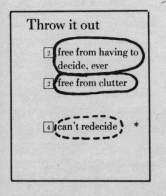

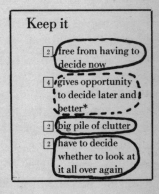

* It's not surprising that Louise will be willing to let these drop out completely. She doesn't *want* to have to decide—now *or* later!

Louise's diagram boiled down to just a few Golden Nuggets. But she found herself in the middle of an impossible Dilemma: "I want the freedom from having to decide now, and I want the freedom from having to decide later." Louise was in a painful, unstable, inescapable *Ricochet Romance*.

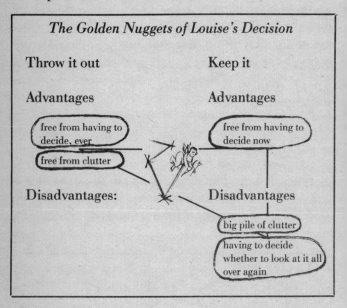

The Golden Nuggets of Louise's Decision

Throw it out — Keep it

Advantages — **Advantages**

(free from having to decide, ever) — (free from having to decide now)

(free from clutter)

Disadvantages: — **Disadvantages**

(big pile of clutter)

(having to decide whether to look at it all over again)

Strategy Four: Do Research. Not applicable. There is nothing to find out.

Strategy Five: Take the Tiger to Tea. Not applicable. No circumstance, no situation, and no person (outside herself) needs to be won over. She needs to win over herself, to understand and overcome her fears of commitment, responsibility, and disapproval.

Strategy Six: The One-Year Plan. Louise was in a tizzy five minutes after the mail arrived. She found it impossible to get through those five minutes. At this point, to think one year ahead was a total absurdity.

Strategy Seven: Settle. In Louise's life, we could easily substitute any event, any happening, any piece of information for "a piece of mail." Life, like the postman, simply refused to leave her alone. Life asked her to make *constant* decisions. Events, just like letters and catalogues, needed to be absorbed, judged, evaluated, and acted on. Not only Louise's house, but Louise's *mind*, was filled with clutter—the noisy, confusing, depressing clutter of unfinished business.

Louise grew up in a household where standards of behavior, even standards for thoughts and feelings, were rigidly determined. She was never allowed to *practice the art* of decision making—evaluating information, trying things out, making mistakes, changing her mind, trying something else, and *discovering* what made her feel like an important, competent, worthwhile person. When she finally broke out of the mold, she stepped right into marriage with a man who was perfectly willing to take charge and make all the decisions. She needed this, and he provided it. But now her head is full of clutter, and she can hardly think *at all*, much less make decisions.

There are cases of indecisiveness so severe and overwhelming that they will be helped by any action, any action whatever. Life plus inaction equals depression and anxiety. Louise could not *act* by settling for one of the alternatives. Basically, she continues to keep the mail, and once in a while, when she feels rested and energetic, she manages to go through some of it. She always feels virtuous and competent when she finally gets a bit more organized, but she cannot keep up the effort for long. And the depression continues.

Gradually, Louise is gaining the courage to make *some* decisions on her own, knowing that some of the time they will not turn out to her benefit. She will make "mistakes," and she is gradually learning to accept that. If anything, Louise is settling for the possibility of failure, for the impossibility of knowing in advance what is going to turn out best, and for the admission that her decisions are *hers* and hers alone. In a nutshell, Louise, whose Troublemaker is *Protection Seeking* is beginning to accept *responsibility* for her decisions, therefore for her actions, and therefore for her *life*.

‹ You may notice that I have not yet included examples having to do with one of the most troublesome Troublemakers of all: *Pleasing*. It is one of the most troublesome because it goes beyond being frustrated, disappointed, or afraid. Wanting (overly) to please others usually gets you *hurt*. If not now, then later. It hurts because your intentions are *good*. It hurts because your actions come out of caring and love. All you ask is to be cared about, cared for, and loved in return. Instead, you get kicked in the stomach. Why does this happen? Why are you *letting* it happen? What might *you* be doing to set yourself up for getting hurt?

I could go through the *Pleasing* examples, showing how Curtis, Bonnie, and Carmen resolved their Dilemmas. But *Pleasing*, as a Troublemaker, is too important to be left up to me. It is *you* who need to struggle with these issues, to figure out—from the inside—what *Pleasing* is all about, and to learn to bring your needs and the needs of others into better balance.

I have selected three situations for you to practice on. *It doesn't matter a twig what the people involved actually decided to do!* There is no right or wrong in decision making. There are only possibilities. If you choose Alternative A, you will receive certain *information* afterward. If you choose Alternative B, you will receive *different* information afterward. Because there are usually Advantages and Disadvantages on both sides, both alternatives have value. And the information you would get from either one is important.

Now, it's time to discover what is most important to *you*. Each of these *Pleasing* examples is taken from real life, exactly as the person stated it. Each situation involves the same basic dilemma: how to find a balance between the need to stand up for oneself versus the desire to please or to avoid trouble.

> *Curtis*, age twelve, is trying to decide whether or not to fight back when he is provoked at school.

> *Bonnie*, age thirty-six, is trying to decide whether to say "No" to the man she is dating when she doesn't want to go along with his plans.

> *Carmen*, twenty-eight, is trying to decide whether to act in order to please her mother or in order to please herself.

I will ask you to treat each example *as if it were your own*. Try to put yourself in the other person's place. If one of your Troublemakers is *Pleasing*, these situations will feel familiar. You will understand the conflicts and tensions these people are experiencing. But you are also different from these people, and that's why I have not included their circles. While many of the same items would be important to you, you might have additional items, or they might be circled in a different way. After the examples, I have provided a brief review of each of the steps needed to resolve a Decision Dilemma. Do keep in mind that you will be learning about *yourself* and how you can learn to resolve your *own* dilemmas which involve *Pleasing* others.

Curtis

Choice: Fight back	Choice: Do not fight back
Advantages:	**Advantages**
boys will respect me more	might not get hurt
won't be pushed around so much	stay out of trouble at school
can use karate training	stay out of trouble with father
can show that I'm tough	

Disadvantages:

- get hurt
- get in trouble with teachers
- get in trouble with father
- guys will expect me to fight all the time
- gets boys mad

Disadvantages

- boys will think I'm a sissy
- get pushed around a lot
- I'll feel like a sissy

Bonnie

Choice:
Say "No"

Advantages:

- feel good about myself
- he would increase his understanding of the situation
- things I need to do
- have more time to do things for myself and children

Choice:
Give in

Advantages:

- want to please him
- avoid getting the third degree
- keep him from getting angry

Disadvantages:

he'll scream at me
will get the third
    degree
he may leave perma-
    nently
afraid of his temper

Disadvantages:

have to put off things I
    want or need to do
little or no time for self
    and children

Carmen

Choice:
Act in order to
please mother

Advantages:

would get approval
    (maybe eventually)
sometimes saves the
    day
avoids a confrontation

Choice:
Act to please me

Advantages:

would make me
    stronger in the
    future
eventually show
    mother her behav-
    ior isn't working
    any more
gain respect for self
eventually be resolved,
    I think

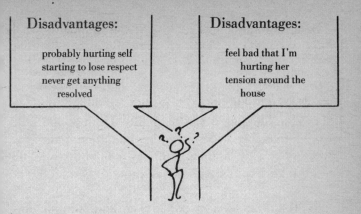

Disadvantages:	Disadvantages:
probably hurting self starting to lose respect never get anything resolved	feel bad that I'm hurting her tension around the house

1. Look at the items until you are thoroughly familiar with them. Can you think of any other reasons why *you* would or not choose each alternative? Put them in! Make this the best learning experience you can for *yourself*.

2. Do the relaxation procedure you like best. Have a pencil ready, and turn the book face down.

(a) Visualize a quiet, peaceful scene, with some rhythmic movement in it—flowing water, surf on the beach, trees or flowers waving in the breeze. Stay with the scene, eyes closed, for sixty seconds.

(b) Breathe steadily and slowly, eyes closed. Use four counts to inhale, four to exhale. Inhale through your nose, exhale through your mouth. Imagine the breath coming in through the soles of your feet, in a light, bright color. The breath gathers up fragments of stress and tension, and releases them as you exhale. Count to yourself,

"One-2-3-4, out-2-3-4; two-2-3-4, out-2-3-4; three-2-3-4, out-2-3-4, "until you've finished" "ten-2-3-4, out-2-3-4.""

(c) Picture the national flag, outlined against a bright blue sky, with puffy white clouds moving by. The flag is waving gently. Hum to yourself, preferably without words, the national anthem. (The U.S. anthem [Oh, say, can you see . . ."] takes about sixty seconds.)

3. Turn the book or paper over, and let your eyes wander gently over the items. In a little while, you will find your eyes being pulled or drawn to certain items. Circle these.

4. There are four SECTIONS in the *Road of Life* Diagram:

- Advantages on one side

- Advantages on the other side

- Disadvantages on one side

- Disadvantages on the other side

Put your pencil in the middle of any SECTION that has one or more circles, and draw a line to every other SECTION that has one or more circles.

5. Identify your personal Decision Dilemma:

(a) *Monkey Bottles*
    Advantages(s) connected to Advantage(s)

(b) *Railroad Tracks*
    Disadvantage(s) connected to Disadvantage(s)

(c) *Tiger 'Neath the Tree*
   Advantage(s) connected to Disadvantage(s) on
   the *same side* of the diagram

(d) *Ricochet Romance*
   Any triangle

(e) *Cat's Cradle*
   All four sections connected

6. *Strategy One: Find Out Where You Are.*

Place (1)— You MUST be in one of the alternatives.

Place (2)— You could be in the *Shadow Road*. You could *do neither.*

Place (3)— You are waiting for something to happen; then you MUST be in one of the alternatives.

Place (4)— You are waiting for something to happen; then you could be in the *Shadow Road.*

7. *Strategy Two: Look for Mirror Images.* Look on the *diagonals* for items that are talking about the same thing. For example, in Curt's diagram, one *Mirror Image* is: "won't be pushed around so much" / "get pushed around a lot." Let your eyes go back and forth along the diagonal. One side of the *Image* will feel "heavier," more "powerful," more "demanding." Leave the powerful one in. Erase or cross out the weaker one. Don't worry about finding all the *Mirror Images*. They are not always easy to figure out! Any

ones you miss should show up in the *Quick Rating*.

8. *Strategy Three: Do a Quick Rating.* Change every "might" to "probably would." Change every "might not" to "probably would not." Change every Advantage which means "get rid of XYZ" or "no more XYZ" to, "free from XYZ."

For Advantages:

1 —I could not survive without this.
—I cannot continue to survive without this.

2 —I could live without this, but it would hurt a lot or be extremely uncomfortable.
—I could continue to live without this, but it will hurt a lot or be extremely uncomfortable.

3 —I could live without this, but I wouldn't like it.
—I could continue to live without this, but I won't like it.

4 —I guess I could live without this if I had to.
—I guess I can continue to live without this if I have to.

For Disadvantages:

1 —I would find this absolutely intolerable.
—I am finding this absolutely intolerable.

2 —I could live with this, but it will hurt a lot or be extremely uncomfortable.
—I could continue to live with this, but it will hurt a lot or be extremely uncomfortable.

3 —I could live with this, but I wouldn't like it.

—I could continue to live with this, but I won't like it.

☐4 —I guess I could live with this if I had to.
—I guess I can continue to live with this if I have to.

- Erase or cross out all items rated ☐4.

- Try hard to erase or cross out all items rated ☐3.

- Leave in all items rated ☐2.

- Draw *another* circle round all items rated ☐1.

The items remaining are the Golden Nuggets of your decision. They are the essence of your Decision Dilemma—what it is all about.

9. *Strategy Four: Do Research.* Try to find out as much as you can about the outcomes *before* making a commitment.

Try experiencing both alternatives side by side.

Try experiencing one alternative most of the time, while you experience the other part of the time.

Try experiencing one alternative full-time for a while, then try the other one full-time for a while.

Go to the library and ask the librarian how to find out what you need to know.

Ask friends, family, or professional experts about what you need to know.

10. *Strategy Five: Take the Tiger to Tea*. Minimize the effects of an important Disadvantage by: talking things over, learning a skill, preparing for the worst.

11. *Strategy Six: The One-Year Plan*. Ask whether in one year you: want to feel the way you feel right now, want to be treating others the way you are right now, want to *be treated* the way you are being treated right now.

12. *Strategy Seven: Settle*. Would you be *willing* to give something up or to accept some discomfort in order to get what you want *most*?

You have already seen from the previous examples in this chapter that not every Strategy needs to be used, or is appropriate, in every decision situation. Sometimes, only one or two Strategies are needed to resolve the dilemma into a Leaning Ladder. At other times, little resolution is possible, and there is nothing left but to *Settle*. The difference, of course, is not in the *situation*. It is in *you*. The more you are willing to give up, and the more discomfort you are willing to live with IN ORDER TO GET WHAT YOU WANT, the more easily you will be able to make up your mind.

Tough Decisions 5: Love, Sex, and Intimate Relationships

Not a one of us has totally escaped the disappointment, frustration, and sorrow of failing to establish or maintain a satisfying intimate relationship. It may have been with our parents, our dating partners, our spouses, or our children. Some of us remember being hurt or disappointed as far back as when we were in kindergarten. And as long as we are alive, most of us will crave the kind of intimacy that comes only from loving and being loved. Love does not even have to come from another person. It can come from a deep sense of purpose, from the arts, or from God. But if it's not there for us to give to and receive from someone or something, we will shrivel up and die.

I have chosen examples which deal with intimacy between people, because these are some of the most difficult and painful situations I see in therapy. The samples deal with: establishing intimate relationships, maintaining them, and leaving them. Uncertainty, anguish, and the potential for suffering seem no different for sixteen-year-olds than for forty-nine-year-olds: "Should I call him or wait until he calls me? What if she/he says no? Does he/she expect me to go to bed with her/him? If I do, will I measure up? Should we continue to see each other? How can I break this off without hurting him/her too much?" And so on.

There is no end to the number of situations and therefore the number of examples that could be used. I have selected some that I think will be useful and will feel familiar. You now have a grasp of the dilemma types and Strategies so we no longer have to move in a step-by-step fashion. I will present each decision situation first in its complete form, but with the items circled and rated, and with the little figure where it really belongs. Then I'll show you how the decision boiled down to the Golden Nuggets, after removing some of the *Mirror Images* and the items *Rated* ③ or ④. In each case, *one* of the Strategies turned out to be the most helpful. This is the one

Strategy we will explore. Finally, I will let you know what the person decided to do.

Quick Rating

Tracee and Joyce had each resolved their Decision Dilemmas by the time we finished the *Quick Rating* Strategy:

Tracee's Complete Diagram

(Question: If Dave asks me to the dance, should I say . . .)

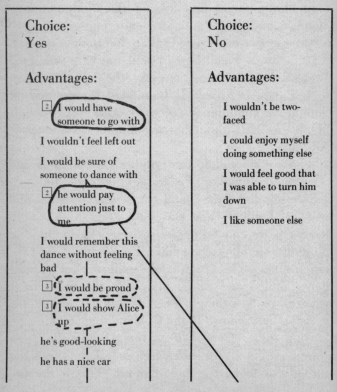

Choice:
Yes

Advantages:

[2] I would have someone to go with

I wouldn't feel left out

I would be sure of someone to dance with

[2] he would pay attention just to me

I would remember this dance without feeling bad

[3] I would be proud

[3] I would show Alice up

he's good-looking

he has a nice car

Choice:
No

Advantages:

I wouldn't be two-faced

I could enjoy myself doing something else

I would feel good that I was able to turn him down

I like someone else

334

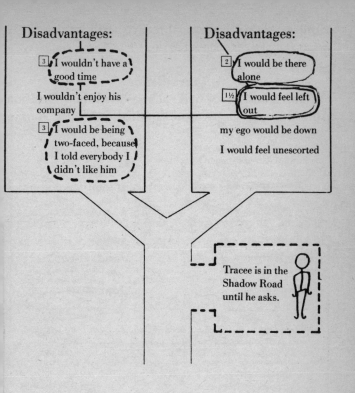

Disadvantages:

3 I wouldn't have a good time

I wouldn't enjoy his company

3 I would be being two-faced, because I told everybody I didn't like him

Disadvantages:

2 I would be there alone

1½ I would feel left out

my ego would be down

I would feel unescorted

Tracee is in the Shadow Road until he asks.

Tracee discovered that *feeling left out* was something she could barely tolerate. She decided to say "Yes" *not* because she liked Dave and would enjoy his company. She decided to say "Yes" in order to *avoid* being left out. She knows in advance that she will probably not have a good time, but by making her decision for the reason she did, she loses the right to complain about *that*.

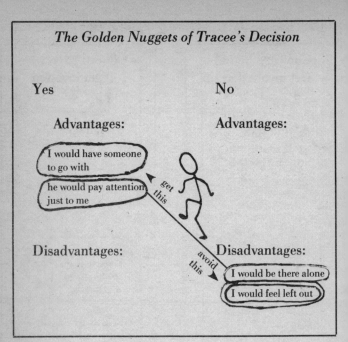

The Golden Nuggets of Tracee's Decision

Yes

Advantages:

I would have someone to go with

he would pay attention just to me

Disadvantages:

No

Advantages:

Disadvantages:

I would be there alone

I would feel left out

get this

avoid this

Joyce

Joyce worked in the D.C. area but maintained ties with a former boyfriend in New England, where she regularly went to visit her family. On her most recent visit, the friend had talked seriously about wanting her to move back to the area and maybe "get involved" again. Joyce's mind was thick with possibilities, and she asked me to help her work through them.

Choice: Get involved again

Advantages:

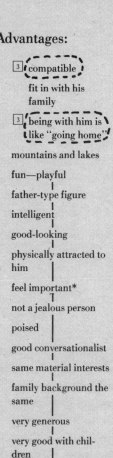

[3] compatible

fit in with his family

[3] being with him is like "going home"

mountains and lakes

fun—playful

father-type figure

intelligent

good-looking

physically attracted to him

feel important*

not a jealous person

poised

good conversationalist

same material interests

family background the same

very generous

very good with children

Choice: Not get involved again

Advantages:

no items

* a kind of reflected importance, due to his social position and contacts

athletic interests the
same

cultural interests the
same

Disadvantages:

sometimes feel like an
intruder

no longer close to our
other friends

have my independence

plays emotional games

doesn't need an inti-
mate relationship

1 hurts those closest
to him

don't trust him sexu-
ally

2 no conception of
time

1 unreliable

no career or apparent
goals
not an adequate
support system for me

Disadvantages:

no items

At this point in her life, Joyce did not have a clear idea what she wanted or who might provide her with the intimacy she wanted (*seemed* to want?). But there was certainly no doubt now about what she did *not* want.

Joyce had no items at all on one side of the diagram. This happens when one alternative is very clear, but there is no other specific alternative being considered. It happens from time to time, especially in decisions involving intimate relationships. It means that you are not sure whether you want to get, or stay, involved with this particular person, but you have no other particular person in mind.

Because there were no items at the *top* of the Ladder, Joyce's decision was to *avoid* or *escape* something, not really to move *toward* something desirable. The same would be true for you if the items at the bottom of your diagram were all rated higher than the items at the top. Basically, what you want to do is *avoid*.

Considering the number of items Joyce began with, the boiling down produced amazingly few. That's why it is never wise to base your decision on *how many* items there are in any section. It is their *importance* not their number that counts.

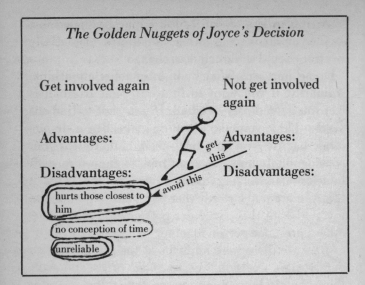

The Golden Nuggets of Joyce's Decision

Get involved again

Not get involved again

Advantages:

Advantages:

Disadvantages:

Disadvantages:

get this

avoid this

hurts those closest to him

no conception of time

unreliable

Research

Most decision dilemmas, on any subject, cannot be resolved just by *Quick Rating*. In intimate relationships, *Research* is a particularly useful Strategy. In fact, the whole purpose of *dating* is to do research! In societies where marriages are arranged, dating is unheard of. Because young people here are free to make this choice, they are strongly encouraged to "date around," "play the field," not get "tied down" too soon. Still, our whole being seems to point us toward an eventual relationship with *one* person.

Both the desire to be free and the desire to settle down with one intimate partner are natural and powerful. Some people clearly head in the direction of freedom of choice (forever). Others head in the direction of settling down. And some people find themselves in an endless war first with one desire then the other. Regardless of which desire may be uppermost at the moment, the other is always potentially stronger should circumstances change.

Doing *Research* is tricky in intimate relationships. Ordinarily, if you want to find out what baseball is like, you go and play baseball. If you want to find out about pottery, you take a pottery class. But a strange thing seems to happen when you try to do *Research* in intimate relationships. Somehow, when you're with the person, you find yourself thinking about what it would be like to be *free*. And when you're free, you're wondering what it would be like to be with the *person*! The challenge is to observe how much you enjoy being with the person *while you're with the person* and how much you enjoy being free *while you're free*. Clear-headed *Research* is the way to do this.

Anthony and Gloria resolved their Decision Dilemmas basically by doing good *Research*.

Anthony

Anthony's dilemma was somewhat like Eddie's—the young man who was dating two women at the same time—except that Anthony had no particular second person in mind. His was a, "This-person-versus-freedom-to-choose-another" dilemma. He met Maura at a party and had been dating her once or twice a week for about four months. She didn't knock his socks off, but she wasn't bad either. Still, he thought he might be able to do better. Unfortunately, Anthony was the type of person who finds it difficult to date more than one person at the same time. He liked to direct all his attention to one relationship, then, if it didn't turn out, direct all his attention to another one. Anthony's complex Decision Dilemma was a typical one—trying to balance a desire for companionship and intimacy with the desire for freedom and the fear of the uncertainty.

Anthony's Complete Diagram

Choice: Continue to data Maura

Advantages:

(3) blond, pretty

affectionate

usually fun to be with

[1] good in bed

enjoy her friends

[2] nice to have someone

[2] she really likes me

share some interests

Disadvantages:

(3) a little overweight

[2] doesn't like active sports

[2] puts me down sometimes

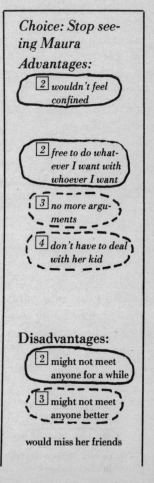

Choice: Stop seeing Maura

Advantages:

[2] wouldn't feel confined

[2] free to do whatever I want with whoever I want

(3) no more arguments

(4) don't have to deal with her kid

Disadvantages:

[2] might not meet anyone for a while

(3) might not meet anyone better

would miss her friends

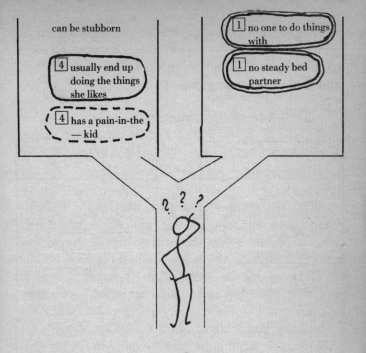

can be stubborn

4 usually end up doing the things she likes

4 has a pain-in-the — kid

1 no one to do things with

1 no steady bed partner

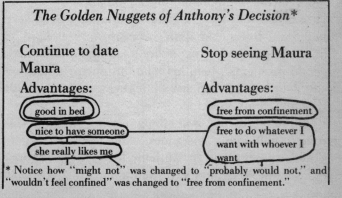

The Golden Nuggets of Anthony's Decision*

Continue to date Maura

Advantages:

good in bed

nice to have someone

she really likes me

Stop seeing Maura

Advantages:

free from confinement

free to do whatever I want with whoever I want

* Notice how "might not" was changed to "probably would not," and "wouldn't feel confined" was changed to "free from confinement."

343

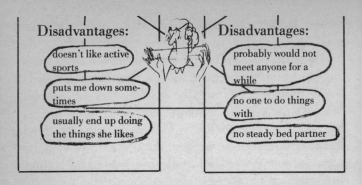

Disadvantages:
- doesn't like active sports
- puts me down sometimes
- usually end up doing the things she likes

Disadvantages:
- probably would not meet anyone for a while
- no one to do things with
- no steady bed partner

While the number of items in Anthony's diagram was considerably reduced, you can see that he still had a *Cat's Cradle* going. He had to do *Research*. He needed to have his eyes wide open all the time he was with Maura. He was going to give the relationship his best shot *while remaining fully aware* of his feelings about it.

Anthony had learned which things about the relationship were most important to him. On the positive side: sex, certainty, and being wanted. On the negative side: interests not shared, being criticized, and being overpowered. Anthony learned a great deal more during the three months he did active *Research*. He learned that while a good sex life was indeed very important to him, he didn't want to work as hard as he thought would be necessary to solve the communication problems. Also, his relationship with Maura's son deteriorated, and his willingness to put up with the child diminished.

Anthony learned something else he hadn't suspected, although a closer look at the Golden Nuggets would have revealed it. Anthony learned that he was more attracted by how well Maura met *his* needs than he was by her own personality. He wanted someone good in bed. She was. He wanted someone to do things with. She would. He wanted to be wanted. She did want him. As he realized that these specific needs could probably be met by any number of people, Maura's qualities as a unique individual became less relevant, and eventually he broke off with her. Had Anthony found Maura more interesting, or had he been willing to put more effort into making things work, they might well have stayed together.

Gloria

Gloria, thirty-four, was much further along in her relationship with Warren. The question of marriage had come up from time to time, but each sensed that the other was not quite ready to take the question seriously. Gloria was divorced and had two daughters, one four, the other six. In her early thoughts about remarriage the children's needs rated high on her list of priorities:

Gloria's Complete Diagram

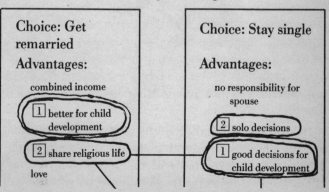

Choice: Get remarried	Choice: Stay single
Advantages:	**Advantages:**
combined income	no responsibility for spouse
1 better for child development	2 solo decisions
2 share religious life	1 good decisions for child development
love	

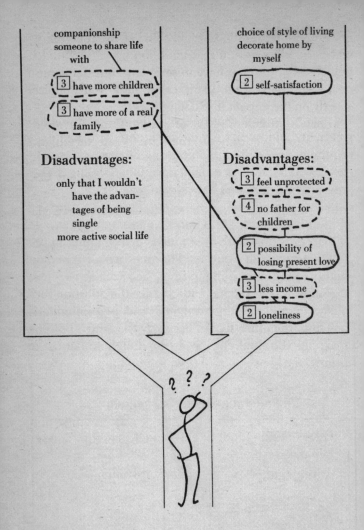

companionship
someone to share life
with

3 have more children

3 have more of a real
family

Disadvantages:

only that I wouldn't
have the advan-
tages of being
single
more active social life

choice of style of living
decorate home by
myself

2 self-satisfaction

Disadvantages:

3 feel unprotected

4 no father for
children

2 possibility of
losing present love

3 less income

2 loneliness

Gloria used different words, but you can see that the Advantages she found in staying single are similar to those Anthony listed under "Stop seeing Maura." They imply a desire for freedom, especially freedom of choice. Gloria adds the element of responsibility, which is, in essence, a restriction on what feels like a free choice. Now you have to seriously consider someone else's needs too. You can't base your choice strictly on the impact it will have for you.

Gloria's strongest sense of responsibility involved her children. Not only did these items rate very high, but her main worry about marriage was that a stepfather would not use the child-rearing methods she believed were correct. She even dropped the item, "no father for children," feeling that it had to be qualified. In her opinion, no father was better than a poor one. The same held true for, "better for child development." In her mind, the item was qualified by ". . . provided he treats the children properly."

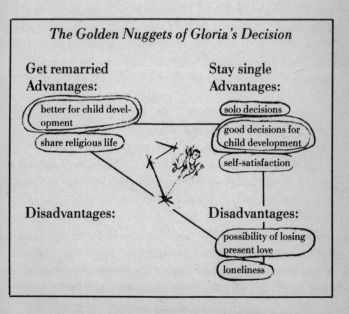

The Golden Nuggets of Gloria's Decision

Get remarried
Advantages:

- better for child development
- share religious life

Stay single
Advantages:

- solo decisions
- good decisions for child development
- self-satisfaction

Disadvantages:

Disadvantages:

- possibility of losing present love
- loneliness

Warren had had practically no experience with young children, and this contributed greatly to Gloria's Decision Dilemma. He read the books she wanted him to read and attended classes she wanted him to attend, but when push came to shove, would it work? Could he actually carry out these high-minded methods, especially if the children resented his demands on their mother's attention? That remained to be seen.

The phrase, "That remained to be seen," *is Research*. It means you will try something out, you will give it sufficient time to produce results, and you will be *looking* at those results as they unfold. Most of all, you will be thinking, "Here I am in the middle of this experience. How do I feel? Am I peaceful? Calm? Excited? Happy? Irritated? Embarrassed? Unfulfilled? Worried? Bored? Disgusted? Lonely? Afraid? Inspired? Comfortable? Tense? Depressed? Elated? Do I wish I were somewhere else? Would I like this experience to continue? Would I like to find myself in this experience again tomorrow? If yes, *why*? If not, *why not*?

This is Research. Not a judging or an evaluation of what is going on, but a constant, aware monitoring of your own personal *reactions* to what is going on.

The most accurate feelings will arise when the *Research* situation is already one of the decision alternatives, or when you can create a setting as close as possible to the alternative you are considering. A married couple contemplating divorce, for example, might agree to a trial separation. They have already had the experience of doing *Research* on being married. The separation could give them some of the experiences of being single, if they use it with awareness and sensitivity.

Gloria's case was the reverse. She was having the experience of being single (and liking it). Could she find a way of doing *Research* on being married? Yes. It is becoming increasingly common for people considering marriage to live together for an extended period of time before making this major commitment.

Gloria and Warren decided to take this step, planning in advance for a trial period of at least six months to no longer than one year. At that point they agreed to decide one way or the other. Warren sublet his apartment for the remainder of his lease and moved into Gloria's house. It would have been to their advantage to rent or buy a third place, so that one would not be living on the other one's "territory," but finances would not permit it.

There was an initial period of turmoil, which lasted about four months. (If the children were older, this could have taken quite a bit longer.) The girls' relationship with their mother changed considerably, particularly the older daughter's, as Gloria began to share time, attention, and decision making with Warren.

Warren was agreeable to trying Gloria's child-rearing methods, which tended to be more permissive and "equal" than he thought proper. His natural inclination was to tell the children what to do, expecting them to obey quickly and without hesitation. Had the children been brought up in this fashion, they might have felt comfortable with that approach. But they had not. From the time they were three or four, Gloria had included them in decisions and had worked with

349

them to find agreeable compromises on their major disagreements. They would not have accepted a do-it-because-I-said-so approach.

Adjustments also had to be made to accommodate Warren's work schedule and his running workouts. Wisely, the family waited until all these changes had become settled routines before starting *Research* in earnest.

Both Warren and Gloria (and the children too, eventually) sensed their commitment was growing, and they were pleased with their ability to work through conflicts in the "spark" stage, that is, before they became raging infernos. Most of all, they were able to agree (through constant communication) on ways of handling the children that were satisfactory to both of them. Warren became a little more relaxed and trusting about letting the children make mistakes and live through the occasional unpleasant consequences of their decisions. Gloria, on the other hand, tightened up and no longer insisted on "checking with the children" on every little thing. She *discovered*, by observing herself closely when she did it, that she had been turning to the children in this way partly to involve them, but partly to provide *herself* with needed companionship.

Research showed Gloria and Warren that their marriage had a good chance of succeeding. (No guarantees . . . ever.) They were married a year and a half after deciding to live together.

The One-Year Plan
All decisions take the future into account, because all behavior is intended to bring increasing happiness

and self-fulfillment. But in many cases I have observed, the One-Year Plan is *the* idea that mobilizes people into action. When the realization sinks in that not one iota of pain will be diminished in one year, *unless* one moves *now*, things start to happen. This particular Strategy seems to produce a firmness and certainty of purpose unlike any other. I've seen shy people speak up, angry people quiet down, silent people start to communicate, and domineering people start to listen. They all said, "This is my life, and I don't like the way it's going. I intend to be happier one year from this date than I am right now."

Many people know what they need to do to make themselves happier. They are just afraid to do it. The *One-Year Plan* often gives people the courage they need to begin creating a better life for themselves.

Lily and Alexis each made a move that was totally "out of character," after encountering the *One-Year Plan*. It took enormous courage for each of them to face—and *overcome*—powerful fears of rejection and loss.

Lily

Lily, fifty-one, was married, with three grown children—two who had finished college and one who was a senior in high school. Two months previously, out of the blue, her husband had said he was thinking of asking for a divorce. She hadn't even suspected there were problems! Needless to say, her shock and depression were enormous.

John said he had been unhappy in the marriage for a long time and had been seeing another woman for over a year. He hadn't wanted to hurt Lily and the children, so he had tried to live in both worlds. He was asking Lily to give him time to "get his head together" until he could see his way clear to making one decision or the other.

John and Lily went for counseling and began to deal with issues that had remained buried for years. Each had to decide whether there was enough left to make the marriage worth fighting for. John had to make his own decision, to be sure, but marriage is not a spectator sport! Lily had her own vital decisions to make, and she needed to make them fast.

By the time I saw her, Lily had decided to allow John to stay in the house. Her dilemma was whether to allow him to stay there for an unspecified time or to give him a three-month time limit, at the end of which he would either have to make a commitment to the marriage or leave the house.

To you, perhaps, this would be no dilemma at all: "Throw the bum out," you would cry indignantly. But Lily was different. She was a kind-hearted, agreeable person, who disliked putting people on the spot. She was often considered "too good" for her own good. Telling her to "throw the bum out" would have been like asking her to wrestle with Godzilla. Still, she was willing to consider the three-month time limit as a vague possibility.

It took over an hour of discussion for Lily to come up with her "Yes-But" List. She had a particularly hard time thinking of any Advantages for insisting on a three-month time limit. In the end, her *Road of Life* Diagram was much like Joyce's; a large number of important items boiled down immediately to the *essential* few.

Lily's Complete Diagram

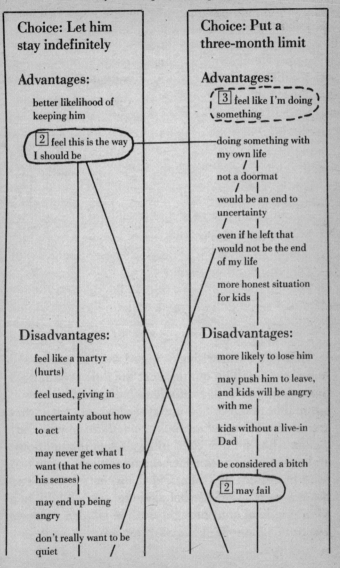

Choice: Let him stay indefinitely

Advantages:

better likelihood of keeping him

[2] feel this is the way I should be

Disadvantages:

feel like a martyr (hurts)

feel used, giving in

uncertainty about how to act

may never get what I want (that he comes to his senses)

may end up being angry

don't really want to be quiet

Choice: Put a three-month limit

Advantages:

[3] feel like I'm doing something

doing something with my own life

not a doormat

would be an end to uncertainty

even if he left that would not be the end of my life

more honest situation for kids

Disadvantages:

more likely to lose him

may push him to leave, and kids will be angry with me

kids without a live-in Dad

be considered a bitch

[2] may fail

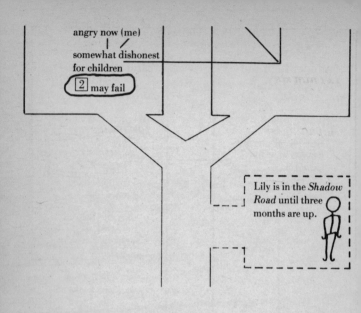

angry now (me)

somewhat dishonest

for children

2 may fail

Lily is in the *Shadow Road* until three months are up.

This was a surprising result. Lily was afraid she was going to fail no matter what she did! We changed those *possibles* into *probables*—"may fail" became, "probably would fail"—and discussed at length what she wanted to be *feeling about herself* in one year. Lily couldn't handle this right away. It was too unknown and threatening to consider changing the way she had lived her entire life. She folded up the diagram and put it away. I didn't see her again for two weeks. Then she came back and brought out the *Golden Nuggets* Diagram. There was a major difference:

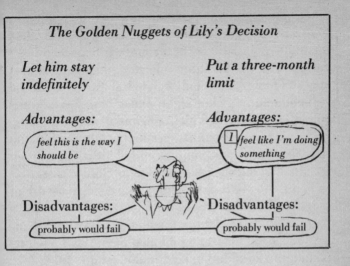

The Golden Nuggets of Lily's Decision

Let him stay indefinitely

Advantages:

feel this is the way I should be

Disadvantages:

probably would fail

Put a three-month limit

Advantages:

1 feel like I'm doing something

Disadvantages:

probably would fail

"It took me a long, hard time to come to this decision," she said, "but when the idea that I would probably fail in either case finally got through to me, I decided that by God one year from now I wanted to look back and say I *did* something about it, that I didn't just sit there waiting and 'taking it.' It became very important for me to take a stand, so I changed the rating from a ③ to a ①, and it was clear what I should do."

John *did* leave, and the marriage did dissolve. Lily occasionally wondered whether things might have been different if she had let him stay indefinitely, but she doubted it. He seemed really to have had his mind made up from the start. She guessed that had she chosen differently, she would have lost him, *and* time, *and* self-respect in the process.

Alexis, age twenty-nine, used the One-Year Plan for what was easily one of the most difficult and painful decisions of her life—informing her parents that she was gay. Alexis had married at twenty and had two children, a girl of eight, and a boy of six. Alexis was a very attractive girl, personable and outgoing. She was a good friend to people but always felt that her friendship could only go so far. Other people felt close to her, but she never felt deeply close to them.

When Alexis had been five years old a next-door neighbor had sexually molested her. As is typical in these cases, the neighbor threatened to hurt her if she told anyone. This fear, combined with Alexis' own reluctance to speak up or to question adults, led to four years of abuse. The experience left her sexually numb and deeply fearful of intimacy.

Ironically, her sexuality expressed itself outwardly, so that she was playful and seductive to men, but they could never get beyond first base. Her husband, Dan, was a quiet, passive man whom Alexis did not find threatening. She had never enjoyed sex, but she felt that it was her lot in life to submit. Basically, Alexis had gotten married because she wanted children. She loved her children deeply and was a dedicated, devoted mother.

After six years of marriage—passable for him, just tolerable for her—Alexis became friendly with one of her female co-workers. Conversation over coffee extended to lunches, then to drinks after work, and finally to outings on weekends. The long and short of it was that Alexis fell in love with this woman. Both women were reluctant to enter into an intimate relationship, but gradually they did, and were filled with shame, fear, and guilt.

The true nature of their relationship remained a secret for over a year. Alexis tried hard to keep her marriage going, but it crumbled to bits before her eyes. Both she and Dan became irritable and depressed, and because she would not reveal the truth of the matter, nothing could be resolved. The only thing Alexis could bring herself to say (and this was honest) was "Dan, I'm just not happy." They separated, and after two years Dan remarried.

For almost twenty-five years, Alexis had kept secrets. But some secrets have a way of growing, like mold, until they cover and spoil one's healthier thoughts. Her decision to *tell*, at last, grew out of a need to *survive*. The secret was killing her.

Alexis had not even reached the diagram stage of her decision, although the question, "Should I tell my parents or not tell them?" had been raging in her mind for at least two years. She was due to visit her parents in a few weeks and she felt that the time had come, but she was terrified. As soon as I asked, "Alexis, do you want to be feeling these exact feelings one year from now?," she was transformed. She looked straight at me for ten or fifteen seconds, without speaking. Then, she said, "No." That night, she composed and sent this letter. I think you will be able to pick out all the items that would have gone into a diagram: the fear of rejection, the impact on her life, the need to be "clean" and whole. It is one of the most touching letters I have ever read.

357

Dear Mom and Dad,

Today is Dad's birthday. Dan has remarried, and in a couple of hours I will be going to see my therapist, who has been helping me deal with the sexual abuse that has caused me so much pain, hurt, shame, guilt, and loneliness throughout my life.

The things I have been finding out have been very painful for me. They include:

1) To keep control over the emotions I was feeling, I almost totally blocked out feeling from my life. The normal feelings that people take for granted, I am only now beginning to feel again. The one that hurts me most is loneliness—the emotional loneliness that prevented me from getting close to people. (They could get very close to me—many people did and still do—but I never allowed myself to get close to them).

2) My life has been a continuous saga of keeping secrets because of the guilt and shame only I knew about. And I am at a point in my life that I want all the secrets to stop. I want people to accept and love me for me—not who they think I am. As my friend so aptly puts it: my closets are so full of skeletons, there is no more room for me anymore.

3) Because I could never come and tell you about the sexual assaults (yes, there were many), I, *in my eyes*, also lost my parents—their love and the caring that *I wanted and needed so desperately*. I was so lonely and so hurt and so full of shame.

4) Consequently, as a little girl, I made a pact with myself to never let people close to me. I gave up the idea of trust.

5) Each week, another part of how I view the world

has become clear. I'll try to list those for you:

a) I never told about the assaults, because to do so would have caused tremendous trouble.
b) I never felt I could try to stop the assaults, because children don't question what adults tell them to do.
c) I did not like to wear a dress, because I felt unsafe in one—seen as a female.
d) I felt that sex was to be endured—it was not fun.
e) To me sex was scary, no one told me it was fun, was enjoyable.
f) My normal childhood sexual exploration filled me with shame and guilt and became a terrible burden I hid from everyone.

Each week I have relived scenarios that helped me understand how I formulated these ideas that have influenced and ruled my life.

The devastating result of all this is that I punish myself by not allowing myself to have any sexual pleasure (that is so to this day). That was a major factor in the destruction of my marriage to Dan. I really am happy for Dan and his new marriage, and I wish him real happiness. For me, happiness comes from the fact that I have Scott and Kara as a result of that marriage.

The two things I am no longer willing to go without are the love I want from you, my parents, and the love of someone who knows about all the skeletons in my closet.

I have now found the second type of love, and that has come from a woman. For the first time in my life I have felt love, and I want to keep giving love to her.

But, as you can imagine, to do so has the potential for causing much hurt because of the way our society views such things. I am willing to endure any hurt that may result.

The thing I am no longer willing to endure is any secret that will keep me from having the open, free-of-secrets, love I want from you. I now want the accepting love from my mother and father *that I never allowed myself.*

I know in my heart, Mom and Dad, that as you are reading this letter you are probably crying. I am crying also. But for me that has got to stop. I am too lonely to hide things from you anymore. I want to be happy now. I want to be loved and accepted. I'm sorry for the burden I've just placed on you, but the secrets have to end. If you cannot accept the fact that I want to love a woman and that I want her to be accepted and loved also, I will understand, and I will accept that because it is even more important to me that there be no more secrets.

If you still want me to come home on the fourteenth, I will do so with the understanding that you accept me and the fact that I love a woman. If you don't feel that you can do this, you must tell me not to come home, because I will sense how you really feel about the whole thing if you do tell me to come home although you cannot accept me as I am.

Please let me know your decision by the fourteenth, whatever you decide.

I love you very, very much!

Love,

Alexis

Chapter IX. Sarah: Does She Stay in Her Marriage?

There is one major Strategy left, and you all know what it is. It is clearly the most successful of all the Strategies, yet it is the one we try to avoid at all costs. It is to *Settle*, to accept a compromise, to give up from your life something very desirable—willingly—and to accept *into* your life something unpleasant or painful—willingly. Sarah had to do some settling, because in the end some of her decision conflicts could not be reduced or resolved. She couldn't make *things* be different, so in some respects she had to make *herself* be different.

Sarah's dilemma incorporated almost all of the issues that can cause you to have difficulty making decisions: work, money, changes, Troublemakers, intimacy, responsibility, moral standards, and the desire to avoid hurting others—especially children.

The Background

Sarah and her husband, Douglas, had married right out of high school. They came from the same social and religious background, had many interests in common, and found each other physically attractive. The marriage had worked well—even beautifully—for eight years, until their son was born. A daughter was born two years later. Jason was now five, and Jennifer was three.

Doug complained that Sarah had changed completely when Jason was born. She had become preoccupied with the child, shut Doug out of her life, and was generally disagreeable. Sarah, in turn, complained that Doug couldn't stand not being the center of attention any longer and was harsh and dictatorial with the children. Sarah retaliated by withholding sex, and Doug retaliated by criticizing and arguing with her. Basically, the two had gotten into a serious power struggle. She said, "When I try to talk things out, he just yells at me." He said, "When I try to talk things out, she gives me the silent treatment."

This pattern had escalated steadily over the past five years until the event that brought them into counseling occurred. It began in a harmless, innocent way, as these things usually do. Doug had asked Sarah to get a baby-sitter so they could visit friends that evening. Sarah said she didn't want to. Doug began to argue with her, dragging out the usual arsenal of weapons. "You never want to be with me. You never want to do anything I want to do anymore. You never want to leave the children with a sitter. You're no fun to be with (the Machine Gun). I don't know why I married you in the first place" (the Nuclear Missile).

Not to be outdone, Sarah counterattacked. "You never think of anyone but yourself. Why should I want to be with you when you treat me so badly. I get more satisfaction from the children than from you (the

Machine Gun). I don't know what I'm sticking around here for" (the Nuclear Missile).

Doug responded, "Well, if you're so miserable, why don't you just get the hell out!" With this, he went up to her and pushed her on the shoulder. She stumbled back against the wall, slipped, and fell down. Sobbing, she got up, grabbed a bottle of aspirin out of the closet, and locked herself in the bathroom. Doug banged on the door until she let him in. She hadn't even opened the bottle. She was subdued but in control. Without looking up, she pushed past him, saying quietly, "I've had it."

Doug managed to persuade her to go with him for marital counseling, and it was in this setting that I met them.

The Decision

I would like to take you through Sarah's Decision Dilemma slowly, step by step, and with a lot of explanation. Each step made the issue *clearer*, though not necessarily more *comfortable*. By the time the Golden Nuggets emerged, Sarah had a great sense of relief, because both she and Doug now knew what she wanted and needed *most* out of life and how she could best focus her efforts to get what she needed.

There is a kind of peace of mind that comes from having things calm and orderly, being free of friction or discomfort. Sarah did not have this. Instead, she had the peace of mind which comes from being *clear* about values, *clear* about goals, and *knowledgeable* about how those goals might be accomplished. In a way, it was more *strength* of mind than peace of mind. How did it happen? Let's review each step to see how

Sarah finally became able to Settle.

Back in Chapters II and III, you saw how Sarah was able to stop her mental merry-go-round by writing her thoughts down spontaneously, as they occurred. We called this the "Yes-But" List:

marriage is supposed to last forever

the children's lives would be very disrupted

it's terrible living with someone I don't trust

doesn't support me in the way I discipline the children

I don't have many skills for a good job

I think I could make it if I had to

I was able to take good care of myself in the past

my friends would be supportive

divorce is against the teachings of my religion

it would be hard for my parents to take

it would be very hard for Doug's parents to take

end constant fighting in front of the children

never listens to what I have to say

walking on eggs all the time

could avoid turning everyone's life upside down

might never meet anyone better

my standard of living would be lower

don't know if I could handle it

no one to do things with

I'm lonely and afraid in my own house

big hassles—legal and otherwise

lots of turmoil

he's making me lose my self-respect, which was never terrific

could have a change for greater happiness

stability for children

I love my house

I enjoy being a mother and homemaker

would hate to admit to my mother that I'm having problems

at least I know what I've got

has hit me and has threatened to hit me again

if I stay, I could avoid dealing with the turmoil

I love him (I think) but I don't like him right now.

Sarah took time to walk around with her list, sometimes stopping and staring blankly into space, as she *visualized* herself in each situation with its various possibilities. While she walked, she added these items to her "Yes-But" List:

I'm afraid to be on my own

children love him

tired of putting up with the way he treats me

feel like he doesn't love me

I can't ever seem to win

criticizes me in front of his parents

don't know what to expect

Sarah had a tremendous amount of information to deal with, not only because of the sheer number of the items but because of their emotional weight. It is literally impossible for the human brain to make sense of a decision that is allowed to remain in this form. It *must* be organized or categorized in some meaningful, and hopefully simple, way.

My next step with Sarah was to put her items into the *Road of Life Diagram*. First of all, we tried to reduce each item to no more than four or five words. (Sometimes, this is not possible. The whole story has to be told.) Then we placed each item into its proper category. One item had to be split and put into two different places: "I love him (I think), but I don't *like* him." The first part—"I love him (I think)"—was an *Advantage* of staying. The second part, "but I don't *like* him," was a *Disadvantage* of staying. I also separated another item, "lonely and afraid," into two separate ones. Sarah's diagram, with the items shortened, now looked like this:

Choice: Move out

Advantages:

- think I could made it
- able to take care of self in past
- friends would be supportive
- have a chance for greater happiness
- end fighting in front of children

Disadvantages:

- children's lives very disrupted
- few skills for a good job
- against my religion
- don't know if I could handle it
- hard for parents to take
- very hard for Doug's parents to take

Choice: Stay at home

Advantages:

- marriage supposed to last forever
- stability for children
- love my house
- enjoy being a mother and homemaker
- know what I've got
- avoid turning everyone's life upside down
- avoid dealing with the turmoil
- I love him (I think)
- children love him

Disadvantages:

- has hit me—threatened to again
- terrible living with someone I don't trust
- never listens to what I have to say
- walking on eggs all the time
- lonely
- afraid
- making me lose my self-respect

standard of living lower

no one to do things with

big hassles—legal and otherwise

lots of turmoil

hate to admit problems to mother

afraid to be on my own

don't know what to expect

afraid he might hit me again

don't like him right now

doesn't support my discipline of the children

tired of putting up with the way he treats me

feel like he doesn't love me

can't ever seem to win

criticizes me in front of his parents

Sarah had to go through the relaxation/circling procedure twice. The first time, nothing in particular seemed to stand out. She said, "I could circle the whole thing." The *incident* was still clouding her thinking, and in her agitated state, she could not sense or feel the subtle "pulling" of the critical items. We put this diagram away and went through the entire relaxation procedure again the following week. By this time, she had settled down, and it took only a few minutes for the items to pop out.

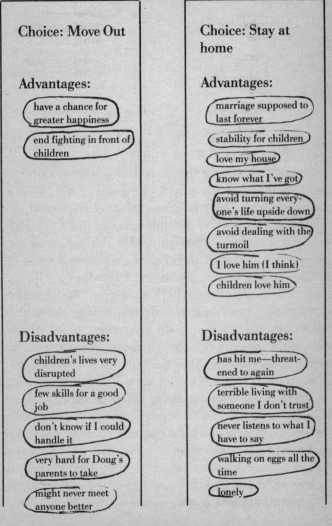

Choice: Move Out

Advantages:

- have a chance for greater happiness
- end fighting in front of children

Disadvantages:

- children's lives very disrupted
- few skills for a good job
- don't know if I could handle it
- very hard for Doug's parents to take
- might never meet anyone better

Choice: Stay at home

Advantages:

- marriage supposed to last forever
- stability for children
- love my house
- know what I've got
- avoid turning everyone's life upside down
- avoid dealing with the turmoil
- I love him (I think)
- children love him

Disadvantages:

- has hit me—threatened to again
- terrible living with someone I don't trust
- never listens to what I have to say
- walking on eggs all the time
- lonely

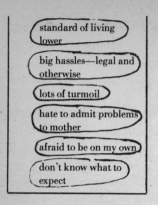

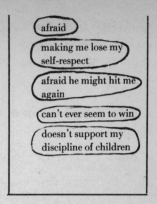

What were Sarah's main concerns?

I suggested earlier that it is useful, but not necessary, to discover what types of desires and fears—WISHES and WORRIES—are most important to you. You can use the *Mini-Manual* in the Appendix to learn whether, in this particular decision, you are most concerned with such issues as: practical matters (Brass Tacks), keeping your word (Pledges), self-fulfillment/self-development (Enhancers), or possibly one of the Troublemakers. Before moving on to the Seven Strategies, let's pause a moment to see which categories are represented among Sarah's *circled* items. (Remember that you may find an item expressed as a WISH ("I want more independence") or as a WORRY ("afraid of being independent").

BRASS TACKS: practical matters; such as, employment, money, or education

few skills for a good job
standard of living lower

370

COMPANIONSHIP: wanting to be with others, or wanting more privacy

    lonely

PLEDGES: wanting to live up to your word, meet obligations

    marriage is supposed to last forever

PLEASURES AND COMFORTS: wanting smoothness, stability, certainty, order, beauty, fun, mental stimulation, variety

    love my house
    lots of turmoil
    avoid dealing with the turmoil
    big hassles—legal and otherwise
    children's lives very disrupted
    stability for children
    don't know what to expect
    know what I've got

ENHANCERS: self-acceptance, self-confidence, self-respect, honesty, caring for and about others, mutual support, finding/maintaining intimacy, mastery, freedom of choice, meeting moral standards

    have a chance for greater happiness
    end fighting in front of children
    don't know if I could handle it
    might never meet anyone better
    afraid to be on my own
    I love him (I think)
    children love him

terrible living with someone I don't trust
never listens to what I have to say
walking on eggs all the time
afraid
making me lose my self-respect
has hit me—threatened to again
afraid he might hit me again
doesn't support my discipline of children

*TROUBLEMAKERS: Prestige Seeking, Power
Seeking, Pleasing, Protection*
(*Troublemakers* are normal desires or fears which
have gotten out of hand. In their moderate state, they
are usually *Enhancers* or *Pleasures and Comforts*.
They become Troublemakers only when you *must*
have them at all costs, especially when you sacrifice
other people's needs to obtain your own, or sacrifice
your own needs to fulfill someone else's. The items
listed below seem likely to be operating as Troublemakers for Sarah.)

very hard for Doug's parents to take (Pleasing)
hate to admit problems to mother (Protection)
can't ever seem to win (Power)

Some of Sarah's Enhancer items could turn into
Troublemakers if she goes to extremes with them, for
example, if she would do almost *anything* to avoid
confrontation, if she would do almost *anything* to
avoid making someone angry, if she would do almost
anything to avoid failure. These are the Enhancer
items that *could* become Troublemakers for Sarah:

afraid to be on my own (Protection)

never listens to what I have

walking on eggs all the time t.

afraid (Protection)

afraid he might hit me again (Prot.

The Seven Strategies

Strategy One: Find out Where You Are. Sarah is married and living at home. She is in Place (1)—solidly inside one of the alternatives, experiencing *all* the Advantages and *all* the Disadvantages of "Stay at home." She might say, "I'm thinking of leaving," but she is still in that place. She might say, "I am definitely leaving," but she is still in that place. She might say, "I am definitely leaving on Sunday," but she is still in that place. She will *be in that place* until the very moment she *leaves that place* physically. Then, and only then, is she in the other place: "Move out."

Strategy Two: Look for Mirror Images. One of Sarah's items, "have a chance for greater happiness," is a *Mirror Image* of *all* the Disadvantages under, "Stay at home." Those Disadvantages are the specific reasons why she was unhappy. Because Sarah wanted to *learn* more about those specifics, she chose to eliminate, "have a chance for greater happiness."

These were the remaining *Mirror Images* (remember to look only along the *diagonals*):

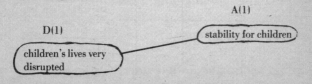

373

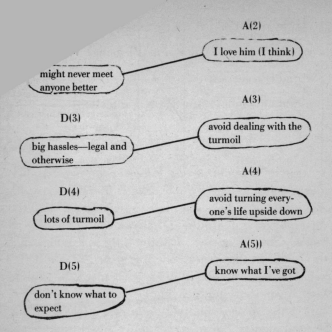

A(2)

I love him (I think)

might never meet anyone better

A(3)

D(3)

avoid dealing with the turmoil

big hassles—legal and otherwise

A(4)

D(4)

avoid turning everyone's life upside down

lots of turmoil

A(5))

D(5)

know what I've got

don't know what to expect

Sarah could feel no difference between D(1) and A(1). She had to leave them both in. She then selected A(2), D(3), D(4), and D(5). After selecting her *Mirror Images*, Sarah had somewhat less information to deal with.

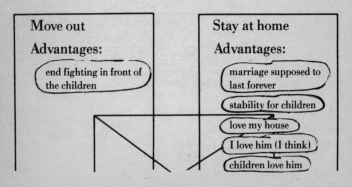

Move out	Stay at home
Advantages:	**Advantages:**
end fighting in front of the children	marriage supposed to last forever
	stability for children
	love my house
	I love him (I think)
	children love him

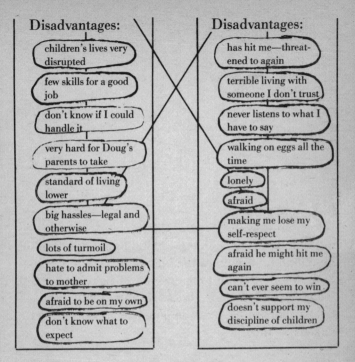

Disadvantages:	Disadvantages:
children's lives very disrupted	has hit me—threatened to again
few skills for a good job	terrible living with someone I don't trust
don't know if I could handle it	never listens to what I have to say
very hard for Doug's parents to take	walking on eggs all the time
standard of living lower	lonely
big hassles—legal and otherwise	afraid
lots of turmoil	making me lose my self-respect
hate to admit problems to mother	afraid he might hit me again
afraid to be on my own	can't ever seem to win
don't know what to expect	doesn't support my discipline of children

But she still had almost three times as much information as her mind could possibly process. Because the number of items was still excessive, I asked whether she would be willing to try to combine two or more items into one statement or idea that expressed the same thing. For example, the *idea* of disruption/turmoil/hassle was expressed in three different items. Sarah felt she could combine them:

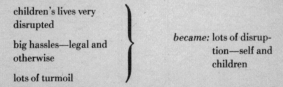

children's lives very disrupted

big hassles—legal and otherwise

lots of turmoil

became: lots of disruption—self and children

has hit me—threatened to again—terrible living with someone I don't trust walking on eggs all the time afraid afraid he might hit me again } *became:* afraid of his explosive temper

never listens to what I have to say can't ever seem to win } *became:* doesn't respect my opinions

Before Sarah could use the *Quick Rating*, we needed one more small item change. "End fighting in front of the children" expresses the idea of *being rid* of something. We changed it to read, "free of fights in front of the children." Before *Quick Rating*, then, with all items collapsed as much as possible, Sarah's diagram looked like this:

Move Out	Stay at home
Advantages:	**Advantages:**
free of fights in front of the children	marriage supposed to last forever
	stability for children
	love my house
	I love him (I think)
	children love him

Disadvantages:

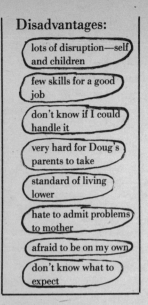

- lots of disruption—self and children
- few skills for a good job
- don't know if I could handle it
- very hard for Doug's parents to take
- standard of living lower
- hate to admit problems to mother
- afraid to be on my own
- don't know what to expect

Disadvantages:

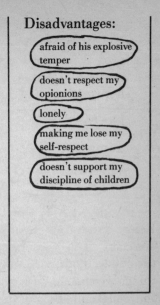

- afraid of his explosive temper
- doesn't respect my opionions
- lonely
- making me lose my self-respect
- doesn't support my discipline of children

Strategy Three: Do a Quick Rating. Sarah and I thought through the worst possible scenarios of the various Disadvantages. I asked her to *picture* scenes—scenes of disruption: informing the mother and in-laws, being yelled at (maybe hit), having her opinions contradicted, etc. And we visualized scenes of the harmonious, loving relationships she wanted. I even asked her to do one week of *Research* before *Quick Rating*, to live through each day observing how much she enjoyed the Advantages, when they occurred, and how painful the arguments were. The week was calmer than usual, but Sarah hadn't forgotten the pain of five years of conflict. She returned the following week and did her *Quick Rating*. (She had some trouble matching the *Quick Rating* statements with: "marriage supposed to last forever" and "children love him." For the first, I asked her to say to herself, "I want to live up to my moral/religious standards." And for the second, I asked her to say, "I want to see to it that my children are happy.")

After *Quick Rating*, her diagram looked like this:

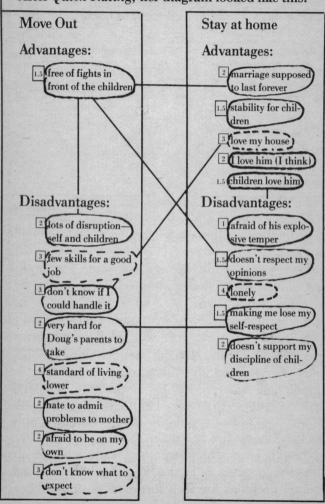

Move Out

Advantages:

1.5 free of fights in front of the children

Stay at home

Advantages:

2 marriage supposed to last forever

1.5 stability for children

3 love my house

2 I love him (I think)

1.5 children love him

Disadvantages:

2 lots of disruption—self and children

3 few skills for a good job

3 don't know if I could handle it

2 very hard for Doug's parents to take

4 standard of living lower

2 hate to admit problems to mother

2 afraid to be on my own

3 don't know what to expect

Disadvantages:

1 afraid of his explosive temper

1.5 doesn't respect my opinions

4 lonely

1.5 making me lose my self-respect

2 doesn't support my discipline of children

Alas, there were still too many items and no sign of resolution.

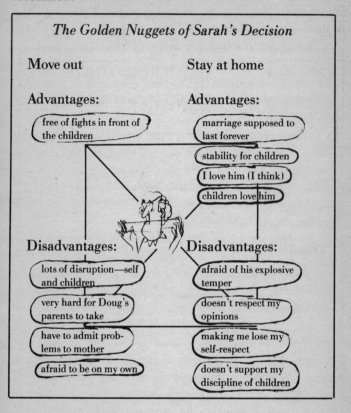

The Golden Nuggets of Sarah's Decision

Move out

Stay at home

Advantages:

- free of fights in front of the children

Advantages:

- marriage supposed to last forever
- stability for children
- I love him (I think)
- children love him

Disadvantages:

- lots of disruption—self and children
- very hard for Doug's parents to take
- have to admit problems to mother
- afraid to be on my own

Disadvantages:

- afraid of his explosive temper
- doesn't respect my opinions
- making me lose my self-respect
- doesn't support my discipline of children

Sarah looked at her diagram and sighed, "So this is what it all boils down to. You just can't win, can you?" "No, Sarah," I said, "you can't. Choosing isn't winning. Choosing is choosing."

Strategy Four: Do Research. People who are in counseling or therapy at the time of making critical personal decisions are in a fortunate position. They have the advantage of being able to experiment with ideas and behaviors in a safe place, under the guidance of a neutral but concerned party. They can display feelings ordinarily kept hidden, they can role-play desired behaviors, and they can practice communication skills, knowing that the situation will not get out of hand. Meanwhile, they have the advantage of practicing these skills in real life and getting feedback on them.

Sarah's diagram showed three very important areas where *Research* could be done: admitting to relatives that she was having difficulty, behavior management of the children, and the distribution of power, that is, deciding who had authority to do what, and how disagreements should be handled.

The first step in any kind of good, scientific research is *observation*. I asked Sarah and Doug to observe closely *exactly* what was happening that made them tense or angry. I especially wanted to know how angry interactions got started: what were their expectations, who said or did what, what did the other person then say or do, etc. I also asked them to review the course of their marriage to see what was different about their interaction now, as opposed to their interaction during the first eight years.

In about a month, the patterns were clear. Doug had been the oldest child in his family, and the only son. Like many first-born children, he was given—and took—a great deal of responsibility for the care and supervision of his younger sisters. He was kind, devoted to his parents, and dutiful, but he did not expect his authority or his decisions to be questioned. On the whole, his judgment was good, and he was respected in the family and in the community.

Sarah was also a first-born child, with one younger sister. She grew up in a "traditional" home, where her mother was a homemaker, and her father was relied on to make most of the decisions. Sarah had taken a leadership/supervisory role in relation to her sister but a subordinate role in relation to her father, the only male in the household.

When Doug and Sarah met, their expectations of each other were well matched. Doug expected to be in a position of authority, a position he handled with both sensitivity and competence. And Sarah expected to be in a position of compliance, a position she handled comfortably and agreeably. In fact, according to Doug, the one word which best described Sarah during the early years of their marriage was "agreeable," and to Sarah, the word which best described Doug was "strong."

Then Jason arrived. *Sarah's feelings of being responsible and in charge surfaced*. In the past, she may have disagreed with Doug, but she saw no point or justification in opposing him. It was easier and "righter" to go along with what he wanted. Their earliest disagreements centered on the handling of Jason: Should he be fed on demand or on schedule? Should he be picked up or allowed to cry? Should he be confined or allowed to roam freely? Should he be left with a sitter? Should he be spanked? How much freedom should he have to do what he wanted? Etc. Because Doug had also been in a "parental" role with his sisters, he felt he had as much competence and experience to make these decisions as Sarah had.

Sarah found herself in a bind which is not unusual.

Since she respected Doug's judgment, wanted to please him, and was used to dealing with men in a somewhat submissive, subordinate way, she often asked his advice (What do you think I should do?"), asked for agreement or approval ("Is it O.K. what I did?), and let him make decisions ("Well, all right, if you think so."). But at other times, she contradicted him, criticized him, blamed him for having too quick a temper, and tried to prevent him from taking over her handling of situations.

When Sarah and Doug did *Research* on their interactions, they discovered a typical interaction pattern:

(1) Sarah would ask Doug for advice or an opinion.

(2) Doug would give it.

(3) Sarah would disagree and say why.

(4) Doug would defend himself and get angry.

(5) Sarah would get angry in return, and the conflict would move into full swing.

(6) Sarah would withdraw in anger.

(7) Sarah would think it over and decide maybe he was right.

(8) Sarah would change her mind and tell Doug so.

(9) Doug would begin to take some action based on the opinion.

(10) Sarah would suddenly feel she had been "bull-

dozed" into something and would change her
mind again.

(11) Now the fight was really on, and the situation
would deteriorate rapidly with name-calling,
much use of, "You never," or "You always,"
and of course the inevitable dredging up of
every grievance that had occurred for the past
thirteen years.

Research taught the couple that much of their conflict and much of Doug's supposed disrespect for Sarah's opinions was initiated by Sarah's own actions!
By asking for agreement, she was delivering the message, "What I think and do cannot stand on its own.
It needs your stamp of approval." Then, by complying
with decisions with which she did not agree, and *especially* by changing her mind back and forth, she deliv-
ered the message, "I don't respect my own opinions
enough to stand up for them or to stick by them."

What was the problem in this marriage? The problem was that Doug was receiving those messages accurately and acting on them! Sarah's lack of confidence
stimulated Doug to take over and be strong. When she
changed her mind, he felt betrayed and helpless. Her
vacillation *stimulated* him to get angry in an attempt
to pin her down and force a conclusion to the issue.
Once Sarah and Doug understood the history and dy-
namics of their interactions, the next task was to experiment with changing them, so the next stage of
scientific research consisted of manipulating the elements operative in their interactions and observing
what happened.

Since most of the arguments centered on child management, we decided to undertake an intensive program of parenting training, along with training in assertiveness skills. Sarah and Doug were able to come a good deal closer to agreeing on principles of child management, but some serious disagreements remained. For example, Doug did not feel he had to explain *why* he was asking (telling, really) Jason to do something, while Sarah felt Jason needed some explanation.

They agreed to try this approach: each parent would refrain from intervening in the other's handling of a disciplinary situation, if the other had already begun it; and neither would disagree with the other's handling of such a situation in front of the children. Meanwhile, areas of serious disagreement would be brought to the counseling sessions for review.

Assertiveness training was another matter altogether. The couple had married under a strong contract: "Doug makes good suggestions, and Sarah agreeably goes along with them." Now, it was Sarah who wanted to change the contract. But did she really?

If she did, would she be able to carry it off?

If she carried it off, would Doug be willing to go along?

If he were willing to go along, would he be *able* to relinquish his more powerful position?

These questions could only be answered in time, so the answers were not available at the time Sarah was trying to make this decision. She would have to make up her mind one way or another *without* having some vital information. No matter which alternative she chose, she would be *taking a risk*. *Research* helps, but it can only go so far.

Strategy Five: Take the Tiger to Tea. Sarah was an agreeable person who tried to avoid friction in general, but between people in particular. The thought of facing the pain and hurt, maybe even anger, of her mother and in-laws was terrifying. To her knowledge, Sarah had never indicated to them that her marriage was less than completely satisfying.

But Sarah had to have realistic expectations. Few parents, when confronted with the threat of a breakup in their child's marriage, are going to say, "Well, now, that's just fine. We understand everything and wish you all the luck in the world." *There is going to be pain*. For everyone. But if a painful decision is not yet absolutely final, especially if some action is being taken to try to work things out, parents and in-laws can be most supportive.

Parents love their children! Your parents don't want to see you suffer any more at the age of twenty-five, thirty-five, or fifty-five, than they did when you were five. Sometimes it's even harder for parents to deal with an adult child's pain, because they feel so helpless. Trust that this caring and concern is there for you to draw on . . . if you will do so.

Doug and Sarah each agreed to inform their own parents as best they could that the marriage was in trouble, possibly big trouble. They agreed to make it clear to their parents that *they did not want advice*. They only wanted to inform them about what was happening and to ask for their understanding and patience. Doug was more comfortable doing this, perhaps because he was not so afraid of confrontation, perhaps because of his own inner strength. But it was not so easy for Sarah. It was rare for any member of her family to bring a problem out into the open, especially one this serious.

It may have been cowardly, but Sarah chose to speak first to her mother alone. She used the diagram as a starting-off point, describing the problems in as much detail as she could without violating the deepest privacy of the marriage. She added that she and Doug were in counseling and were trying to work things out. Finally she said, "I just wanted to let you know what's been going on." Sarah's mother had only one comment: "I've known for a long time that you weren't happy. Let me know if there's anything I can do."

Doug's parents were more upset. They had strong feelings about the sanctity of marriage and didn't believe divorce was a realistic answer to marital problems. They were less sympathetic to the position of either party and felt that both should be willing to compromise more in order to make the marriage work. If Sarah were eventually to leave, she would have to take into account the relative certainty of criticism from her in-laws. This could be an ongoing factor if Sarah assumed any personal responsibility for maintaining contact between the children and Doug's parents.

After about eight weeks, we took another look at Sarah's diagram. By this time, many of the issues regarding discipline of the children had been settled. The most important and successful agreements were:

(1) to discuss disagreements out of the children's presence, (2) to allow the party initiating a disciplinary action to carry it out without interference from the other, and (3) to support the other's action later if necessary, by saying to the child, for example, "This problem is between you and your (father/mother). Why don't you talk it over with (him/her)?"

By that time, Sarah had also *Taken the Tigers to Tea* and had found out that one of them (the upset of Doug's parents) was real—they were not interested in *Tea*—but the other (the upset of her own mother) had never existed.

The third major disruptive factor in the marriage—poor communication and an unbalanced power relationship—was slower to improve. It would require major changes in each partner's style of interacting as well as a major change in the original (unspoken) marriage contract.

Strategy Six: The One-Year Plan. Of all the Strategies, Sarah found this the most helpful in resolving her Decision Dilemma. In fact, the decision itself *became* a One-Year Plan. Sarah felt that if she and Doug could not put the marriage on a new footing in one year, it would probably never happen.

There was one, and only one, item in her diagram which had rated a clear and unambiguous $\boxed{1}$: "afraid of his explosive temper." No matter how much she was afraid to be on her own, no matter how much she craved stability for herself and the children, no matter how much she and the children might love Doug, Sarah *knew* that she could not and would not allow herself to be physically abused—or even threatened with physical abuse. True, she had learned that she was often provocative and irritating, but not every person who is provocative gets hit! Mostly, Sarah was no longer willing to put up with the fact that Doug had assumed he had the *right* to hit her, no matter what the circumstances.

Sarah decided to stay in the home for one more year. It would be, she knew, a year of hard work, as she and Doug struggled to give up or rework ingrained behavior patterns of long standing.

At the time of her decision, Sarah's diagram looked like this (Note: One item, "marriage supposed to last forever," had dropped in rating to a ☐3 and was omitted.):

Sarah's Final Diagram

Choice: Move out	Choice: Stay at home
NOT BEING CONSIDERED AT THIS TIME	**I REALIZE THAT IN ORDER TO HAVE THIS:**
	stability for children I love him (I think) children love him
	↓
FOR ONE YEAR, I CAN AVOID THESE CONSEQUENCES:	**I WILL HAVE TO ACCEPT THIS RISK FOR ONE YEAR:**
lots of disruption—self and children very hard for Doug's	afraid of his explosive temper doesn't respect my

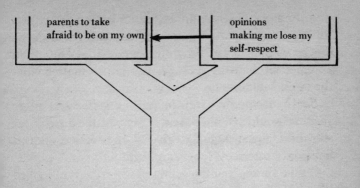

parents to take	opinions
afraid to be on my own	making me lose my
	self-respect

Strategy Seven: Settle. Sarah Settled—not for a certainty, but for a risk. Had she known, beyond any doubt, that the Disadvantages of staying in the marriage would definitely continue, she would have left. She Settled in the HOPE that *she* could learn to communicate more clearly and confidently, that *she* could learn to respect and stick by her own opinions, that *he* would be willing to live with a person who did not always agree with everything he said and did, and that *they*, together, could forge a new relationship based on equality of power and mutual respect.

Chapter X. You

Decision making is always somewhat uncomfortable, because a *decision* is required only when there is *conflict*. Only when you have a pull in two directions at once do you have the makings of a decision.

The *Road of Life* technique leads to a *way of thinking* about decisions. It doesn't tell you *what to do*. (Who has the right to do that?) But it does show you exactly *why* you are having trouble making up your mind, by pointing the way to the knots that keep you tied up in doubt, fear, and longing.

You now know that balancing and trade-offs are *part and parcel* of every important decision. Instead of being preoccupied with the "rightness" or "wrongness" of the decision, you can begin to use decisions for the amazing *learning* tools that they are—the only real means to gather accurate information about life and about yourself.

You are the artist of your life. With your decisions, you literally *create yourself*, just as an artist paints a picture—a dab of paint here, a dab of paint there—by a move in this direction, a move in that direction. Only, unlike a painting, *you* are never finished. Your decisions don't make you complete, or perfect, or better, or worse, or right, or wrong. They only make you more *definite*, more *real*, more *alive*. They make you . . . YOU!

Three Cardinal Rules of Decision Making

(1) Making decisions is a way of GETTING IN-FORMATION.

(2) Each alternative is likely to have very important ADVANTAGES *and* very important DISAD-VANTAGES.

(3) You will never be able to tell whether a decision was beneficial until AFTER you have made it and had a chance to EXPERIENCE the out-comes.

Chapter XI. Questions and Answers

Q. I can't always limit myself to only two alternatives. Sometimes there are three or more. What should I do then?

A. One of the reasons the *Road of Life* succeeds is that it reduces the amount of information you have to look at *at one time*. To begin with three alternatives would defeat that purpose. Instead, I suggest you use two alternatives to start with. Then, select the "winner" of the first two to match against the third, and so on, always moving two at a time.

There is this one caution: the pattern of circles may change from comparison to comparison. Therefore, begin each diagram fresh, with no circles at all, and work through the decision in the usual way.

Q. Do I need to draw out the whole diagram, or can I just make two lists—the pros and cons under each alternative?

A. *Any* writing down of your items will help, and organizing them into pros and cons will help even more. But only the diagram shows clearly that when you (represented by the little figure) *move* into one alternative, you give up *all* of what is in the other alternative (the good and the bad). The complete diagram shows how your two alternatives are connected to, and dependent upon, one another.

Q. What if there are no items at all in one or more categories?

A. No problem. Treat it like a "no circles left" category.

Q. When I did my diagram, I had over eleven Advantages on one side, but only three on the other side. Shouldn't I go with the one that has more items in it?

A. No. The most important consideration is the *weight* or *value* of the items. This is something that can only be *felt* and only *you* can feel it. One Disadvantage, for example, could easily outweigh dozens of Advantages if it's *important* enough to you.

Q. I got circles in only one category and couldn't connect them to anything to get a pattern. What should I do?

A. Circles in only one category should be treated like a Leaning Ladder. It means your decision is clear, but one end of the Ladder is more important than the other. If the circles are at the bottom, it means that you want very much to AVOID something. Choose the *other* alternative. If the circles are at the top, it means that you want very much to GET something. Choose *that* alternative.

Q. When I did the relaxation exercise and opened my

eyes, nothing at all seemed to pop out, so I didn't get any circles. What does this mean?

A. *Sometimes*, the amount of conflict in a decision produces so much anxiety and confusion that you cannot feel subtle differences in the way the items "pull" at you.

Sometimes, your eyes will be drawn immediately toward something you don't want to admit or don't approve of, and your conscious mind will quickly pull them away.

Sometimes, people have a desire to *hide* their values and attitudes. If you never reveal what it is you want or what you're afraid of, people can't hurt (manipulate) you by withholding what you want or by making you afraid.

A *no-circle* pattern usually suggests a high level of fear or tension and a strong desire for safety.

If nothing popped out, I suggest you fold up the diagram and put it away for at least three days. Then, take it out and repeat the relaxation procedure, using double the amount of relaxation time: two full minutes. When you open your eyes, let the "pulling" happen, but don't try to force it. Think of this exercise simply as an opportunity to learn about yourself. No one is going to pressure you into *doing* anything.

If this is not successful, skip the circling procedure altogether and move right into the *Quick Rating*. *Quick Rating* produces somewhat the same results, but without using the important element of intuition.

Q. I noticed that some of the people in your examples used intervals between numbers for their *Quick Rat-*

ing, like 1.5. Doesn't this make things more complicated?

A. One of the major obstacles to successful decision making is that people have a poor understanding of what is *more* important to them, and of what is *less* important. *Quick Rating* is a way to make these judgments fairly easily.

The point is to discover, dealing with any two items, whether they are equal in importance to you or whether one is *much* more important, *somewhat* more important, or just a *tiny* bit more important than the other. If you want to rate one item with a 2.7614^8 and the other with a 2.7614^9, it shows you are aware of a slight difference. That's the basic idea.

Q. Don't we need to take into account the *probability* that something might or might not happen? After all, if something is not very *likely* to come about, maybe we should ignore it.

A. People who do laboratory research on decision making have discovered something fascinating: people detest figuring out probabilities, and they are very poor at doing it. For example, if I were to put nine red marbles and one blue marble in a bag and ask you to estimate the probability of drawing out a blue marble, you, like most people, might stubbornly hold to a probability of fifty-fifty, even though the chances are clearly only one in ten.

I have deliberately chosen not to include probability estimation in the *Road of Life* procedure, believing it to be one more large burden in a task that is difficult enough as it is. However, I *have* addressed the question of probability in a simpler way. I ask people to change *complete uncertainties* (may, might, can, could, afraid that, don't know whether) into *moderate certainties* (probably would, or probably would not). This not only removes the emotional tension that usually accompanies feelings of uncertainty, it enables people to get a better grip on the decision. If they can live with the *moderate certainty*, they can definitely live with the possibility.

Q. The examples you use never seem to be exactly like the problem I have. Am I doing something wrong?

A. If I used sixteen-thousand examples, I could never come up with one exactly like yours, because no other person is *exactly* like you. This book is more like a road map than a photograph. It can point out the gravel roads, superhighways, and detours, but it can't tell you where to buy gas. Your decisions will be the result of a *unique mix* of your past experiences, values, fears, and hopes for the future. And only you know what these are.

Q. I was taught always to put others ahead of myself. Isn't what you are suggesting self-centered and selfish?

A. I believe that people have a good sense of what is right for them, even when they are not fully aware of what that is. When they go against this "natural knowledge," they feel uncomfortable and unsettled. Some people are truly comfortable putting the needs of others ahead of their own. Actually, in doing so, they *are* meeting *a need of their own*—a need to give and to sacrifice in order to feel like a good, worthwhile person.

Others are *trying* hard to be comfortable with sacrifice, but—face it—they're not. They are trying to live up to a standard which is not right for them. These people would probably be happier in the long run if they accepted the evidence that is in front of their eyes: *for them* a more nearly equal balance between their needs and the needs of others may be necessary.

Q. I can see all of the Troublemakers operating in me at one time or another and sometimes more than one at a time. Is that possible?

A. In order to appreciate the meaning of the Troublemakers, I think of each one as contributing something to a woven, plaid fabric. That fabric is your personality. All the colors (the Troublemakers) are there, woven together to make a whole. But, for each person, the particular *pattern* of colors is unique, with one or two of them wider, brighter, or stronger than the others.

Therefore, in any *Road of Life* Diagram (or decision situation) which contains one Troublemaker, you may see elements of the others, but they won't *dominate* the whole. For example, in a Prestige situation, there are often elements of Pleasing. And in a situation where Pleasing is important, there are often elements of Protection. Another common combination is Prestige and Power. In fact, these two often switch back and forth in importance, depending on the specific situation. But in each situation, one will be dominant, the other more subdued.

Q. I am not happy with the idea that children can *choose* to misbehave. I was brought up to respect my parents, and I expect my children to respect me when I tell them to do something. When you point out why children don't do what they're supposed to, it sounds like you're giving them permission to disobey. Are you?

A. I have always loved words, and one of my favorite activities is to look up their history, to discover what they were originally intended to mean. The word *respect*, as in this question, has *come* to mean *obey*. But its real, original meaning was "to look back at," and even the current dictionary definitions have *nothing* to do with obedience!

Children respect and take the advice of people who act in accordance with their own moral principles and who think of children as good, competent people, doing the best they can with the experience they've had. When parents and children get into a power struggle, respect disappears, and all that's left is "winning." I am neither giving nor withholding "permission" to disobey. I am only describing what I see, and why some people, including children, may *choose* to disobey.

Q. I can hardly even get *started* on making a decision. I'm an anxious person anyway, and the whole idea of having to make up my mind makes things even worse. I find it hard even to name alternatives. Is there some way I can overcome this?

A. It may help if you understand an important connection between your mind and your body. Physiologists have discovered that when people watch or think about an activity, their muscles *perform* that activity at a microscopic level. In fact, this subconscious muscular activity can sometimes raise a person's heartbeat almost to the same level as that of the people actually performing or playing!

When you *mentally rehearse* an action—any action—your muscles will begin to move ever so slightly. Most of this activity is in the form of anticipation. Your body will produce chemical and structural changes which prepare you to act. If the action is never carried out, your body must get rid of those chemicals and try to reverse the neurological and circulatory changes that took place. This causes cellular irritation and fatigue.

One of the primary causes of anxiety is a body that is kept in readiness to act but never acts. That's why people who are tense and anxious often find relief through vigorous exercise.

Ask yourself whether some of your anxiety might be due to *inaction*. Are you constantly creating problem situations, for which your body obediently *gets ready* to act, and then not allowing yourself to carry anything out? If so, you may find relief through exercise or from taking *some* small action, *any* action, to dissipate this muscular energy and to allow your body to return to its resting state.

Regular practice of sound relaxation techniques is another way of reducing overall anxiety and increasing mental clarity. From personal experience, I can recommend transcendental meditation. Good results have also been obtained from such practices as progressive relaxation, biofeedback, hypnosis, yoga, rhythmic activities like swimming or jogging, prayer, or other meditative techniques with or without a spiritual component. Take time to investigate and practice various techniques, until you find one that suits your natural inclinations and your lifestyle.

Q. *After* I have made up my mind, someone will come along and start to question or criticize my decision. I find that I can't stick to my guns, so I begin to get mixed up all over again. Once I've made up my mind, how can I *keep* it made up?

A. When someone questions, criticizes, complains about, or argues with one of your decisions, even with the best of intentions, you should know that you are about to be manipulated. *If* you have presented your decision as a trial—for example, "I'm thinking of this," or "How would you feel if we did this?"—then you have *invited* comment. And you'll surely get it.
But *if* you have stated your decision as firm and final, you have *not* invited comment, have you? *If you change your mind in response to pressure*, you are saying, loud and clear, to those around you: "Hey, folks, I don't *really* believe in the worth or value of what I have just said. Please argue with it, and if you are persuasive enough, you'll probably get me to change my mind."

Gaining respect for your opinions, and therefore for yourself, *can* be accomplished in time. It takes work, because the techniques you need may be unfamiliar to you. And it takes time, because both you and those around you will want to slip back into the old, familiar patterns.

I am going to outline a plan for you which *will* lead to increased self-respect and increased respect from others. It's not easy. *And*, it assumes that the decisions you want to hold to are reasonable, wholesome, life-supporting, and meant to increase your well-being as well as the well-being of those around you.

Are you ready? Here we go.

STEP 1: People who let themselves be talked out of what they believe is right are almost always in the grip of a Troublemaker—usually *Pleasing* or *Avoidance*. They want to avoid someone's anger or to avoid confrontation in general. Standing up for what you believe often makes other people angry. *To increase respect for yourself, you must first be* willing to take the risk *that someone will get mad at you*. If you *cannot* take this risk, stop reading here, and go on to the next question.

STEP 2: The most typical scenario for "giving in" involves being asked to do something, or asked by someone else for permission to do something, such as, "Would you serve on the committee?" or "Can I stay out past midnight?"

Get input before you make a final decision. Ask the person making the request to *explain* why they want what they want or why they think the way they do. When they have finished replying, you can ask, "Is there anything more you'd like to tell me?" or "Do you have any other reasons?" Ask questions if you are unclear about any of the information.

STEP 3: Don't answer right away if you don't have to. You can say, "Let me think about it for a half hour (a day or two, until next week, until the next meetings, etc.).

STEP 4: (Assuming you want to say "No") Return to the questioner with a statement that follows either of these lines: "I've given a lot of thought to your request, but (GIVE A GENUINE REASON) or (GIVE A GENUINE FEELING)."

Examples of REASONS:

> *I think the food is overcooked here.*
>
> *I'm too tired.*
>
> *I don't have time to take on another responsibility.*
>
> *You did not come home on time last week.*
>
> *It costs too much money.*

Examples of FEELINGS:

> *I don't like* _____ .
>
> *I don't enjoy* _____ .
>
> *I don't feel comfortable about* _____ .
>
> *I prefer not to* _____ .

Here Comes the Pressure

Pressure will come in three forms:

(a) the person REPEATS an opinion on, or reason(s), why you should do what he or she wants, usually more vigorously

(b) the person makes a CRITICAL comment

(c) the person asks a QUESTION . . . which is not really a question

How to Respond

Step 5: Respond to a REPEAT by hearing the other person out, then repeating the same reason (either the factual REASON or the FEELING) that you gave in STEP 4. Add a statement at the beginning to show that you understand the other person's point of view, for example, "I appreciate what you're saying (I understand your position, I see your point), but I don't have time to take on another responsibility," or "I know you like that place, but I think the food is overcooked there," or "I know your friends can stay out, but I'm not comfortable about *you* staying out past midnight."

You are under NO OBLIGATION to respond to a critical comment, such as, "That's no reason!" "That's the silliest reason I ever heard!" "Well, I don't agree with you!" However, you can answer such comments with a calm silence, or you can say, "I'm sorry you feel that way."

When asked a question that is not a question—repeat, is not a question—but is a criticism in the *form* of a question ("Why?" "Why not?" "Why won't you?" "How could you?"), please try to understand what these "questions" are really asking of you. They are asking you to justify your decision, to give a reason for your decision (to hold up a target) so they can attack it (take a shot at it).

How can you tell whether a question is a genuine one or an attempt to manipulate you? Do this. Give your genuine reason or reasons one more time. Don't forget that *feelings* are genuine reasons which don't have to be justified or explained. Now . . . listen carefully to the very *next word* that comes out of the person's mouth.

The Secret Word

If the word is "*but*," you are being manipulated.

STEP 6: If you heard the word "but," the worst that can happen is that you have to start repeating yourself. (Yes, the person will be angry—if you've read this far, you were prepared for that.)

If the person is being fairly reasonable, says "But," and then trots out all the reasons why you should change your mind, use the response, "I understand your position, but (once again, give your original REASON or FEELING)." You might have to say it fifteen times. Eventually, the other person will give up.

If the person says "But," then criticizes or attacks, say nothing or "I'm sorry you feel that way." (Saying nothing is better.)

If the person says, "But why?, Why not?, Why won't you?, etc." say "I've already given my reason(s)." Then, you must STOP TALKING, or you will find yourself in big trouble.

STEP 7: Expect a period of coolness or turbulence. Manipulators have feelings too! They may feel upset, hurt, angry, or defeated. For sure, they won't be too happy with you for a while. BUT THEY *WILL* GET OVER IT. And so will you.

The Respect Progression

For the first few weeks or months, they'll be *angry*:
"Who does he/she think he/she is! I'll show him/her."

For the next few weeks/months, they'll be *confused*:
"Why isn't this working?"

For the next few weeks/months, they'll be *cautious*:
"Maybe this person isn't so easy to manipulate after all."

In the next few weeks/months, they'll be *convinced*:
"This person can't be manipulated."

And, finally, they'll be *considerate*:
"I respect that person."

Q. What should I say when people ask, "Are you *sure* you're making the right decision?

A. Say, "No."

Appendix I. Mini-Manual for Pinpointing
Your Wishes and Worries

CATEGORY ONE: THE BRASS TACKS

A. *Finding, Keeping, and Advancing in Jobs*

more job opportunities

get set in business for life, maybe

would be afraid of getting fired

come out with good references (recommendations, credentials)

more assurance of a good job

would establish good business contacts

better chance of promotion

have to train someone to take over my job

B. *Education: in School/through Experience/Training on Your Own*

has the courses (does not have the courses) in the area I need good preparation for college

need the work experience

gives real-life experience instead of being in school

find out what history (forestry, working with children, doing office work, working with my hands, etc.) is like

chance to learn Spanish (photography, pottery, scuba diving, to play the piano, etc.)

C. *Getting, Earning, and Spending Money*

earn a good (fantastic, so-so, terrible) salary

tax advantage (good/bad investment)

price is right (costs too much)

afford it better later on

high cost of repairs

don't want to get in debt (worry about paying off the debt)

good fundraising idea

D. *Using Your Time*

more (less) time for other things

less travel time

no time for other activities (unspecified)

takes too long

may be a waste of time

E. *Finding a Place to Live*

gives me a guaranteed place to stay

would have to break the lease

would have a hard time finding a place to live

might have to move too soon

F. *Maintaining/Repairing/Keeping Up*

less maintenance and upkeep of car (house, property, tools, machines, possessions, etc.)

more (less) dependable (reliable, durable)

likely to need major repairs soon

good (poor) service record

G. *Getting Around*

near public transportation

would have (would not have) a way to get around

hard to get to

public transportation unreliable (unavailable)

H. *Being Practical (in General)*

it's practical

it's useful
frivolous (wasteful, unnecessary)

does the job (doesn't do the job)

needed it for a long time

CATEGORY TWO: COMPANIONSHIP

A. *Having Company/Having Friends*

afraid of being alone (isolated, cut off, left out, out of place)

would feel more like part of a group that I like (admire, want to belong to)

get to meet lots of people

chance to be with my friend (friends, family, parents, relatives, buddies)

could lose (gain) his/her/their friendship

comfortable (uncomfortable) with those kinds of people

B. *Getting or Being Involved*

enjoy being involved with (doing things with) other people

have someone around to discuss problems (ideas, thoughts) with

able to participate in things with my husband (wife, children, friends, co-workers)

give me a chance to get to know her/him/them better

enjoy friendly competition (team sports)

C. *Enjoying Being Alone*

see what it's like to be (live, do it) alone

need some space (time to think, to get my head together)

feel like being alone (rather go alone)

seeing too much of each other

gets me away from him (her, them) for a while

CATEGORY THREE: THE PLEDGES

Giving Your Word

I promised (said I would, gave my word, made a vow)

agreed to take on the responsibility

wouldn't be able to follow through

paid (registered) for it

counting on me to finish in time (be on time)

CATEGORY FOUR: PLEASURES & COMFORTS

A. *Enjoying a Smooth Flow of Events*

wouldn't have to think too hard (worry about it, make decisions, keep track of things, keep things in order)

have to adjust to a new neighborhood (set of friends, school, job, boss, co-workers, routines)

easy to do (get, accomplish, organize, keep clean, keep running smoothly) peaceful (quiet, settled, no pressure)

too hectic (complicated, fast-paced)

would be a hassle (would avoid a hassle) with him/
her/them/it

tired of the rat race

B. *Knowing What's Going to Happen*

already know what to expect (the people, the
"ropes," the setup, the best parking places, etc.)

have someone to count on being (going out) with

would have a good chance (or be sure) of getting
the type of sofa (car, stereo system, teacher, washing machine, lover, etc.) I've been wanting

would know (would not know) for sure what's going on (what's going to happen, what he/she/they
have in mind)

C. *Herbs and Spices*

fun, entertaining

mentally stimulating (a challenge, fast-paced)

boring after a few minutes (hours, months, years)

would be an exciting (different, new) experience
(person, school, place to visit, thing to do, thing to
have)

D. *Personal Preferences*

like the wide open spaces (climate, sun, mild winters, snow, mountains, view, privacy, size of the rooms)

feel crowded, cramped, boxed-in (too many people, rooms too small, too much clutter, too much traffic)

like (don't like) my boss (studying, the atmosphere, my mother-in-law, that kind of music, vegetarian food, my boyfriend's dog, etc.)

time to do fancy cooking (fix up the house, build model airplanes, garden, decorate, read, putter around)

he/she is fun to be with (lively, interesting, funny, good in bed, outgoing, nice to people, easy to get along with, etc.)

he/she is cold (stubborn, selfish, nasty to my friends, stingy, argumentative, moody, etc.)

In General

$$I \begin{Bmatrix} love \\ like \\ don't\ like \\ hate \end{Bmatrix} the\ way \begin{Bmatrix} it \\ he \\ she \\ they \end{Bmatrix} \begin{Bmatrix} look(s) \\ feel(s) \\ sound(s) \\ taste(s) \\ smell(s) \\ work(s) \\ act(s) \end{Bmatrix}$$

CATEGORY FIVE: THE ENHANCERS

A. *Respecting Yourself*

would begin to accept myself as I am

respect myself more (lose respect for myself)

others would respect me more

wouldn't get pushed around so much

more comfortable with self

feel worthwhile (feel like a s—t)

B. *Respecting Others*

accept them as they are

show respect for their right to choose

change to hear what they have to say

gives him/her/them the benefit of the doubt

leaves him/her/them free to decide

doesn't put pressure on him/her/them

C. *Expressing Yourself Honestly*

it's the real me

not what I really feel (fake, hypocritical)

can have my say (let it all hang out, clear the air)

want to express my ideas (opinions, thoughts, feelings)

D. *Caring for and About Others*

don't want to hurt her/him/them

would show that I care (a considerate, kind thing to do)

would be a tattletale (get someone in trouble)

a way to say thanks (pay back a favor)

doesn't get people all fired up (upset) for no reason

don't want to make him the bad one and me the good one

E. *Finding/Maintaining/Losing Intimacy*

gives me (does not give me) emotional support

could find (develop into) real love

share my thoughts (activities, feelings, weekends, life) with someone

potential for closeness and trust

way to show my love

may never find someone to love

F. *Accomplishing/Mastering/Resolving*

find out whether I can really do it

able to try my wings

gain self-confidence (learn to be independent/self-sufficient)

stand up for myself (not play into someone else's game)

trust my own judgment

be my own person (explore my own interests, make my own decisions)

H. *Making a Meaningful Contribution*

like to help out

feel needed (feel useless)

chance to use education (training, skill, talent)

can teach (share) what I know (what I can do) with others

it needs to be done (I want to be sure it gets done)

feel like a responsible person

I. *Creating*

chance to create (make) something new (beautiful, useful)

good atmosphere for developing creativity

stifles creativity

helps me be more flexible

gives me creative ideas

J. *Feeling Free to Choose*

free to decide on my own

free to fix it up any way we want

have total personal freedom

don't want to be confined (tied down, inhibited, restricted, pressured)

might get stuck (trapped) in a job (school, neighborhood, relationship, marriage) I don't like

K. *Protecting and Improving Physical and Mental Health*

lots of tension

good way to use up extra energy (get rid of tension)

get needed rest

get (stay, get over) feeling angry (hurt, sad, depressed, hopeless)

get (stay in, get out of) shape

safe (dangerous, could get hurt, cause permanent damage, die)

fattening (clogs up the arteries, slimming, cleansing, nourishing)

make me feel/look better (younger, handsome, healthy, pretty)

L. *Meeting Moral Standards*

the right thing to do (what people are supposed to do)

not right (bad, not nice, doesn't feel good/right)

would feel guilty

my civic duty

feel like a good person

against the rules

against the law

against my religion